MICHELLE FACOS

An American in Pandemic Paris

A Coming-of-Retirement-Age Memoir

Award-winning author Michelle Facos fell in love with Paris while stationed daily as a child in front of a French language-learning program on public television. Despite living in New York during her years as a paralegal and as a PhD student at New York University's prestigious Institute of Fine Arts, Facos's fidelity to her first city-love has never wavered. The City of Light inspired her career as an internationally renowned art historian and rewarded her devotion with an extended stay during the early days of the COVID-19 pandemic, a gift of inestimable value. Visit michellefacos.com. For photos relevant to individual chapters, see the author's Instagram highlights.

Although the characters and events in this book are true, some names and details have been altered.

ISBN 979-8-218-00902-1

Book design by bespokebookcovers.com

POUTHIER PRESS

Contents

Prologue

I arrived in Paris in March 2020, fresh from an eight-week, solo, soul-searching retreat that took me from the frozen, snow-bedecked forests of Quebec to the cloud forests of Costa Rica. Shortly thereafter, I found myself stranded and without income in a series of incremental incidents that transformed my carefully planned near-future. I had intended to stay in Paris for two months of dancing, dining, music, and wandering, followed by May in Warsaw to lecture, June in Copenhagen to conduct research, and July in Shanghai to teach. Afterward, I had planned visits to Germany (Greifswald, Hainewalde, Potsdam), and to Stockholm to visit my daughter, Hanna, before returning to the U.S. to teach by August 20th. Instead, I was gifted eighteen months of unfettered freedom, albeit radically constrained and intensely local. Before, I only knew Paris well, but during my stay our relationship progressed to one of intimacy.

Earlier, in September 2019, I visited Hanna in Stockholm. We chatted about spirituality, self-love, Law of Attraction, soulmates, and, more pragmatically, where I would spend my Spring 2020 sabbatical. Although my toxic if thrilling relationship with Trocadéro Man hadn't officially ended, I sensed the writing on the wall. My inner voice advised solitude and recuperation, 'wintering'. I resolved to get my shit together once and for all, emerging, I envisioned, like a free and beautiful butterfly from her psycho-emotional cocoon. My propensity for detrimental romantic relationships in which I persevered with the determination of a religious fanatic had to end.

In sixth grade, I portrayed a middle-aged Philip Nolan in a dramatization of Edward Everett Hale's *The Man Without a Country.* The lines that have stuck with me come from William Ernest Henley's poem "Invictus:" "I am the captain of my fate; I am the master of my soul." That's what I had lost along the way; I felt tossed about like a sailboat in the waves. I wanted to regain the natural confidence of toddlers and animals that I vaguely remembered possessing in my childhood. I never questioned the wisdom of capturing pollywogs in the field behind our house or building castles in my Daddy-built sandbox around whose perimeter he had painted a garland of red hearts joined by cursive script that read 'I love you'. But half a century of serial monogamy—anxiety-ridden, lonely, overburdened, and preoccupied—combined with who-knows-what traumas from my childhood had transformed me into a psycho-emotionally dependent cripple, as tentative as an abused animal.

Six weeks in Costa Rica before heading to Paris seemed a salubrious solution, a kind of tropical wilderness retreat for neophyte explorers of spaces interior and exterior. For a cathartic six weeks, I slept in sea-level jungles, explored high-altitude cloud forests, and lay on white sandy beaches—eating when hungry, sleeping when tired. I spent waking hours as a child might: studying disciplined armies of leaf-cutter ants, sloth-spotting in the forest canopy, listening to waves lap the shore and crash against rocks, and observing the antics of howler monkeys as they swung with terrifying ease from branch to branch of the arboreal canopy with the insouciance of aerial acrobats. I also meditated, watched Abraham Hicks videos, tapped with Brad, and read Eckhart Tolle and a smattering of other self-help gurus with the avidity of a spy looking for a secret message; I cried inconsolably as torrents pounded the tin roof of my one-room rain forest cabin.

By the time I arrived for a ten-day stay on an isolated beach south of Tamarindo on Costa Rica's Pacific coast, the therapeutic benefits of an immersive engagement with nature had generated peace and contentment. Mission accomplished? Perhaps. Mornings, I lounged on 'my' solitary beach under the protective shade of palm trees and enjoyed the graceful ballet of pelicans in the sky and the busy determination of tiny hermit crabs on the beach as they searched for and fought over tender morsels of fallen mango. When the shade vanished, I trekked back 150 yards through the jungle to my spacious dwelling, the tile floor cooling my sizzling soles. Afternoons, I lazed in the hammock suspended from my porch overhang from whose comfort I observed lizards ambling, sunning, or darting about the garden. I reread *The Wind in the Willows* and *A Moveable Feast*, an appropriate prelude to my upcoming stay in Paris.

Was I done? I cherished my simple solitary life doing as I pleased when I pleased. I experienced no compulsion to gratify others. Still, as the days wore on uncertainty grew. Maybe I hadn't finished, maybe my inner harmony was situational not permanent. Who wouldn't feel relaxed where the sun always shines, ripe avocados and mangos drop from the trees, and one falls asleep to the sound of waves ebbing and flowing on a tropical shore?

My inner voice spoke: *get down to business, you're leaving in ten days*. Back to friends, responsibilities, urbanity. I understood her message: I should take an ayahuasca journey. I had long been curious about this plant medicine, and several friends had attended transformative ceremonies. Perhaps such a psychotropic jolt would realign me with my path. Based on LSD trips taken back in the day, I felt sufficiently grounded to venture into this uncharted territory, one where relinquishing all conscious control is fundamental to a positive experience. I searched the internet, located an association of shaman, perused its website, and found Erick. He ran a small retreat at his home, perched on a lush mountainside overlooking a verdant valley with the cloud forest at the horizon. This is exactly the kind of luminous, breezy, expansive environment in which I thrive. I shuddered at the thought of being tossed among a gaggle of fellow explorers vomiting and tripping in a dank hut under the dark sweaty canopy of a tropical rainforest, the kind of place where such experiences often unfold.

Erick listed only a phone number, and several days of phone tag left me exasperated. Two nights before departing my Pacific paradise for a few days in Tamarindo and then San Jose, the capital, I called one last time. If he answered I'd go, if not I'd assume the universe didn't intend for me to have this experience at this moment. Erick answered. He posed questions to evaluate my preparedness physically (did I have heart problems?) and psychologically (did anything weigh on my mind?). I was ready. I knew I was. I rearranged my travel with just one night in San Jose and spent three days as Erick and his small staff's only guest.

I swam in the refreshing water of his pool and relaxed in a hammock enveloped by perfume-emitting flowering plants. I napped and listened to the chirping of birds and their buzzing wings as they flew by; I gazed at the hazy blue mountain landscape and received the best massage of my life in an ayahuasca-covered hut perched on the hillside, caressed afterward by gentle mountain breezes. Erick and I dined together at every meal, for which his chef prepared organic delicacies that conformed to the obligatory pre-ceremony diet. Paradise. Erick described the serendipity of finding this property at just the moment he decided to pursue the shaman business independently after the shaman he had assisted for six years returned to her native Peru. He explained that for those tuned into the correct spiritual channel these kinds of opportunities present themselves regularly and obstacles melt away. After hearing this, I was more eager than ever to learn the lessons ayahuasca offered. He suggested reading Don Miguel Ruiz's *The Four Agreements*, which I did that afternoon in the hammock. I concluded that a civilization governed by these simple principles would be far more humane than any subjected to the Ten Commandments or any other laws proffered by Western monotheistic religions.

My first 'journey' was profound. The second, on my fourth day, was a tale of horrific gut-wrenching nausea barely tempered by complete immersion in the mysterious *icaros* songs that traditionally accompany the ayahuasca ceremony. That time, my body and my mind/spirit had conflicting experiences, whereas in the first journey they fused seamlessly. The first journey taught me a lot. I arrived at the wall-less building that doubled as the outdoor living/dining area in the cool, fragrant air as the sun set. At the far end, a gentle fire blazed. Erick awaited, accompanied by two silent helpers. One, a voluptuous young woman with fine, waist-length, black hair and a sincere smile, seemed the embodiment of the earthbound feminine principle. She nurtured me at the beginning of my journey.

The other, a tall, ripped young man with shaved head, smooth chest, and the kind of tats I've seen in *National Geographic* photos of male members of Amazonian cultures, wore nothing except a sarong. He carried a staff and functioned as a kind of warrior-guardian. He remained silent and spent most of the evening/night squatting by the fire, his muscular profile silhouetted against the pale night sky. Late, after Earth Mother and Erick retired, he stood or sat patiently and silently beside me. All through the night. Never—at least since childhood—have I experienced such a profound sense of well-being, fully confident that my caretakers kept me safe from whatever threats—exterior or interior—might menace.

I sat at the spot prepared for me: a mattress positioned against the end of a short wall in case I wanted to sit with back support facing the flickering fire and pale blue mountainscape beyond. Pillow at the head, blanket at the feet, and to the right, a glass of water for quenching thirst and a bowl for vomiting. Erick retrieved a small cauldron containing ayahuasca tea, a mixture of many plants from his own garden and brewed on the premises. He hung it over the fire, chanting and waving his hands over it like a conductor directing a mellifluous musical passage.

Quietly at first, the recorded *icaros* music began. Guardian kept time with a rain-stick. Erick approached with a mug of ayahuasca tea and crouched beside me as I swallowed, suppressing the urge to wretch. Undoubtedly the foulest thing I've ever tasted. I thought, *it tastes like poop juice*, although I hope never to gather the necessary evidence to make a scientific comparison. I sat up, leaned against the little wall, and gazed at the sun setting behind the mountains, glowing orange before slipping quickly beneath the horizon, as it does near the equator.

Now, the waiting game. I remembered it well from my

psychedelic youth. Waiting for that sensation that something coursed through me. A tightening of the neck muscles below my ears, for instance, or a tingling in my limbs. Or a perceptual change. I had hoped to see the network of shimmering colors—the energy fabric of the universe—that I had seen in documentaries evoking the visual experience of ayahuasca. The music increased in tempo and intensity, or were my senses suddenly more acute? It was hard to tell, as with so much else when one is tripping. I remembered how the experience makes one appreciate uncertainty and fosters patience.

For the first hour, I suffered severe, ghastly nausea. The *icaros* sung in a low and melodious voice by Earth Mother pulsed through me. She approached holding large leaves smoldering at the edges and emitting a pungent, acrid odor that permeated my body and brain. I assumed their purpose was to facilitate purging. She did this repeatedly, continuing after my second cup of ayahuasca tea. The first, as often happens, produced no cerebral transformation. After each visit, she applied a lemony balm to her hands, rubbed them together furiously for a few seconds until warm, and then opened them like a book before my nose, allowing me to inhale the pleasant, citrusy aroma.

I purged a bit. I desperately wanted to vomit the way Hanna always does when ill—bountifully and without restraint—but I've never had that capacity. I always considered this inability an insignificant genetic trait, like rolling your tongue or wiggling your ears. In that moment, however, I wondered if it were a physical manifestation of repression, a reluctance to release constraints that impeded my recuperation of self. Or perhaps there was a third explanation.

Soon (time had ceased to be measurable and anyway I had left my watch in my room), something began to happen. That familiar opening of the sluices of consciousness. To avoid a 'bad trip' one must maintain them open until the journey's end. Like a devout novice, I submitted to the journey Mother Ayahuasca led. You're advised to bring a conscious intention and to contemplate it before embarking but I didn't. I thought wishing for something specific might limit my experience after Erick related the maxim, 'You can ask Mother Ayahuasca for what you think you want, but she will give you what she knows you need'. Humbled in the presence of this powerful earth force, my conscious intention was simply *Mother Ayahuasca, show me, teach me.* I would happily embrace whatever wisdom she imparted.

Powerful emotions began to wash over me, and I lay down to minimize resistance—physical or mental—to the unfolding journey. First, tremendous gratitude welled up. I acknowledged my privileged life: health and fitness, a perfect daughter, loving and supportive friends and family, extraordinary experiences. My thoughts then turned to my parents. I marveled at their limitless love and support. They never questioned my dropping out of high school to attend a college that, had I waited to graduate, would have been Plan B or C. They never questioned my sudden decision a month before college graduation to marry four months later an admirer they had never met. Nor my decision to work as a waitress when I moved to New York. They supported me no matter what and without question. Few people had parents like that in the 1970s. I was lucky.

Then, thoughts turned to my father. A traumatized World War Two veteran who returned home with three purple hearts, a Bronze Star with two oak leaf clusters, and undiagnosed PTSD. He dreamed of becoming a writer, artist, or university professor but allowed his sense of duty rather than his inner voice to guide him. I have long recognized that it's no accident that I became an art history professor and writer—my father's dream fulfilled but tragically not by him. I envisioned him connected to me by a giant tube attached to our respective abdomens. It gushed emotional pain from him to me. The tube had been there since my infancy, and I had no way to halt the flow. This open conduit had no floodgate.

For both of us, this situation was involuntary and unconscious. My father loved me more than life itself, as he told me so many times, and would never have harmed me had it been within his power. His torrent of psycho-emotional pain formed me. I cried as I recognized how profoundly he would have regretted the unintentional suffering he caused and because I couldn't fully alleviate his pain. Then, the scene shifted, and my father morphed into a past long-term partner. A kind man but like my father shaped by an emotionally abusive childhood. His past traumas became my then-present ones, flowing into me unstoppably, even long past the end of our relationship. I cried because I couldn't relieve his pain either.

And finally, Trocadéro Man, another victim of childhood trauma. That pain flowed unstoppably into me, too. I intuited that it resulted in actual physical harm delivered indirectly. During the eighteen months of our relationship, I was crazy in love and plagued by more health problems than I experienced during my entire previous life. In that short time, I suffered my first bone breaks (a foot then two toes), a compromised immune system after falling ill on Zanzibar, and sudden-onset gluten intolerance. I couldn't fix him either, of course. I knew one must first identify one's need for help and then initiate the self-healing process, as I was doing.

In my tripped-out state, I had a life-changing realization. Mother Ayahuasca showed me what I needed to know. I would never have connected these three men who had been in my life under varying circumstances and at different periods. She revealed that I absorbed their profound emotional pain like a sponge, never reducing their suffering but augmenting my own. I woke in the morning feeling as if curtains had been drawn back from my consciousness and sunlight and elation rather than worry and pain streamed in. The sluice closed while the sponge dried in the Latin American sun. I felt capable of spotting warning signs that would protect me from becoming an emotional dumpster in future relationships. I left Costa Rica a few days later, celebrated my sixty-fifth birthday with friends in Cleveland and New York, and flew to Paris, ready to process the wisdom of the previous months and enjoy all the magic that Paris has to offer.

Chapter 1
Arrival

I arrived in Paris on Sunday, March 1, 2020. I had looked forward to this moment since October when I bought my plane ticket, intending to stay, ideally, with my beloved Trocadéro Man in his glorious penthouse apartment. Every moment since our first meeting in March 2018 had been pure bliss, and now, with his 'soon-to-be-ex-wife' (as he referred to her publicly) ensconced in her own apartment, our opportunity to test cohabitation had arrived. In October 2019, we rendezvoused for a romantic long weekend at the Venice Biennale, and I had hoped he would join me at his chalet in the snowy Quebec wilderness at New Year's. He didn't. And suddenly it was March.

Emerging from the RER B—the suburban train from Charles-de-Gaulle Airport—onto the boulevard Port-Royal, I squinted into the blinding sunshine and inhaled deeply the crisp, late-winter air, happy to bask in familiar surroundings. Families headed to the Luxembourg Garden (*le Luco*, to locals) for Sunday recreation, couples sipped after-lunch espresso at the window tables of restaurants, bibliophiles browsed the outdoor bins of bookshops. Paris has always felt like home—a comfortable and reassuring locale—but this time it also feels somewhat new. After an absence of a year, I am back under healthier circumstances, free (I hope) from the thrall of my exhilarating yet psycho-emotionally detrimental relationship with Trocadéro Man. No regrets, however. If sent back in time, I would make the same choices. The romance and its aftermath provided a fortuitous albeit brutal opportunity for personal growth —tough love from the universe. For that I am grateful. I think.

I turned right, dragging my electric blue Samsonite suitcase behind me and crossed the Esplanade Gaston-Monnerville, named after the Guyanese politician Gaston Monnerville (1897-1991). *Bonjour Marshal Ney*, I greeted under my breath as I passed François Rude's patriotic bronze sculpture. I have taught it many times in my art history classes. Loyal to Napoléon, Ney was executed by the restored Bourbon monarchy in 1815 following the Battle of Water-loo. He refused a blindfold and gave the firing squad its order to shoot. He was forty-six. Rude portrayed him at a happier moment: in the heat of battle, having just drawn his raised sword from its scabbard, Ney twists backward, mouth open, shouting orders as he leads his troops into battle.

My temporary home lies a few blocks further west, on the rue de la Grande-Chaumière, a name which translates as 'the large, thatched cottage', a rustic vestige now long gone. It's in the Sixth Arrondissement, snuggled halfway between le Luco and Tour Mont-parnasse. One of those block-long streets saturated with Parisian-ness. Old four- and five-story buildings line the street, with shops or restaurants occupying ground floors distinguished by soberly painted facades of navy blue, forest green, black, maroon, and, in the case of the tiny, pocket-size shoe repair, orange. From the end of the street, it looks like a row of giant wooden building blocks.

Residential apartments begin on the second floors, a reassuring situation considering greedy entrepreneurs have transformed numerous Parisian residential buildings into boutique hotels and apartments into offices or AirBnBs, a practice that has sent real estate prices skyward. At the north end of the street lies a branch of Paris's most famous art supplier, Sennelier, its window filled with cheerful, creativity-inspiring pastels and watercolor boxes. Next door, the Paris headquarters of the Anthroposophical Society displays books that invite passersby to cultivate their spiritual humanism and to learn more about the teachings of anthroposophy's founder, Rudolph Steiner, whose theory of life unfolding in seven-year stages seems curiously applicable to my own.

Down the block on the same side is La Wadja, a traditional, pierogi-serving Polish restaurant beside the orange shoe repair and next door, an art book shop whose holdings must be subterranean because from the window one sees only a circular staircase winding downward. In the middle of the block, a commemorative plaque marks a building once housing the art school run by early twentieth-century sculptor and Rodin student Antoine Bourdelle. At number 8, a plaque indicates the location of Paul Gauguin's apartment and studio utilized prior to his final departure for Tahiti in June 1895; he shared it briefly with Czech painter Alphonse Mucha, who later moved to number 13. After World War One, the Italian painter Amedeo Modigliani lived in the same building. The only current artsy enterprise on 'my' side of the street is a frame shop. Otherwise, there are two more restaurants (Parisians love dining out) and two small hotels, appropriately named Villa des Artistes and Académie des Artistes. Even the most unassuming block-long streets in Paris house such small thriving businesses. It's one thing among many I miss about 'old' New York, where I lived on West End Avenue during the 1980s.

My walk-up apartment occupies half of the third floor of a courtyard building whose entrance is next door to Esttia, a restaurant run by a trio of young Italian-food enthusiasts. The small but sufficient apartment has semi-depressing views of a blank wall on the kitchen and bathroom side and on the bedroom and living room side, a courtyard with a lone, currently leafless, tree. Usually, I like leafless trees in the wintertime because they don't obscure the land- or cityscape beyond. But here, my vista consists solely of an unwanted view into the apartment of a young couple, barely veiled by a screen of branches. I look forward to the tree sprouting leaves so I don't feel like a voyeur each time I glance out the window.

Although I'm on sabbatical and should be choosing my location based on the availability of research resources—Copenhagen would be the logical choice, with the security of tenure and a sense of sufficient professional accomplishment I have become too hedonistic to find professional considerations motivating. After all, what good is money and freedom if—while attempting to better the human condition—one doesn't enjoy the remarkable experiences life offers?

Besides the city itself, which radiates an enchanting quality easy to discern but difficult to articulate, music and dance draw me to Paris. Specifically, swing dancing at Caveau de la Huchette, located in the cellar of a sixteenth century building on the rue de la Huchette, a dozen steps from a majestic view of Notre-Dame's flying-buttressed south side and in the thick maze of Greek and Indian restaurants crammed between place Saint-Michel and the rue Saint-Jacques. Over the centuries, Rosicrucians, Templars, Freemasons, and French revolutionaries have conspired under Caveau's low subterranean vaults, which bear traces of Romanesque sculpture.

I discovered Caveau during my Fall 2017 stay and have since become a devotee, reveling in live music—from big band to blues—and dancing several of the seven nights a week it's open. Had it not been for Marian, a swing-dancing friend visiting from New York, I might never have gone. I've realized that when I plan activities intended to please others I usually find myself enriched in the process. Although I didn't dance, Marian did, with Jean, who later became my favorite dance partner and a friend.

At that time, I lived in the Ninth Arrondissement near Métro Bonne Nouvelle, whose name translates to 'Good News'. The only good news it offered to the legions of homeless living under the overhangs of the post office there or camping in tents and appliance cartons on the surrounding side streets was living unharassed by the authorities. The musicians at Caveau pack up at 1:30 a.m., and I have trouble tearing myself away earlier. Most customers depart in time to catch the last metro, which stops running during the wee hours. Occasionally, I walked home via the pont Saint-Michel and the pont au Change, past the Tour Saint-Jacques, and up the deserted boulevard de Sébastopol to the boulevard Saint-Denis. It felt less creepy walking on wide, semi-trafficked boulevards than on narrow side streets.

Near Bonne Nouvelle, prostitutes of every imaginable physical description lingered in doorways or leaned brazenly against the entrance to the KFC at the corner of Sébastopol and Saint-Denis: obese ones oozing out of sports bras designed for pre-pubescent girls, wrinkly-faced, knobby-kneed ones wearing fishnets visibly attached to garter belts and teetering on glittery platform shoes, young shapely ones wearing vinyl miniskirts that revealed a lack of underpants—black, Asian, and white. I never felt threatened though; Paris, like many European capitals, feels safe almost everywhere. And no civilians carry guns, a detail that makes Europe automatically safer. Still, by Caveau's closing time, I was often sweaty and exhausted and crawled into one of the taxis waiting on the quai Saint-Michel.

The second factor motivating my visit to Paris is Rodolphe Raffalli. I may be the only person on earth who decides where to stay in Paris based on easy walking distance from a heavenly evening of extraordinary guitar playing. But then, I have a history of making decisions others have found puzzling: turning down a full scholarship to Stanford, for example. Rodolphe has absolutely no idea who I am despite my erratically regular presence much less how devoted I am to his music: I own all his CDs. His modest YouTube presence doesn't capture the sublime live experience.

Rodolphe sits on a stool in a corner of the back room of the Piano Vache, a student dive-bar plastered with deteriorating, decades-old performance posters, situated in the shadow of the Panthéon, the final resting place of the Great Men (and a few Great Women) of France. There's no cover charge, and the first set starts at 9:30 p.m. By that point, it's crowded with students and tourists. You won't hear better jazz at the Blue Note in New York. The vigilant manager, more concerned with the musical experience than revenue, darts about with admirable discretion and persistence chiding guests talking loudly enough to disturb serious listeners.

When I'm not in Paris and it's Monday evening, regardless of where on the planet I am between 9:30 p.m. and 1:30 a.m. Paris time, I visit Piano Vache in my imagination. I know when each of the three sets begins and ends, what kind of jazz they play during each, how the musicians and their friends huddle together in the dark, narrow, block-long lane smoking cigarettes during breaks. I know how the crowd thins by the last set—mostly songs—which begins at 12:30 a.m. David Gastine, the always smiling, curly-haired comp guitarist, often sings Charles Trenet's "Menilmontant," and a lovely, dark-haired Gen X woman with a bob and bangs who radiates groundedness and rapture often contributes a song or two by Edith Piaf or Léo Ferré. Other musicians come to listen or play. This trio exudes euphoria, and it's endearing when Raoul, the brawny, double bass-playing brother of David, chuffs like a tiger when he's deep in the groove. By the third set, rarely more than ten devotees linger, and, if I have not moved up previously, I do then, sitting so close that I could touch Rodolphe's guitar.

Thus, the Fifth or Sixth Arrondissements offer the best logistical solutions to my Parisian nightlife preferences. From Grande-Chaumière, I can walk home from both Caveau and Piano Vache in twenty minutes compared to the forty-five it takes me to walk to Bonne Nouvelle. Suddenly, two months in Paris seems too short, even if I haven't been in town more than eight hours.

And I survived my first day without thoughts of Trocadéro Man muscling their way into my consciousness. Until now. Today is the two-year anniversary of meeting Trocadéro Man via Tinder the day of my arrival in Paris in 2018. Too embarrassed to reveal this detail to friends and family, this scion of a prominent Parisian family concocted a story I validated about our meeting on the advice of a mutual friend I supposedly encountered at a party in New York a few days earlier. Trocadéro Man's Tinder presentation, with an array of photos similar to mine—on sandy, Mediterranean beaches, skiing on snow-blanketed slopes, leaning languidly against ancient ruins, nattily dressed (in a suit and tie and wearing a shirt whose French-cuffed sleeves peeked an appropriate half inch from his jacket sleeves)—was appealing. I interpreted this as a signal that he was my kind of guy. So different from the hordes I had left swiped: late middle-aged men who erroneously consider wearing wife-beaters or lounging shirtless an enticement.

Trocadéro Man was professionally accomplished, loved music and nature, and was proud of his children. That evening, he invited me to the Russian Cultural Center for what turned out to be more an adult talent show than a music and dance cabaret. We rendezvoused on the Left Bank side of the nearby pont de l'Alma. I arrived first and identified him at a distance, strolling with carefree confidence from the Right Bank. He wore a navy cashmere coat and a brown fedora that he wore pretty much year-round except in the most oppressive heat of summer.

Trocadéro Man smelled like springtime and fresh laundry, spoke English, German, Spanish, Chinese, and Russian, was easy to talk to, and seemed to find my snide remarks about the entertainment amusing. We dined afterward at a café across avenue Rapp, sharing a salad and each ordering a fragrant, steaming bowl of pumpkin soup and a cosmopolitan. When he asked me what I wanted to drink, I—always erring on the side of modesty—declared that water was fine, but he ordered a cosmopolitan and I said I'd like one, too. Since cosmos were the drink of choice for the *Sex and the City* ladies and perhaps also because they're pink, I'd always pegged them as a chick drink. I was surprised this charming and accomplished businessman-engineer-mathematician-pilot-philanthropist ordered it. I would have expected a smoky scotch or a glass of Viognier or a Cab. But I liked that he did as he pleased.

I admired his untroubled, child-like impulsivity, but in retrospect I'm pretty sure it was more a manifestation of rank having its privileges. At dinner, Trocadéro Man told me he was a 'player', but I interpreted this confession (evidently mistakenly) as a sign of self-deprecation. He impressed me as intelligent, perceptive, and spiritual. I accepted his invitation to go horseback riding in Rambouillet Forest on Sunday desperately hoping the year of refresher English-seat riding lessons I had recently taken back in Purgatory, Indiana, where my day job is, prepared me adequately. As it turned out, barely.

On the following dismal, misty Sunday, Trocadéro Man picked me up on the rue Mouffetard, where I stayed in Spring 2018, a meandering street dating back to Roman times now lined with food shops, crepe stands, and boutiques. I climbed behind him onto his *moto*, a familiar experience I had missed since my divorce two years earlier; motorcycle adventures had been one of our great pleasures. I clenched the passenger handles below my thighs as he whisked us to his mother's *gardien*-protected property south of Paris to borrow her car so we would not be drenched before our riding adventure began.

A petite welcoming raven-haired woman with enormous kindly blue eyes, Mother had prepared lunch for us. Well, this was a first: meeting Prospective Boyfriend's mom on the second date! Afterward, I borrowed her oiled cotton jacket, and we headed to the stable in her shabby Renault. There, I mounted a petite Landais appropriately named Rodin. I had never heard of a horse named after an artist, and I doubted either the stable owners or Trocadéro Man knew that in the mid-1980s I had curated an Auguste Rodin exhibition at The Brooklyn Museum. An expert equestrian, Trocadéro Man took off ahead of me but soon slowed, so we could ride side-by-side. He transferred his reins to his outside hand, removed his glove, and reached out to me, and I, understanding the intent behind the gesture, did the same. First physical contact. We held hands as our horses sauntered through the forest, sheltered from the light rain by a canopy of trees.

"Isn't this romantic?" he asked.

"Yes," I cooed.

After an hour, we dismounted at a crossing by a centuries-old stone marker, and he drew me toward him. His firm, gentle embrace warmed me inside and out. We stood there for a timeless silent moment, feeling the contours of each other's backs for the first time and our rapidly beating hearts through our thick clothing. My head nestled against his chest. It was one of those perfect instants when time stands still. Then he pulled his head back, looked into my eyes, already shouting 'yes, yes!', and kissed me. A wonderfully gentle yet passionate kiss in the misty rain in the middle of Rambouillet Forest.

For me, that day and all the subsequent ones in his company unfolded pretty much as in a fairy tale or Rom-Com, my skin surface barely capable of containing the exhilaration that yearned to burst forth. We remounted, him giving me a leg up. After a stretch of cantering on a narrow hilly path with scratchy branches swatting me in the face, I doubted my equestrian competence. After a two-hour ride, I returned to the stable in one relieved piece, my slightly abraded cheeks visible souvenirs of my deficient equestrian skills. And thus, in the most marvelous way, the romantic adventure began. And thus it would continue, when we were together and often when we were not and had to rely on video-chatting for distanced togetherness.

An unsettling thought just dawned on me: did I secretly hope Trocadéro Man would reenter my life, sweep me off my feet, and apologize for ghosting me during the three-and-a-half months since our last romantic rendezvous at the Venice Biennale? Did I wish that I would again have the run of his penthouse, sip Veuve Cliquot on the terrace, and cuddle between soft linen sheets, enjoying the tactile contrast between his baby soft skin and the springlike curls of his chest hair? I thought the revelations of my ayahuasca journey a few weeks earlier had provided closure to the Trocadéro Man affair, enabling its transformation into a bittersweet memory. But had it?

Chapter 2
March: Should I Stay, or Should I Go?

Monday 2 March

Today, I grocery shopped and explored my neighborhood. Two organic stores, Naturalia and Bio c'Bon, are within a five-minute walk on—or just off—the boulevard Raspail, with its welcoming benches and tree-lined median strip. Rodin's *Balzac* stands sentry on his pedestal at the intersection of Raspail and the boulevard Montparnasse, holding for eternity his erect penis. If only passersby knew what those hands were doing beneath his bronze robe, although the sculpture's phallic silhouette and the English pronunciation of his name—'ball sack'—do provide hints. I learned about *Balzac* from one of the great American Rodin scholars, Kirk Varnedoe, while working on my PhD at New York University's Institute of Fine Arts. He asked the class what they thought the great writer's hands were doing before advancing to the next slide, an image of Rodin's *F-Athlete*, a headless, nude young man standing in a contrapposto position and holding an erection—a study for *Balzac*. Giggles and gasps.

The choice made sense considering Rodin's options. Showing the nineteenth-century writer in a conventional pose—sitting on a chair, perhaps with his hand resting on a pile of books or thoughtfully holding a pen—would have seemed banal, uninspired.

Showing Balzac as a youth, before public recognition of his eminence and without his signature lion's mane of hair, would have required an identifying inscription. It would also have failed to embody the vigor of this prolific writer's achievement. So, Rodin cleverly combined the mature mastery of the author—signified by his easily recognizable, middle-aged head—with a suggestive yet discreet visual metaphor for his literary potency.

Rodin was heavily invested in the *Balzac* commission because he, too, first achieved success in middle age. Varnedoe also mentioned a passage in Balzac's writing in which the author compared the creative act of ink streaming from a pen with the procreative act. I feel a very different affinity with Balzac because like him I find that Parisian life—no matter how banal—fascinates with poetic intensity.

Balzac must have seen Ernest Hemingway. He lived a few blocks away on the rue Notre-Dame-des-Champs in 1924 and frequented the two still-thriving brasseries at the Montparnasse-Raspail intersection: La Rotonde and Le Dôme. Around the corner from Le Dôme is the rue Delambre, a typical Parisian shopping street, equipped with a butcher, fish store, Greek deli, fancy fruit stand, cheese shop, wine shop (the chain Nicolas), and a generic grocery (Franprix). Down the block lies a hotel where Gauguin—and later, the Surrealist André Breton—lived temporarily.

My American colleague Ben was in town and came for dinner. He had no choice about the evening's activity since it was a Monday. He left Piano Vache after the second set, but I remained until the bitter end. David, who triggered in me a state of euphoria when he sang "Menilmontant," recognized me during the last set, and we exchanged a few pleasantries about mutual friends in New Jersey, where he attends the annual Django-a-Gogo festival. Thirty-six hours in Paris and I already feel like an insider! The evening filled me with such joy that I skipped part of the way home on the lamplit, deserted streets of the Fifth and Sixth Arrondissements, passing the Panthéon in surroundings bewitchingly vacant and illuminated in its majestic Neoclassical splendor. As I walked past le Luco, gated nights for security reasons like all Paris parks, I could smell the earthy scent of things growing.

Thursday 5 March

Last night, I went to Caveau de la Huchette. Despite my two-year absence, the same fellow manned the bar and joked with customers and the same good-humored woman who drives home to the suburbs nightly after her very late second job shift checked coats. I recognized the regulars: the portly, swarthy man who barely moves his feet and pushes and pulls his always-younger partners, directing their movements like a fisherman reeling in and casting out; the lonely, bald fellow who sits hunched on the padded bench in front of the stage and watches shyly as couples dance. I imagine him wishing he had the nerve to ask a woman to dance but never actually doing it. Year after year. A curious man. Does he regret not dancing? I have never seen him dance although he is there pretty much every time I go. A lover of live jazz in any event. I danced a few times with IT Man. I have no idea of his name or what he does, but he looks like the kind of bespeckled forty-something introvert who might wear a pocket protector and keep his cell phone in a belt holster. He's a kind and gentle dancer who thoughtfully adjusts his moves to the skill level of his partner. I suspect he danced with me because the good female dancers weren't there.

Sadly, my preferred dance partner, Jean, was absent. He's the best swing dance partner I've experienced. Despite his limited repertoire of moves, Jean has the uncanny ability to make his partners look and feel like Cyd Charisse. Awkward young men often ask him to dance with their dates. Despite his small stature—he's my height and can't weigh much more than one hundred pounds—Jean is a gently authoritative lead. His clear signals—hand pressing against your back, adjusting the placement of your clasped hand—make even inept women feel the competence and confidence of a *Dancing with the Stars* contestant.

My mind strayed into the past as I zig-zagged home at 1:30 a.m. Traversing the empty streets, I envisioned random famous people— Albert Camus, Gertrude Stein, Emile Zola, Descartes, Danton, Benjamin Franklin, Amelia Earhart, Mozart, Mark Twain, Napoléon—wandering the vicinity, as well as anonymous citizens throughout the centuries going about their business. In Paris, I am always vacillating among the actual moment, memories, and an imagined past.

I read plaques. I don't know of any other city where you can learn as much about its history by simply stopping to read. I noticed numerous memorials to Resistance fighters at the spots where they were killed by occupying German forces between the 19th and 25th of August 1944. What a thrilling and terrifying week that must have been: more than fifteen hundred Parisians died trying to liberate Paris. My gut tightened as I mulled over the contrast between this serene night and the surging adrenaline of combatants who trod the same sidewalk during those critical days.

Robert Bottine fell on the northwest corner of the boulevards Saint-Germain and Saint-Michel on August 19th, Robert Houvre died on the rue Vaugirard just west of the boulevard Saint-Michel on August 22nd. Jean Monvallier-Boulogne was twenty-four when he was shot on August 25th outside what is now le Luco's entrance to the RER B. In fact, there must have been intense fighting along the boulevard Saint-Michel side of le Luco: Jean Arnould, one of General Leclerc's bodyguards, Jean Bachelet, Pierre Bounin of the Moroccan Regiment, Lieutenant Jules Martinet, Jean Revers of the Second Armored Division, and Raymond Bonnand all were killed within one hundred yards of each other on August 25th. Vive la France; their memories are a blessing.

Friday 6 March

This morning, the sun shone as I wound my way through the cobblestone streets of the Sixth Arrondissement to the Seine, first along le Luco on the rue Guynemer, a street named after World War One flying ace Georges, executed by the Germans after his plane crash-landed behind enemy lines in 1917. Amazingly, the Germans honored him with a hero's funeral in deference to Guynemer's impressive record. Then, onto the rue Tournon, which becomes the rue de Seine on its downward descent toward the river. I turned right onto the bustling rue de Buci, packed with food shops and crowded restaurants that spill onto the sidewalks, and continued after it turned into the rue Saint-André des Arts, with its falafel joints and trinket shops. It ends at place Saint-Michel, home of Paris's most recently built wall fountain. Although resembling the kind of Baroque confection one sees in Rome, with its monumental figure of Saint Michael vanquishing Satan, it's a vestige of the urban renewal project initiated by Napoléon III that transformed the city into its modern self during the second half of the nineteenth century. There's always something to see in the square: musicians, fire eaters, pickpockets, people waiting to meet friends.

I turned my attention to Notre-Dame, still a construction site after the tragic fire of April 2019, with wooden frames supporting the arches of the flying buttresses and plastic sheets stretched where stained-glass windows once glimmered. This is the first time I've seen it in its damaged state. Still majestic, its blocky twin towers never adorned with spires confer on it the authority of an architectural mountain at the heart of the city. The plaza in front of it— usually a gathering place for tourists, skateboarders, and drug dealers—is now roped off and inaccessible. Restoration continues apace with completion slated for Spring 2024, in time for the opening of the summer Olympics.

I continued along the Seine until the pont de la Tournelle, which led me to Île Saint-Louis, home to a harmonious architectural ensemble constructed during the seventeenth century. I descended one of the stone stairways leading to the water and rested on a stone bench under the shade of a tree on the quai d'Anjou, where the artist Honoré Daumier lived in the mid-nineteenth century. I thought of the laundresses he portrayed plodding up these steep stone stairs—bleary-eyed, with a heavy load of clean, damp laundry slung over one shoulder and holding the chubby hand of their toddlers with their free hands. In the nineteenth century, laundering was a desirable—if poorly paid —job for stay-at-home moms whose children were too young to enter the work force.

Throngs of ghosts infiltrate one's consciousness in Paris. And the better you know the city's history, the more ghosts you encounter. Down the block from Daumier's apartment is the studio sculptress

Camille Claudel occupied after losing the child she had conceived with her lover-mentor, Rodin, who rebuffed her desire for a more committed relationship. To her great disappointment, Rodin remained true to the illiterate Rose Beuret, his faithful companion of thirty years, marrying her in 1917, within months of their respective deaths.

Claudel suffered a fate typical of strong independent women of the day: the moment her supportive father died in 1913, her brother, the writer Paul Claudel, committed her to a mental hospital from which he refused to allow her release despite heart-wrenching pleas by Camille and the medical staff. Sadly, she made almost no art during her thirty-year incarceration. Does the quai d'Anjou feel melancholy to those unfamiliar with her and Daumier? I like the tree-lined quays of Île Saint-Louis because they are tranquil and have unimpeded views of both the Right and Left Banks depending on where you sit. And the stone benches are cool in the summertime.

This evening, I had my first date from the site I signed up with before arriving in Paris. Although I considered it a reasonable strategy for improving my French while closing the emotional door on Trocadéro Man, I wonder if I'm deceiving myself. Is this a covert admission of romantic neediness? Should I be alone for a while or longer? Am I searching for a partner? Or a place to call home? I've never much liked living in Purgatory, where I've been stalked and bullied, gaslit and deceived. I rarely spend more time there than necessary.

I miss my Swedish life in Tolg and the cottage I chose and called home for almost fifteen years, now inhabited by Philandering Ex and his new missus. I miss the forest, the lakes, my rowboat, the mossy stone walls, and picking blueberries in the woods behind the house. I miss the scent of the lilac wall surrounding the cottage, the huge jasmine bush beside the kitchen window, and my now one-hundred-year-old neighbor, Adine. What remains of my Swedish life—antique furniture, clothing, skis, books, the spice chest my parents received as a wedding gift, my grandmother's silverware, the silhouette portrait of me that my mother had made at a Buffalo department store when I was six—is packed away in a storage room in the basement of my daughter's Stockholm apartment building.

Guy suggested meeting at the Hotel Meridian at porte Maillot, which I found odd. He couldn't possibly live around that commercial no-man's-land, and the Meridian is not one of Paris's charming or classy hotels. But with a puzzled if open mind, off I went in the early evening darkness. Guy was white-haired, blue-eyed, and wore a blue blazer and grey flannel pants. We sat in the lobby and ordered drinks. When I questioned his choice of venue, he explained that it was convenient for him (he lives in Puteaux, a suburb of mostly very modern buildings next to the government stronghold, La Défense, where Trocadéro Man works) and because there was a very good Italian restaurant next door. OK, that made sense, although evidencing concern for his date's convenience rather than his own would have been thoughtful. Is this a red flag?

Sometimes, I feel relationship color-blind. But the first step went well, and dinner, a risotto with scallops, was delicious. I agreed to a second date partly because he suggested taking me to Chartres, which I've been wanting to revisit since my first and only trip there during the All Souls' Day holiday in 1974, while spending my junior year in Siena, Italy. At that time, I took the night train from Milan with my new friends, Harriet and Frank. It was packed with gregarious Italians smoking and chomping on salami long into the night. I remember wondering why the crowded platform on which we stood suddenly emptied, and then noticing a few tracks away a horde piling onto an extremely long train. Frank ran to the end of the platform to investigate and realized our departing track had changed. We sprinted, breathless and with hearts pounding, barely making it onto the correct train before it inched away from the station. Off to the City of Light for the first time!

Tonight, the news mentioned that the COVID-19 virus has arrived in France and is spreading. When I was in New York last week, no one talked about it, and suddenly it's a thing. It seems extremely contagious and life-threatening, so perhaps I should wait before returning to Caveau de la Huchette.

Sunday 8 March

Yesterday, I walked almost ten miles (fifteen kilometers), according to my phone's health app. The weather was glorious. I explored the Sixth, Fifth (Latin Quarter), and Fourth (the Marais) Arrondissements, savoring the people, the architecture, and the scent of buttery croissants wafting from corner *boulangeries*. In the evening, I walked to l'Entrepôt near Métro Pernety in the adjacent Fourteenth Arrondissement to see a salsa band. Alone, I enjoyed a mojito (well, two) and fond memories of listening to salsa bands there with daughter Hanna and Trocadéro Man during prior visits. Listening to the pulsating music and observing skilled dancers of all ages— older couples who had perfected their choreographies decades earlier and younger ones exhibiting enviable athleticism—reinforced my urge to improve my own salsa dancing. I would prefer to learn with a romantic partner; will the Law of Attraction work for that?

Today was grey, and I met Guy at porte Maillot. He was annoyed that I had waited at the 'wrong' spot, asserting that he had given me clear directions, which he obviously had not. Red Flag Number Two. I feel my relationship color perception improving. I did like hopping into his Audi A6: comfortable, safe, familiar. I brought him a five-hundred-gram box of chocolate from Mococha on the rue Mouffetard, my favorite *chocolatier*, which he tossed into the back seat without a 'thank you'.

Off we went to his 'farm' near Chartres. I figured he introduced it as a kind of Wild Kingdom display to impress a potential mate— like a male peacock opening its stunning fan. It was a judicious move on Guy's part, because the choices people make—those fortunate enough to enjoy the luxury of options—reveal a lot about them. Seeing how they live gives potential partners the opportunity to discover whether living conditions are compatible. I found his home cozy. Perhaps I had assigned red flags too precipitously?

Guy's centuries-old half-timber farmhouse with adjacent buildings lovingly restored according to Guy's design form a square around a courtyard of still-dormant rose bushes. It was tastefully furnished with worn leather sofas, comfy armchairs upholstered in cream-colored chintz with trapunto birds and flowers, a seven-teenth-century library table from a monastery decommissioned during the French Revolution, and just the right number of assorted antiques, mementoes, and artworks, including a tabletop Barye bronze rabbit and a Barbizon painting by Narcisse Díaz of the forest at twilight. Guy had retained the living room's enormous open fireplace, almost big enough to stand in, which most French homeowners remove for some mysterious reason. In Paris, although lighting fires indoors is illegal, removing them seems an act of archi-tectural desecration. Guy lit a fire to take the edge off the chill in the unheated house. The ground level has hexagonal terracotta tile floors, and I wondered if they were a reference to the nickname for France, '*Hexagone*'. Such floors are common in older, provincial French homes. Walls and ceilings have exposed beams. The place has exactly the kind of perks I adore: a twenty-meter-long swim-ming pool, a tennis court, a sauna in the pool house, and a beautiful garden. Along the edge of the property lies an orchard beside a babbling brook, just past a Kate Greenaway-worthy picket fence and garden gate.

I mentally moved in and envisioned a typical day: an early morning swim to the chirping of birds, studying clouds as I slice through the water, completing my one kilometer of backstroke. Then, on the flagstone terrace, a breakfast of fresh peaches, straw-berries (in France, there are at least four varieties to choose from), farm fresh yogurt, and coffee, whose aromas compete with the perfumes of the garden that change subtly as spring yields to summer.

Afterward, a few hours of writing in the shade of the orchard, followed by a lunch of garden-fresh salad embellished by local cheeses or—perhaps more traditionally—a rabbit terrine with Mona Lisa (yes, that is an actual variety) potatoes. Next, salad and cheese, according to French custom, washed down by a glass of wine of whatever hue, chosen from his ample cellar. For dessert, a piece of artisanal chocolate with coffee followed by a nap in the grass under the shade of a fruit tree.

Well rested, I might take a bike ride or play tennis, followed by more writing or reading, and enjoy a light supper on the terrace as the sun goes to bed—as the French say, *le coucher de soleil*—and a pleasant intoxication permeates one's willingly vulnerable body, the consequence of a day lived in harmony with oneself and the world and the wine and perfumes of nature, which intensify with the coolness of evening. Afterward, a game of chess, a film, or a walk, ending with a soothing stint in the sauna, whose intense heat coaxes mind and muscle into a state of soporific relaxation. Finally, the deepest, most tranquil sleep imaginable.

Ah yes, I had the future mapped out in a matter of minutes. Guy showed me around. I wasn't expecting to be accosted without warning while sitting with him on a bed looking at a vacation picture of a younger, more attractive Guy with his four children. Absolutely no romantic lead in—no hand holding, no brushing shoulders, no kiss, NOTHING! What is he, fifteen? I gently rebuffed him, telling him it was too soon, and he, reluctantly if courteously, removed his tongue from my mouth and his hand from my thigh. Again, he seemed annoyed. I didn't expect Date Number Two to be a sex audition. So different from my second date with Trocadéro Man: lunch with Mom and a horseback-ride in the forest.

We went for lunch to a nearby village, sharing melt-in-your-mouth foie gras and relishing steak *à point* with frites while conversing about family and travels. After crème brûlée and coffee, we departed for Chartres, whose cathedral, in the midst of a decades-long cleaning, resembled a sooty black and white cookie. I recalled my All Souls' Day visit with Harriet and Frank and our tour with Malcolm Miller, who had so fallen in love with the cathedral in the early 1970s that he abandoned his partially-written dissertation, rented a cathedral-view apartment across the street, and had since—and to this day, I assume—made a living giving enthralling, pay-as-you-like tours to appreciative visitors. I had not remembered all the headless saints inside, decapitated during the French Revolution; *what became of all those heads*, I wondered. The windows are spectacular. A bible in pictures for illiterate medieval citizens, but without a pair of binoculars one sees only the lowest scenes distinctly. Didn't this bother visitors in the past?

As a sign of friendly encouragement after what for him might simply have been an awkward premature attempt at intimacy, I laced my arm through his as we walked around town, but he was as unresponsive as a corpse. After five minutes or so, I unlaced. No reaction. Good French language practice anyway. I've resolved not to squander my time sending 'smiles' to 'suitable' prospects suggested by the app. Why am I still making an effort to meet Mr. Right? Insecurity? Desperation to conform to societal norms?

Wednesday 11 March

This crisp, sunny morning, I walked through le Luco and up the rue Soufflot, admiring with each step the stately Panthéon looming ahead, an eighteenth-century reincarnation of the ancient Roman monument. Its architect, Jacques-Germain Soufflot, envisioned a majestic, central-plan church, but the anti-clerical fanaticism of the French Revolution transformed it into a resting place for civilian heroes. I passed the café where I used to wait for Hanna after her French class during the fall of her junior year abroad and threaded my way to the open-air market at place Monge, 'my' *marché* while living on the nearby rue Mouffetard in Spring 2018.

The main draw for me is a cheese-stand selling the best aged cow's-milk Gouda and Brie with black truffles I have ever tasted. It is run by a mother and son team. "*Bonjour, Madame, comment-allez vous?*" they inquire even if I have been absent for a year, a greeting that instills a reassuring sense of belonging, even if temporary and sporadic. They both have rosy cheeks and the stolid physiques of food lovers—*gourmands*—a passion they share by offering slivers of cheeses they cut for other customers. Although the pair seems motivated by an impulse to delight and educate, it's a brilliant marketing strategy. In addition to my usual order, I wound up buying an aged Comté, superfluous but too delicious to pass up. They gifted me a small cheese, probably something that needed to be consumed in the near future but a generous gesture, nonetheless.

From there, I traipsed over to the rue Mouffetard and Mococha. I should be on a first—or at least a last—name basis with the soft-spoken woman who owns the shop since I visited weekly in 2018 and will continue to patronize it as long as it exists and whenever I am in Paris. I think of her as Madame Chocolat. Her prices are significantly lower than those at other artisanal chocolate shops, and I love how she carries only delicacies produced by three master *chocolatiers*, judiciously chosen and located elsewhere in France. Their wares entice from three wood-and-glass cases that look like they may once have displayed botanical specimens at the nearby Jardin des Plantes.

As I began to select the chocolates she tenderly arranged in the small brown box, she asked, "do I remember correctly that you like only dark chocolate?" a question that made me happy because it made me feel like a regular.

"Yes, and nothing with fruit or gluten," I added.

After ceremoniously tying the box with a black ribbon imprinted with the shop's name in silver letters and placing my little *boîte* in one of those fancy French bags with rope handles that make every purchase feel luxurious, she offered me a *douceur*, a half-size sample of one of her chocolates, presented via an elegant pair of embossed silver tongs. She logged my name into her computer for future frequent shopper discounts and then—as is her custom—carried my purchase to the door, held it open for me, and handed me my bag.

"Thank you, madame, have a good day. See you very soon."

I never received that kind of reception at Teuscher at Rockefeller Center no matter how often I went.

From Mococha, I headed downhill to La Fontaine aux Vins, owned by a friendly couple and their son. Across the way, there's a wineshop in which I have never set foot; it would feel disloyal. At La Fontaine, one of the menfolk hovers outside amid the bins of cheaper wines, happy to advise if asked. Inside, *Maman* works the register, always appreciative of my purchase, no matter how trifling. They wrap each bottle in tissue paper, a ritual that reminds me of times past at American department stores, which once employed professionals who gift-wrapped for free. My patient mother almost always indulged my wish to transform utilitarian purchases into a festive collection of elegantly papered and beribboned boxes reminiscent of Christmas and birthdays.

I turned east to the Grand Mosque, constructed in the 1920s and inspired by the el-Quraouyyîn mosque in Fes. While living on the rue Mouffetard, I wrote there regularly, sitting either in its tiled interior or its lovely garden, peaceful until *lycéens* arrive for after-school socializing. Today, once installed in one of the garden's tiled and roofed niches and before settling down to work, I daydreamed about my Morocco sojourn with Thor in 2018: the air perfumed by honey mingled with coriander, ginger, and leather, the intimidating maze of thirty-six thousand streets in ancient Fes navigable only with the aid of a native guide, the alluring strangeness of Arab and Berber cultures, the stunning architectural contrast between white-washed walls and colorful, symmetrically-patterned tiles and rugs, deliciously sweet, spicy tagine dinners enjoyed in the safe harbor of exotic and lovingly restored *riads* with only a few steps to a sumptuous bed chamber evocative of *A Thousand and One Nights*.

Today, I wore my favorite red leather coat, acquired in Fes. Thor got it for me in a kind of buy-one-get-one-free-offer. The unexpected gift was more the result of our vigilant tour guide, although I shouldn't impugn Thor's generosity. While Mohammad took a prayer break, he abandoned us briefly to peruse an expansive, multi-story leather shop. It overlooked a courtyard of dye-filled stone vats I remembered seeing pictured in *National Geographic*. The shop overflowed with coats and ottomans, slippers and wallets, and one inhaled the pungent perfume of leather with every breath. Thor found an attaché case and a jacket he wanted. He bargained a bit and paid, satisfied with his purchases. When Mohammad returned, he examined Thor's purchases approvingly and asked to see the receipt. One glance and you could see his blood pressure rise.

"There are too many zeros!" he exclaimed.

Mohammad demanded to see the manager and gesticulated wildly, speaking sternly in Arabic at the rattled fellow. The dispute didn't take long to resolve, and one is never sure how much is theater since I assumed Mohammad received kickbacks for bringing clients. The result was that I got to pick out anything I wanted in the shop for 'free'. Thor seemed pleased by his unplanned generosity. Remembering fondly the red leather jacket I had bought in Stockholm in the 1990s and lived in for several weeks before a thief stole it at the Gävle train station, I selected a knee-length, collarless, form-fitting red coat. It was love at first sight and my best souvenir from a memorable trip to a strange and wonderful land. Mohammad enjoyed our complete confidence from that moment forward.

The mosque waiters circulate with silver trays carrying mugs of hot sweet tea, one of the best bargains in Paris at €2.50. As at all establishments in the land of *flaneurs*, readers, and writers, the waiters allow you to sit as long as you like without inquiring how you are doing or if you would like anything else, questions that always feels like virtual hands shoving me out the door. There, I read articles relating to *Denmark and the Invention of Modern Happiness*, a monograph I have been working on for far too long. For some mysterious reason—perhaps because I secretly think it will provide clues to my own—I decided to return to it after a few years' hiatus during the fall while on sabbatical in Greifswald, a walled, medieval town on Germany's Baltic coast. Now, I am determined to finish it, although there is more research to do first in Copenhagen.

Tonight at 8 p.m., President Macron, Head of State—*Chef d'État*, as he is often referred to—gave a speech broadcast on all channels. Seated at his desk and filmed close up—a tactic conveying the impression that I sat across from him and he was speaking to me directly—Macron announced measures intended to impede the spread of COVID-19. Cases have risen sharply in France, and the World Health Organization has declared a pandemic. As a result, non-essential businesses will close on Saturday the 14th and beginning Tuesday the 17th at midnight, *confinement* (lockdown). Apparently, the virus is spreading everywhere in Europe. Worst hit are Italy and Spain, but it is also running rampant in the Grand Est, the eastern part of France along the German border. *Confinement* will last for at least a month.

During that time, one must remain at home, and all schools and universities will close. No one may wander more than one kilometer from their residence or remain outdoors in public for more than one hour at a time. That certainly puts a damper on my recreational program. The only allowable reasons for leaving home are shopping for necessities (meaning food and medical supplies), jogging and dog walking, doctor visits, and work. All 'non-essential' stores will close, as will theaters, restaurants, cafés and bars, all parks and gardens, and all museums and cinemas. Apparently, wine and liquor stores are considered essential, while book- and clothing stores are not. Maybe alcohol is considered therapeutic. Or an essential beverage, "the blood of the earth," as Renaud sings in *"Hexagone."*

When you venture out, you must bring an affidavit (*attestation*) that includes your name, date of birth, address, and the date, time, and reason for your departure. A printable version is available on a government website, but since I don't have a printer, I hope that neatly hand-written information suffices in the event of a police control. I don't have much paper either, so I plan to simply cross off old dates and times and substitute new ones. Public transportation will run on a limited schedule. Macron also enumerated the *gestes barrières* (hygienic measures) now in force: wearing a mask in indoor public places, keeping a one-meter distance from others, washing hands frequently, and, if that is not possible, using sanitizer.

Impeccably dressed and with a solemn, boyish charm, President Macron opened his address with a reassuring "dear citizens," asserting with the confidence of a coach's pre-game pep talk that together we will triumph over this viral enemy "at all costs." His refreshing 'we're all in this together' attitude demonstrated faith in the public's ability to understand and support his logical if difficult decision. Committed to transparency, Macron detailed the international course of the pandemic thus far and presented the scientific data that prompted government action. He spoke in an inspiring, authoritative manner that made me feel proud to be included in this collaborative effort. I've never felt this way after an American presidential speech nor after a Swedish or German one. He closed with the traditional and rousing declaration, "long live the Republic; long live France!"

How could I leave after that? I'm part of the team; President Macron spoke to me personally and made me feel safe and patriotic because of the concern he evidenced for the collective well-being of the nation under his care. In addition, this unexpected situation feels thrilling and historic. Like when I was in Paris during the Bataclan massacre on November 13, 2015. Hanna was visiting from Stockholm for a few days. We went to the newly re-opened Rodin Museum that sunny Friday afternoon while she played text tag with a friend who lived near the canal Saint-Martin, an ethnically diverse hipster neighborhood where the most blood was spilled in a handful of attacks that ravaged several cafés and, especially, Bataclan, a popular music venue that held a sold-out concert that evening. Her friend Vlad frequented one of those cafés and they could have been dining there together at the moment of the murderous attacks. But in a fortunate case of serendipity, Vlad worked late, leaving Hanna to spend Friday evening with North African friends. I had no idea where they went and spent the evening at my Bonne Nouvelle apartment searching for a French language course that started on Monday because that was the purported reason for my stay. I checked e-mail around 9:30 p.m. and found a dozen desperate messages from Hanna's dad, mentioning the attacks and asking if Hanna were safe. I had no idea.

By then, the self-declared Islamic terrorists were in the process of executing dozens of concertgoers as the band Eagles of Death Metal performed in Bataclan's darkened auditorium. I called Hanna, who had watched the news of the first attacks (three suicide bombers) near Stade de France, where a soccer game had been in progress. She and her friends were at a nearby café and wisely decided to leave. By then, public transportation had shut down, so Hanna called an Uber. Her friends—demoralized by yet another event that would make life more difficult for law-abiding Muslims—kindly waited with her.

Attacks occurred all over the city that evening, seemingly at random, and no one felt safe anywhere in public. It was a nightmarish Friday-the-thirteenth that no one who lived through it will forget. It's France's 9/11. When Hanna arrived home, we found a half-dozen terrified twenty-somethings who had been socializing at a nearby café sheltering in our courtyard. Once upstairs, we called Dad and, on the BBC internet channel, watched together live coverage of the massacre-in-progress. A journalist living in the alley behind Bataclan live-streamed the horrific scenario: concertgoers dragging wounded friends from emergency exits to safety, some lowering themselves and then jumping from second story windows, others helplessly cradling the bodies of friends as life flowed from them.

Surreal frontline war reportage was happening a fifteen-minute stroll from where Hanna and I safely sat. That evening Islamic terrorists shot and killed eighty-six at Bataclan and another forty elsewhere, including at Vlad's café. Although public transportation resumed the following day, public buildings remained closed for days, and Paris became peculiarly, if pleasantly, deserted. Not a soul loitered in the pyramid plaza at the Louvre's main entrance, and few dared occupy outdoor tables at cafés despite the unseasonably warm weather. This post-attack Paris evoked in me nostalgia for the enchanting and relatively tourist-free Paris prior to 1990, before the Internet, airline deregulation, and relaxed travel restrictions for Chinese and Eastern Europeans flooded the City of Light with legions of visitors, making Paris feel more like Disney's Epcot than a European capital with roots dating to ancient Rome.

Despite their vast social differences and fervent political engagement, the French exhibit inspiring social solidarity. Although I won't be able to wander freely during *confinement*—a gentler term than lockdown, a term that suggests concern for citizen health rather than a quasi-military response to a foreign threat—its restrictions feel comforting. I suppose I could leave for Stockholm, the U.S., or Germany, where I have chosen family. Still, although habitually more mobile than most, once I have made plans, I usually stick to them. And with the freedom provided by a European Union passport (thank you, philandering Swedish Ex), I can stay in Europe as long as I like without worrying about visas.

I suppose I won't be dating for a while either. That feels fine after today's late-afternoon disaster: coffee at Les Éditeurs, located at the carrefour de l'Odéon, with Cédric, a shabbily dressed yet impeccably groomed, self-identified intellectual. I thought the place felt familiar then remembered it as the former location of my favorite *choucroute* restaurant, Le Chope d'Alsace. I haven't thought about it for ages, although in the 1980s I went there once a visit even in summer, a season when sauerkraut and pork isn't the kind of heavy-weight comfort food for which one usually has a hankering. The date was weird; he seemed to be interviewing women in public. When I arrived, a woman was getting up from his table, where there were two empty coffee cups. Cédric ordered two more (I wonder how caffeinated he was) and I discovered that he did not even live in this bourgeois neighborhood but over in the Nineteenth Arrondissement, the least fashionable of Paris's twenty arrondissements.

Cédric unselfconsciously asked me financial questions to which I did not respond. After coffee, I accompanied him to the huge Left Bank bookstore Joseph Gibert, where he bought a book. Before we parted ways, he grabbed me and kissed me in a way that felt boundary-violating not to mention unsafe, given what we had just learned about the transmissibility of COVID-19. I stopped by the Delacroix Museum enroute home for a cleansing moment of solitude. Place Furstenburg, the tiny square where it's located—always intimate, charming, and tranquil—never seems to change. It was featured on the very first postcard my parents sent to me on their very first trip to Europe, to Paris.

On the way home, I purchased a thermometer at a pharmacy and took my temperature for the first time in years since an early sign of COVID-19 is fever. Mine registered 36.2 degrees Celsius (97.2 degrees Fahrenheit). Because I have a naturally low body temperature I thought it prudent to start tracking my temperature, so if I do get a fever the doctors won't think my temperature is normal. From now on, I'll check twice a day just to be safe.

Tuesday 17 March

St. Patrick's Day, an ordinary day in Paris. It feels strange though, like an abandoned city, an accurate assessment to judge from my neighborhood, Vavin. *Confinement* and school closings prompted a mass exodus over the weekend; journalists estimate that five hundred thousand people departed Paris. A steady stream of young people headed to the Gare Montparnasse dragging suitcases, and I imagine the same scenario unfolded at Paris's other *gares*. On the surrounding streets, families loaded double-parked cars with suitcases, sporting equipment, pets, and bags of provisions before heading to their *résidences secondaires*. With schools, parks, businesses, and recreational centers closed, pretty much anyone who could, it seems, left town. Now, the neighborhood is quiet, its streets deserted.

The Sixth Arrondissement—and my corner of it especially—has a lot of schools, particularly institutions of higher education (administration, where Macron studied, archaeology, pharmacy, Slavic languages), high schools (*lycées*), and junior highs (*collèges*). Students attending universities and schools of higher education often live in tiny, barely bed-sized *studettes* located in dormitories or in *chambres de bonne* (maid's rooms) on the top floors of apartment buildings, usually without elevators. With classes temporarily online, students with families elsewhere departed in droves. Their decision is understandable: isolation in a cell-like room for an indefinite period would be a psychological and physical hardship in a shuttered Paris. My temperature this morning was 35.7 degrees Celsius.

At 8 p.m., President Macron gave another speech, opening dramatically with "We are at war!" ("*Nous sommes en guerre!*"), a health war in which every citizen has a vital role to play. He reiterated the *confinement* and social distancing measures in force for the coming month and promised to provide updates every two weeks. This reassured citizens that the government would be in constant conversation with all relevant actors to evaluate the situation as it develops and to make appropriate adjustments in restrictions (or freedoms).

Macron announced that—to the extent possible—employers should allow workers to telecommute ('home office', as it's called in Europe). He detailed regulations for partial furloughs and financial compensation for affected workers and businesses privileging culture workers, who find themselves suddenly unemployed. He encouraged social solidarity, which would lead to France's victory in this unprecedented war if everyone did their part by staying indoors or actively saving lives. The government, Macron affirmed, was committed to protecting its citizens and the French way of life, regardless of the financial cost (*"quoi qu'il en coute"*). His thirty-minute speech ended with the traditional declaration "long live France" (*"vive la France"*), an attitude reflecting the core republican principle of the separation of church and state. One will *never* hear a public official in France (or anywhere else in Europe) utter the words "God bless X," since that would violate the foundational idea of secular republics like France and the United States. American public officials who routinely utter those words clearly don't understand how anti-clerical America's Founding Fathers were.

News channels now display banners at the bottom of their screens that announce how many Frenchmen are infected with COVID-19 and how many have died, that day and cumulatively. Today, there were 450 deaths reported and 12,000 total infections. My temperature was 36.1 degrees Celsius. I Face-timed with my graduate student Claire, who will soon leave Stockholm for Oslo in order to continue her dissertation research but will have to quarantine with her Norwegian husband for fourteen days upon arrival. They had wanted to spend those two weeks at a cabin in the mountains, but the government won't allow it, so they will stay in Oslo on the family boat, with family members bringing them supplies.

Monday 23 March

Confinement Week Two begins. I am enjoying it and have established a routine: wake up, look at email and Facebook (I know I shouldn't do that first thing, but I can't help myself), meditate for twenty minutes. Sometimes, I take a mini-nap after meditating. Then, thirty minutes of yoga or exercise, followed by oatmeal eaten while watching the news and doom-scrolling websites: Foxnews, CNN, *Dagens Nyheter* (Sweden), *Le Monde* (France) *Washington Post*, Al Jazeera, *The Guardian*, *The Atlantic*, and *Süddeutsche Zeitung*, the main newspaper of Munich, where I lived for a year in the mid-1990s.

Even though most discussion on French channels concerns the

coronavirus and is repetitive, it's also hard to turn off. I find myself riveted to testimony from politicians, medical experts, journalists, and affected workers. I, the news-averse, am becoming a news junkie while improving my French. All channels frequently repeat the recommended hygienic measures: hand washing, distancing, coughing into one's elbow, mask wearing, and using disposable hankies (I guess a lot of Frenchmen are like me and still use fabric ones).

Now that I can't stray far from home or for long and Paris cannot offer its usual profusion of distractions, I'm digging into my Danish happiness book: reading research texts online, delving into the articles I have scanned, and writing chapters. I haven't been outdoors since Friday and am well-stocked with necessities, so I'll stay indoors for the next few days despite the sunny weather. Luckily, in France there's no lack of toilet paper (or anything else), apparently a pressing concern in the U.S. French TV shows American store shelves emptied of this marginally essential product.

Outdoors suddenly feels fraught with danger—almost like living in a war zone—although thankfully not chaotic and terrifying, as the U.S. appears. Still, every person one passes, every thing one touches, offers the possibility of contagion, and COVID-19 truly seems like a virus one wants to avoid like the plague, as my father used to say. A New Jersey friend related her harrowing return from Manhattan the evening New York began shutting down. After resorting to multiple means of transportation—subways, busses, trains, and finally a ferry across the Hudson—she finally arrived home after many hours, an adventure during which she apparently became infected, communicating it to her husband while remaining asymptomatic. She said physical distancing is difficult while living under the same roof. He doesn't feel well and has lost his senses of taste and smell. Since he's a musician, as long as he keeps his senses of pitch, rhythm, and humor he might not mind so much. And, hopefully, his senses will soon return.

Today, the total number of deaths in France reached 860 with 20,000 infections. My temperature is 35.0 degrees Celsius. I video chatted with Thor in Copenhagen and Hanna, still with her boyfriend, Dani, on Phu Quoc, a virus-free island paradise in Vietnam. I hope it stays that way and they remain in that safe haven until this blows over. Seeing her videos of sunsets over the sea and palm trees wafting in gentle breezes makes me wish I had stayed at Playa Lagartillo, Costa Rica, where I spent two blissful weeks in February. Still, it is hard to complain about Paris even with restrictions.

Unlike my extrovert friends, I am enjoying *confinement*. It gives me structure. Walking the streets of my one-kilometer radius, eyes fixed upward to study the magnificent facades lining the streets without concern for bumping into pedestrians or getting hit by vehicles, is delightful. The big and usually busy intersection of Raspail-Montparnasse is now so sparsely trafficked that one can brazenly jaywalk and gaze impudently down nearly empty boulevards. It's quiet—little noise except for sirens. The boulevards near me provide convenient access to several hospitals, and ambulances carrying the sick traverse them with increasing frequency. Otherwise, one often hears church bells, a phenomenon I've never connected with life in Paris. In small towns, yes, but not in the capital. And the air smells like springtime rather than exhaust. I expected Bev to arrive tomorrow from New Jersey and stay for a week, but that is canceled. Madeleine from Milan intended to visit me in Warsaw during my anticipated, month-long stay there in May, but that, too, will be postponed indefinitely.

Thursday 26 March

Yesterday, I chatted with Marian in New York, Kathy in Bregenz, and Hanna on Phu Quoc. I'm grateful for the Internet, our collective conduit to the outside world. New York seems scary and disorganized, Bregenz seems its congenial tranquil self, although social-distancing and hygienic measures are recommended, and Phu Quoc, devoid of Chinese tourists and where the sole case was rapidly identified and isolated, sounds like paradise. This pandemic experience is fascinating. It forces one to live in the moment with acute awareness of how suddenly the world can change. Today, my temperature was 36.4 degrees Celsius, and there are now 1,696 deaths with 29,000 total infections in France.

The situation in the U.S. appears terrifyingly anarchic, even hostile, with anti-maskers behaving as if forced to wear hair shirts. Video clips of pandemic scenes in the U.S. that appear on European television resemble outtakes of *Idiocracy*. I'm thankful to be in Paris, where the situation feels well-managed, scientific studies inform policy, and people behave considerately toward each other, a reflection of the impressive degree of civility in France. In fact, it's the politest country I've ever visited. I like being addressed as 'madame', and hearing people frequently utter '*pardon*', when they've inconvenienced someone, as when a man crosses the threshold ahead of the women he accompanies. No one in a doctor's office, for instance, would ever address you by your first name, a habit that for me is the verbal equivalent of uninvited touching. In France and Germany, it's considered rude behavior, as it once was in the U.S.

Masks are obligatory only indoors; outdoors, people steer clear of one another. I've taken to walking in the middle of the street. Such freedom! The rue de la Grande-Chaumière is now unusually quiet with restaurants, hotels, and commercial establishments closed. The Franprix grocery on the rue Delambre has hung sheets of thick plastic at the cash registers to protect cashiers from customers. It's probably too late to invest in companies producing plastic, but I imagine their businesses are booming. Most store employees wear gloves as do many people in general, including me, sometimes. And bringing home groceries has become time-consuming, with the imperative to sanitize every surface. Friends in Buffalo have set up a station in their garage where they systematically wipe down groceries with alcohol or Clorox before allowing them into the house. Others leave items outside for a few days before bringing them indoors. Is this necessary? Well, better safe than sorry, I suppose. I've joined the trend, and my fruits and vegetables have never been cleaner.

Paper signs and cloth banners hang from windows and balconies thanking health care and other frontline workers for their bravery and service. All over the neighborhood—in shop windows, on kiosks and newsstands, and plastered on buildings—are signs: "Thank you to the health personnel and all those who take care of us for your courage, solidarity, humility, humanity, empathy, strength, and community spirit." Such a heartening contrast to the U.S., where President Trump refers to COVID-19 as the Chinese virus and does nothing to hinder its rampage. The East and West coasts seem to be trying to enforce—or at least encourage—sensible hygienic measures. New York City is in a terrible state, with rented, refrigerated, morgue trucks storing rapidly accumulating bodies. In France, when one hospital reaches capacity, patients are conveyed to locations with bed space and sufficient personnel by ambulance, train, or helicopter. Thus, it makes sense for me to stay in Europe until the pandemic ends (or at least decelerates significantly) if for no other reason than should I get sick, I would get competent and cheaper treatment than in the U.S., even *with* health insurance.

French *esprit de corps* inspires. Every evening at 8 p.m. people repair to their balconies, terraces, and windows to clap in honor of first responders and essential personnel. I do, too, despite living on a courtyard. This activity performs a reassuring sense of community at a time when many suffer from isolation and loneliness. It also evidences shared values that include wanting to keep each other safe. In contrast, the pandemic seems to have fostered selfish, fear-motivated instincts among Americans at a time when the need for trust is at its zenith.

My ticket to see Anna Netrebko in *Adriana Lecouvreur* at Opera Bastille on April 27 has now been refunded and my teaching gig in Warsaw for the month of May officially cancelled. I guess teaching in Shanghai in June is not going to happen either. Well, more free time. And in Paris! In other news, Guy texted me from his farm to inform me that he had fallen from a ladder and broken a wrist. No 'how are you doing?'. While his accident is unfortunate, it seems weird to reach out for sympathy when he clearly doesn't give a flying how-do-you-do about how I'm faring. I responded with an 'oh no! I hope you're better soon'. No immediate response. Maybe a narcissist? A misogynist? Whatever.

Sunday 29 March

Weeks ago, Marie and Gregoire invited me for a brunchtime celebration of spring today at their home in bucolic Saint Mammès,
where the Seine crosses the Loing, an old, lazy river that winds its
way through the countryside with villages and mossy stone bridges
hugging its parklike banks at intervals. That got cancelled at the
beginning of *confinement*. In the past few weeks, I have cancelled
more plans than I have made. My calendar is empty, and instead of
noting in-person activities I record those with whom I phone- or
video-chat.

COVID-19 deaths in France now hover around 600 per day.
Thus far, there are 2,600 deaths and a total of 40,000 infections.
France has set up drive-in testing sites throughout the country, and
one can also get tested at a local laboratory, which in Paris are as
common as *boulangeries* and *fleuristes*. And still, the three major news
channels carry full-time COVID-19 news. Channel 14 offers *collège*
courses in math, French, and history during the day. I occasionally
watch at lunchtime, hoping to improve my math along with my
French. The virus situation is dire in Spain and Italy, where the
entire nations are 'locked down'. In Germany things seem better,
with each *Bundesland* (state) making its own rules. Christin in Greifswald will soon have a baby whom she will not be able to introduce
to its grandparents, aunts, and uncles until the state of Mecklen-
burg-Vorpommern reopens its currently closed borders. My temperature today is 35.9 degrees Celsius.

I walked by le Luco today and saw the tulips unfurling in yellows
and reds. I envy the gardeners in their gated paradise, cutting grass,
planting flowers, pruning, and tilling. Fortunately, padlocks cannot
prevent the perfumes of nature from inundating the vacant streets
of the surrounding neighborhood, and that I can enjoy.

Chapter 3
April: A Smaller, Quieter Paris and a Final Farewell

Wednesday 1 April

Another pandemic cancellation. I was supposed to dine with Emiliana, a young Polish colleague who researches Scandinavian art and should have been on the way from Warsaw to her boyfriend in Bordeaux via nearby Gare Montparnasse. We met a few years ago, when she was an undergraduate at Warsaw University, where I gave a series of lectures on Scandinavian art. We next met at a conference I organized in Berlin, where she gave a brilliant talk about clouds in Scandinavian painting, charming the other participants by wearing a blouse she sewed herself from blue and white cloud fabric.

Walt in Cleveland hasn't left his house much in weeks, and helpful friends stop by to drop off food. He's one of those cooks for whom nothing goes to waste: not a bone, not a tendon, not a root, not a leaf. If I had to pick the person with whom I would most happily be stranded in dire circumstances—when one must survive for an extended period with a limited food supply—there's no question that I would choose the resourceful and ingenious Walt, secure in the knowledge that I'd be enjoying gourmet meals long after the neighbors were frying worms and making grass salads. The fact that he's a talented musician and has the most interesting library of any of my friends seals the deal.

I'm frustrated by the restriction to shop in my neighborhood despite the ease of finding necessities. Open-air markets are closed, including Marché Monge, although it seems that shopping outdoors would be safer. I'm tempted to venture to the rue Mouffetard just for wine and chocolate but will stay local. I'm not even sure Mococha is open. Do chocolate shops provide essential services? I certainly think so.

My world has shrunk, and I've adjusted. It's a moment when one must invent one's own happiness. I think about my Wednesday shopping excursions to Marché Monge with the same resigned nostalgia that I remember walks in the woods holding hands with my long-deceased father. It's odd the way time can collapse. Once something is beyond reach, it doesn't matter if it is long gone, far away, or a twenty-minute walk during pandemic times. This evening, my temperature is 35.5 degrees Celsius. The French death toll has reached 4,000, 500 more since yesterday, and the number of infections is almost 55,000. Twenty-five percent of those hospitalized are in ICU and of those, thirty-five percent are under forty.

Thursday 2 April

My temperature is 36.2 degrees Celsius, and there are 4,500 total deaths in France. Today, I video chatted with the very pregnant Christin in Greifswald. Her daughter will be a very lucky girl; I cannot envision a more creative, insightful, loving, and patient mother. Mine was just loving and patient. I gave future daughter a pair of my soft, sustainable MooseBooties that I sell on Etsy and a medical sheepskin, an item crucial for Hanna when she was a baby. Because we traveled a lot and took her everywhere, the sheepskin accompanied her, so she would feel safe and 'home' when nestled in it, a strategy that worked beautifully. Hanna even slept soundly when tucked under tables at Slavic Macedonian/Serbian/Croatian or Greek parties, where throngs danced and socialized in smoky rooms animated by deafening live folk music. At one point, Christin excused herself to go to the bathroom. I saw her stand up. She looked at me, astonished, exclaimed, "oh, my water broke," called out for her husband, and hung up. I hope she's OK.

Today, I also talked to Hanna, who informed me that Dani wants to return to Stockholm from Phu Quoc, still infection-free. Now, with the pandemic out of control in Sweden, he wants to leave Paradise? Hanna is happy there, and I wish I were with her. I can't imagine a better place to be right now than a disease-free tropical island with my daughter!

Sunday 5 April

There are currently more than 6,000 dead and 25,000 hospitalized in France. I chatted with Thor in Copenhagen and folkdance friend Mara in Oslo. She's disappointed that the pandemic prevents her from spending Passover in Israel and seeing her daughter and grandchildren in person. European countries except Sweden have instituted similar approaches, usually 'hard' *confinements*—as in France—and often quarantines upon arrival. Sweden stands regrettably alone in its unwavering commitment to the questionable principle of 'herd immunity' on the advice of its overconfident health minister, Anders Tegnell.

I've always had difficulty explaining Swedish hubris to people. Not all Swedes are supercilious, of course, especially not *my* friends, but it's a pervasive national characteristic difficult to explain to non-Scandinavians because Swedes put on such a good, apparently sensible and compassionate, show. Danes, Finns, and Norwegians recognize and are often exasperated by Swedish exceptionalism but now the secret is out, and the rest of Europe—and the world—is taking notice. Incredulous French correspondents roam the streets of Stockholm filming crowded cafés, restaurants, and entertainment venues and questioning smirking Swedes about their non-existent concerns for virus spread.

"What's going on there? Why aren't Swedes taking precautionary measures?" perplexed French journalists wonder.

"We're just a small country," they respond, "and we don't

embrace intimacy in any event," ignoring the fact that cinema goers worldwide have seen Ingmar Bergman films. I'm in favor of non-conformity when appropriate and when it will do no harm, but this COVID-19 pandemic does not seem to be one of those cases. Swedes, unlike their Nordic neighbors, generally lack humility, flaunting an unwarranted sense of superiority on a variety of topics, including war.

"No wars since Napoléon," they like to say, as if they've outgrown them, like diapers or afternoon naps. Sweden considers itself a country that has reached maturity and views the childish antics of other nations with patronizing disdain. Consistent with this egotism, Swedish professionals generally believe that their command of English—spoken and written—is as good, if not better, than that of native speakers and have a troubling passive-aggressive approach to inclusivity. Yes, it does have a policy of accepting refugees from war-torn locales including Chile, Eretria, and most recently, Bosnia, Iraq, and Syria. Still, I have witnessed its mortifying lack of compassion second-hand.

One afternoon in 2007, I was at the public library in Alvesta, a small town in southern Sweden where Iraqi refugees were housed. There, I met forty-two-year-old Omar, an Iraqi, at the computer terminal next to mine. He didn't want to bother me but desperately needed help filling out forms required to appeal the decision excluding his twenty-one-year-old twin daughters from joining him in Sweden along with his wife and sixteen-year-old son. He was beside himself with worry and frustration.

Four years earlier, Omar and his family had enjoyed a comfort-able, secular, middle-class existence in Bagdad. They had well-paying jobs (he, a successful engineer with his own firm that special-ized in bridge building, his wife, a high school math teacher), their children attended top-notch private schools, they owned two cars, had a pool in the backyard, and a live-in housekeeper. The 2003 U.S. invasion threw their lives into chaos. They fled to safety and assumed that either the war would be short-lived and they would soon resume their lives in Bagdad or that once in Syria they would be able to get jobs and refashion them.

Forbidden from working in Syria like all Iraqi refugees, Omar vigorously yet unsuccessfully sought asylum in many countries. After two years, and with a dwindling bank account, he did something he never could have imagined: smuggle himself to the West, to Sweden, with the expectation of arranging for his family to join him. After all, they were middle-class professionals eager to rejoin the labor force, and the entire family spoke fluent English and would learn Swedish quickly. Omar paid €20,000 to smugglers who escorted him to Sweden. He traveled for two long months in the stinky, sweaty holds of ships and in the secret compartments of semis carrying goods across borders. He ran out of water once for two days and thought he might die of thirst. Omar hesitated with noticeable embarrassment as he related this horrific tale. Finally, upon reaching Sweden, he was given a dorm room in Alvesta along with a small food allowance and classes in Swedish language and culture. But the first thing he did upon arrival was to apply for his family to join him.

Omar began to cry as he continued and reached into his pocket for a handkerchief. The Swedish government would allow his wife and son to immigrate but not his two daughters because they were over eighteen. I thought to myself: *How can Swedes think it safe to leave two, young, unmarried women unprotected in a Middle Eastern country where they are not legally allowed to either study or work? What are their options?* Omar could not say the words 'prostitution' or 'slavery', but I knew that was what he feared.

I can't remember ever feeling so outraged and helpless. I finished printing my own insignificant document and helped him formulate his appeal. We spoke English while I typed in Swedish. Omar was extremely, embarrassingly, grateful (as an American I felt semi-responsible for his predicament) and wanted to repay me somehow, so he invited me back to his room for milk and cookies. Literally. This was the first, perhaps only, time in my life when such an offer seemed well-intentioned, and I accepted. To have refused would only have added to his feelings of guilt and powerlessness. After two cookies and a glass of milk, he thanked me profusely, shook my hand, and gave me his phone number. I never called. I should have, because I have thought of Omar periodically ever since, wondering if—hoping—there had been a happy resolution to his heart-rending quandary.

Today, I rose early (4:45 a.m.) to join an international group meditation to end the pandemic; I considered it a gesture that might possibly—but honestly probably not—help. On the one hand, I'm skeptical, but on the other, there are many things I don't understand and can't explain, so why not? If meditation miraculously halts the pandemic, the world will soon find itself in a happier place. I slept afterward and glided through the day in a lethargic fog. In other news, Boris Johnson, the U.K. Prime Minister, has tested positive for COVID-19. He was the other outlier besides Tegnell in Sweden, who naïvely placed faith in 'herd immunity'; I wonder what he thinks now?

A very upset Hanna called today from the dock on Phu Quoc: she and Dani decided to leave Vietnam. They paid the German government to get them out, a plan that entails a bus to the port, a boat to the mainland, a bus to the airport, a plane to Frankfurt, and a second flight to Stockholm. When they arrived at the dock ahead of the designated departure time, they were informed that the boat had left without them. The hot crowded port did not feel safe. I suggested getting a taxi and returning to the hotel, but Dani worried that the hotel might close, and they might have nowhere to live. Or if they waited and the situation worsened, they might be unable to arrange departure until after their visas had expired and could not be renewed. Also, they could be stuck there for a lot longer than they wanted. *Or perhaps not*, I thought. From my perspective, those are far too many maybes for the basis of a decision. My father used to say, 'It's easier to stay out than get out', which I think originated with his terrifying experiences as a frontline medic during World War Two but is a mantra that occurs to me whenever I think about doing something that I suspect might turn out to be a bad idea. How I wish they were staying out of Sweden! Now that they are enroute, I hope it is safe and smooth sailing.

Sunday 12 April. Easter

And on Wednesday, Passover began. Many friends participated in Zoom seders for the first time, often more global and inclusive than live celebrations. This newly seized opportunity to enjoy a meal with friends and family on distant continents may change traditions.

Last week, I left the apartment only on Friday to do my weekly shopping. Sometimes, I venture out earlier in the week if I run out of avocados (nightly dinners consist of guac and chips and a pomegranate margarita) or if the milk turns sour. Thankfully, Hanna arrived safely in Stockholm and returned to her budding singer-songwriter career. Her sing-along, "If You're Alive You're Not Alone," seems perfectly attuned to current conditions.

The pandemic has inspired me to contact friends more regularly. This might also be a procrastination strategy knowing me, but it feels important to affirm connections. I speak weekly with Walt in Cleveland and Marian in New York, and I also recently chatted with friends from high school and college, as well as with an assortment of colleagues and friends elsewhere on the planet. I also talked to my informally adopted German 'parents'. Actually, it was more they who adopted me and began calling me their eldest child, a situation my 'siblings' have embraced.

I met Inge and Jürgen in 1986 on an overcrowded train between Prague and Berlin. I had spent Easter week with my friend Katja in Vienna, having taken the overnight train there from Stockholm, where I was doing dissertation research in the days before intracontinental flights were cheap. On the way back to snowy Stockholm, I decided to spend a few days in Prague, intrigued both by a city of legendary beauty and by my desire to visit behind the mysterious Iron Curtain.

I had never ventured beyond Western Europe, but as a child of the Cold War I had heard much about those dismal, undemocratic countries whose factory-worker citizens could only dream of tropical fruit and freedom of expression and movement. I rented a room in the city center from an elderly widow and wandered the gloomy streets of the Bohemian capital, whose former elegance glowed dimly beneath neglected grey facades of chipping plaster and a dense blanket of coal smoke. I visited in splendid solitude the neglected and deteriorating Jewish Quarter, not yet museumified, and the partially closed and dimly lit National Museum.

Then, I boarded a train to East Berlin's Friedrichstrasse Station, from which the night train to Stockholm departed. Fellow travelers occupied the other five seats in my compartment, and I settled into my seat nearest the door to read an art history book. In German. This piqued the curiosity of the middle-aged man sitting across from me, who began asking me (in German) about my interest in art. He, too, was interested in art and history, as was his wife, who sat beside him, although I soon learned they were physicists specializing in non-linear optics and lived in Berlin's Russian Sector. We exchanged histories, and they found my relatively banal American upbringing as exotic and fascinating as I found their Cold War existence.

Inge and Jürgen were university students in Berlin when the Wall materialized virtually overnight, dividing in two what in the nineteenth century had been Europe's fastest growing metropolis. They contemplated leaving for the West, a step taken by many of their friends and some of their relatives. They had just finished their doctoral studies and had jobs waiting in Stuttgart. The move would have entailed leaving their parents behind, perhaps forever. Time was of the essence since escape became more difficult and dangerous with each passing day. In the end, they stayed.

Jürgen hailed from Hainewalde, a village near Germany's Czech-Polish border. Inge was a refugee from Königsberg, East Prussia (now Kaliningrad, Russia), hometown of many distinguished Germans, including the philosopher Immanuel Kant and the artist Käthe Kollwitz. The entire German population of that city had been forced steadily westward during World War Two; Inge's family ended their exhausting and frightening journey in a southern Berlin suburb. After their traumatic life as refugees, she was hesitant to leave her widowed mother alone. Besides, both she and Jürgen had received outstanding educations that guaranteed them rewarding research positions were they to stay.

I was riveted. Jürgen's tale of intrigue and suspense unfolded like a spy novel come to life. Pre-Berlin Wall, they had traveled in France, Switzerland, and England. They spoke wistfully of those adventures and the fact that in those days they could never have imagined a world in which travel was not possible. They did travel extensively for work to 'communist' locations such as Budapest, Moscow, and Samarkand but clearly longed for the unfettered freedom of travel in the West. The fact that they had refused to join the Communist Party constrained their careers, housing, and vacation opportunities. They asked me to tell them about Stockholm, Paris, and life in the U.S. because they doubted the veracity of carefully filtered news reports. This unanticipated conversation exhilarated me, as if I had encountered extraterrestrials. I had wondered about and imagined Russian and other Iron Curtain citizens but never anticipated meeting any.

The anecdote that most impressed me was how their daughter had wanted to take piano lessons. Music lessons—like any extracurricular activity, notably sports—required bureaucratic approval in the German Democratic Republic. So, Inge made an appointment to obtain it. The official measured her ten-year-old daughter's hands and deemed her unsuitable for lessons because of apparent physical limitations: her finger span bode poorly for a career as a concert pianist. It was that simple; the East German government refused to invest in individuals lacking superstar potential. Curiosity and interest were insufficient. Shocked, I then wondered how much fairer the situation is in countries where personal financial resources determine one's access to music lessons, sports coaches, and court or ice time?

The time between Prague and Berlin flew by. I barely had a chance to enjoy the landscape on that bleak, rainy Monday, although I envisioned minefields, barbed wire fences, and guard towers. We exchanged addresses before parting and promised to write. I had been through that routine before. It usually led to nothing but vaguely remembered, short-term travel companions whom I neither saw nor heard from again. This encounter turned out differently.

When we reminisced about our first meeting a few years back, Inge and Jürgen remembered me taking the initiative, but I am pretty sure it was Jürgen who sent that first letter at Christmastime. In any event, we remained faithful, if sporadic, pen pals until Easter 1996, when I again spent Easter week with Katja in Vienna, this time with our respective husbands and children. We were living in Munich at that time thanks to my year-long fellowship to conduct archival research on nudity in German art.

On the way to Vienna, Hanna, her dad, and I spent a few days with Inge and Jürgen in the latter's ancestral village, Hainewalde, a typical hamlet of slate-sided *Umgebindehauser* nestled in Germany's most charming region, Oberlausitz. A few months later, I spent a week with them in Berlin, and Jürgen, an avid amateur historian, taught me everything he knew about the city and its long history. The highlight was 'Lenin in a Box'. During the Cold War era, the Soviet Union displayed a bust of Lenin prominently on a shoulder-height pedestal in front of its imposing embassy on Unten den Linden, the avenue stretching from the Brandenburg Gate to Museum Island and beyond. Following *Perestroika*, the government had trouble deciding what to do with it. They apparently feared humiliation if they removed it but leaving it would have been an embarrassing reminder of the failure of the Soviet project. Some years later, it disappeared in the night, like a dissident. Jürgen and I traipsed everywhere, and after a long and exhausting day of visiting museums, parks, monuments, and churches, we returned to their spacious apartment with its high ceilings and booklined walls, where Inge had prepared a warm and delicious meal. It was at that moment they announced my informal adoption.

The next time Hanna and I visited, Jürgen, a red rose in hand (a German custom), greeted us at the newly renovated main train station in Berlin. He whisked us off to nearby Potsdam—the Saint Paul to Berlin's Minneapolis—where we met his son, Robert, daughter-in-law, Marita, and their two small children. We got along terrifically, and since that time I've house-sat for them while they were off adventuring for months in Africa and arranged sabbatical visits for Robert in the U.S. They've stayed at my house during summer vacations and taken my car to Duluth. My 'sister', a UN diplomat, spent one Christmas with us in Worcester, Massachusetts sharing a room with my guest-friendly mother.

Since my mother's death in 2008, Hainewalde, where Inge and Jürgen retired, has become my 'parental home', an important anchor in my otherwise peripatetic life. As we chatted on the phone, they wondered when I would visit, inviting me to spend the pandemic with them, which I would consider absent my fear of contagion in transit. I hope to visit in the summer, perhaps for Inge's birthday in July, when we will sit under warm blankets by a crackling evening fire on the garden's stone terrace, sipping glasses of *Weissburgunder*, listening to the frogs croaking their evening song, and watching the sun set behind fields of rye.

April is a spectacular month in Paris; there's a reason for the song Count Basie made famous. I long to visit the chestnut trees blooming pink and white along the Seine and in le Luco. Today was sunny, so I—together with everyone else 'stranded' in Paris—went for a walk. At this point, I no longer need to consult Google Maps to determine my boundaries; it's almost as if I'm equipped with one of those invisible-fence dog collars minus the electrical shock.

One of the wonderful aspects of big cities is its characters. Here, there is a lady I see regularly, dressed from head to toe in white. She has an impressive collection of stunning white hats and gloves and a large white cockatoo that perches with entitled insouciance on the fence on the Esplanade Gaston-Monnerville across from le Luco. Passersby stop to photograph and admire the regal, near motionless bird, sporting its own showy headpiece. Once children begin haranguing it, the Woman in White walks calmly over, the bird hops onto her shoulder, and she strolls home.

On my way back, I paused outside the *boulangerie* at the corner of Notre-Dame-des-Champs and Vavin, inhaling deeply. Ah, the aroma of freshly baked bread! This is the first time I've been to Paris since discovering my gluten intolerance in July 2019. Gluten-free life was easy in Costa Rica with so many rice and corn carbs to enjoy, but in Paris wheat deprivation rises almost to the level of biblical suffering. I salivate at the visceral memory of the taste and texture of Blé Sucré's flawless croissants: how they unravel, oozing butter as one pulls the crispy central tip. The contrast between the lightly browned, crunchy, flakey exterior, and the soft, succulent, yellow interior. The miracle of simple and perfect things. My temperature today is 35.8 degrees Celsius, and there have been 14,300 deaths in France thus far, up 500 from yesterday.

Friday 17 April

Time passes more swiftly in pandemic conditions. I never seem able to accomplish in a day all that I plan, despite a dearth of outside activities. Nonetheless, I'm making encouraging progress on *Denmark and the Invention of Modern Happiness* but approaching the end of what writing I can do without further research. For that I need libraries and archives in Copenhagen, although I can't imagine boarding a plane anytime soon. I'll have to figure out another way to spend my days.

I've explored my Sixth Arrondissement domain in greater depth in six weeks than I did my Upper West Side neighborhood over the course of a decade. There isn't much to remind me of Trocadéro Man nearby, and I've managed to avoid the temptation to listen to his soothing, melodious voice with its faint, endearing French accent in clips available on the Internet. In the early days, when I was ardently in love and separated from him by an ocean, I watched snippets regularly. In any event, he knows I'm in Paris and has made no effort to get in touch, so it seems I'm not even friend material. It's undoubtedly better this way even if it saddens me. We had fun together and what I believed was an authentic connection.

Parisians are adjusting to pandemic life, tweaking their behavior in accordance with newly emerging scientific findings. Food shops now have well-developed protocols. Some allow only a limited number of customers inside. Personnel wear masks and face shields, and most shops have now hung soft plastic sheets to separate cashiers from customers and from each other. The cheese shop permits only two customers at a time and no browsing indoors. Flesh eaters stand in line outside the fishmonger and butcher as well. Some businesses have painted dots or affixed tape lines on the sidewalk by their entrances to indicate the one-meter distance waiting customers should keep. It's interesting because in the U.S. the recommended distance is six feet, almost two meters. Now you can buy masks and hand sanitizer at grocery checkouts, not just in pharmacies.

This week, I received the shipment of one hundred masks that the administration of ARTS—the international journal of which I am Founding Editor-in-Chief—thoughtfully sent from its Wuhan headquarters. Wuhan, birthplace of the virus. My colleagues there have not been outside much since January and write that usually crowded and bustling Chinese cities now resemble ghost towns. I can't envision an empty Shanghai. When I taught there in the summer of 2013, people swarmed everywhere like ants at a picnic, with the enormous, pristine Apple Store near the Bund functioning as the chocolate cake. Stay-at-home restrictions must be nearly intolerable for the legions of poor Chinese who live in cramped, barely habitable spaces. I've seen those who live and work in thirty-square-foot candy shops or crowd their multi-generational families into tiny spaces without running water or electricity under the bleachers of sports fields. The have-nots in urban China often exist under conditions Westerners would consider intolerable, even—at least in Scandinavia—illegal. Most workers have what they refer to as a 9-9-6 schedule, working 9 a.m. to 9 p.m. six days a week, with days off at Chinese New Year.

In a city renowned for its chic women, *parisiennes* are now beginning to look like women elsewhere. While I haven't seen any stooping so low as to venture outdoors in sweatpants, more women are wearing jeans and opting for running shoes over Louboutins. I have even noticed fewer Tods and Clergeries, walking shoes that are practical and stylish albeit pricey. In the absence of a social life, comfort trumps fashion. Even the most unobservant will notice an unprecedented number of unmanicured hands with chipping nail polish and hair with visible roots now that beauty salons are off-limits. I was almost surprised that in Paris these weren't declared 'essential' services. Despite compromised appearances, women still stride the streets with characteristic self-assurance. The women of Paris seem to have entered a tacit collective agreement to temporarily suspend normally reigning codes governing personal appearance, additional evidence of the solidarity that transcends class boundaries in France.

I switched my dating website subscription to the U.S. out of curiosity since meeting prospects in Paris at this moment seems dangerous and impractical, considering geographical constraints, lack of places to meet, and the seeming aversion of French men to exploratory video relationships. I used the same pictures and profile translated into English. The differences between self-presentation on the American versus the French site is fascinating. For instance, unlike Americans, French men never include pictures of themselves standing on docks or on the sterns of boats proudly holding large fish or posing on the golf links or with their fancy car or motorcycle. Who are these guys trying to attract anyway? Other straight men? Are some women impressed by this kind of display? I would rather see where a potential partner resides: house or apartment? What kind of furnishings? What kind of setting? And how does he spend his leisure time? Is there a piano? Does he travel? What pictures are on the wall and what books on the shelves?

There's about the same ratio of selfies in France and the U.S. (although more typical among men with low levels of education). For some inexplicable reason, they're often taken in bathrooms, hallways, or cars. I mean, even if no one ever takes pictures of you, *please* have someone do it for your dating profile. Preferably a selection of images that show various aspects of your life. And, although men may enjoy pictures of scantily clad women (I included one by Hanna of me in a bikini smiling and leaving the water taken at a beach on Paros), I don't think many women want to see selfies of shirtless (or more) men in beds—especially hotel ones—or pools. More well-educated French men do this than do well-educated Americans. I assume these men are more interested in sex than relationships, but I'll never find out, because I won't meet a man who posts this kind of picture. Interestingly, when describing what they're looking for, many French men use the term 'soulmate' (*âme soeur*) but

Americans rarely do. Many French men also specifically seek intelligent and feminine, sometimes thin, women.

As far as dislikes go, what French men do not like, besides infidelity and vanity, is poor hygiene. They have to state this in a dating profile? What is going on with French women's hygiene? Are they referring to bad breath, undesirable body hair, BO, *what*? No American men mention hygiene nor, as French men often do, make references to their interest in philosophy, claim to be learning piano, or spending their time painting or writing music or poetry. Nor do Americans include 'tinkering' or exploring regional nature and history—*patrimoine*—among their hobbies, while French men often do. Also, a surprising number of French men sail and ride horses. Who knew?

I have also noticed interesting (apparent) social class differences. If a man wears a sleeveless shirt, has tats, displays a fuzzy or sideways photo or his motorcycle, he probably doesn't have a college education either, and may well smoke tobacco regularly, enjoy camping, and be unable to survive without his cell phone. There's a definite correlation. American men seem much more willing to commence with a virtual relationship and see where it goes, speaking of which, Guy texted again, informing me of his physical therapy schedule and continuing to refrain from inquiring about me. Why does he even bother? As far as dating is concerned, French men seem to feel that it is either meeting in person or not at all. Perhaps because they want to find out if there is physical allure, although the ones I have test driven, despite appearances, would never win a Don Juan award. From a casual survey of friends, this is an endemic problem with French men, who seem to assume that once they're satisfied so is their partner. It's disappointing to have sex with a fifty-plus man who has all the finesse of a teenage virgin. I'm all for verbalizing one's preferences, but in this situation, where does one begin without sounding patronizing?

Perhaps I should replace man-hunting with another hobby. But I can't seem to shake that nagging urge for a male partner. Is it fear? Certainly not fear of being alone, because I enjoy that. Perhaps fear of not having someone around when I fall and can't get up and then starve to death out of reach of my phone, hearing it ring when my daughter calls but unable to respond, and she doesn't know exactly where I am, or if she does, doesn't know whom to call for help. That kind of fear.

Also, it'd be nice to have a reliable partner to share experiences with—extraordinary musical performances, Aegean sunsets, meteor showers—someone from whom you can learn new things, someone who expresses their appreciation of your efforts and existence, someone who perceives things as you do. And a certain amount of convenience. Like sharing chores, expenses, and driving duties, and having someone guard my luggage while I am off searching for a bathroom.

In recent years, I've rediscovered the joys of being alone: not having to compromise about when and what to eat, who to spend time with, how long to stay at the beach or in the museum. And the freedom to leave my toenails unpainted, permit body hair to flourish, pick my nose, fart, turn the light on to read or watch *The Avengers* reruns at 3 a.m. I also like being able to leave my pile of necessities on the partner side of the bed: earbuds for listening to guided meditations or sounds of the rainforest, bite guard, snacks, books, extra pillows, fuzzy socks in case my feet get cold.

Regardless, there's no substitute for the gentle caresses of—and nourishing skin-to-skin contact with—someone to whom you feel spiritually bonded, with whom you are on the same vibrational frequency. Burrowing into warm sand on tranquil beaches is simply not as satisfying as a perfectly fitting spoon, naked with your beloved, his arm gently pressing you close. Nor does the wind blowing through your hair replace the sublime feeling of your beloved's hand running his fingers through it. Ask any dog.

I'm not actually sure why I'm considering American men when I haven't had an American romantic partner for more than twenty years and have no intention of living in the U.S. long-term. My homeland has simply become too unstable, dilapidated, and dangerous for me, with a burgeoning population of suspicious, lie-embracing, gun-toting, often racist meth-heads and oxycontin or fentanyl addicts, especially in the South and Midwest. And healthcare is unpredictably expensive, whereas in Europe if there's any cost at all, it's easily affordable and a matter of public record. None of this 'we can't tell you how much that procedure will cost'. No insurance companies refusing treatment endorsed by doctors. I guess I'm hoping to unearth an American-born, multi-lingual world citizen who eats organically, lives by the Four Agreements, and is similarly committed to ecological sustainability.

Today, my temperature is 35.7 degrees Celsius and yesterday the death count reached 18,000 in France, rising now at a rate of about 1,000 per day. One-third of total deaths have been in retirement homes. News segments frequently address this tragedy. Family members, forlorn elderly parents, and stressed-out employees express fear and frustration. I think Swedish retirement homes are cleansing themselves of inhabitants at such a furious pace due to COVID-19 that they may soon have an overabundance of vacancies.

Thursday 23 April

Why does time seem to pass more swiftly in *confinement*? It takes me longer than usual to get going in the mornings partly because I'm glued to the COVID-19 news channels, which occasionally report other events, such as the latest antics of Donald Trump. I work in the afternoons: advising, consulting, editing, writing. Next thing I know, it's 8 p.m. and time for dinner and catching up with friends. And I sleep like a baby, which I've finally mastered after twenty-five years of partners who snored violently and experienced abandonment issues when I took refuge elsewhere.

This week, I chatted with Inge and Jürgen, who are beginning to work in their garden, friends in Beijing, Berlin, Bregenz, Chicago, Cleveland, Dresden, New York, and, of course, Hanna. We often chat while she's biking—the wind can be *loud*—or on a walk by the nearby sea in Stockholm, where she lives. She sings me bits of the beautiful new songs she's writing. I love witnessing the process: sometimes she has a riff or a melody, but no words, other times a phrase or stanza requiring development. Today, my temperature is

35.7 degrees Celsius, and the French COVID-19 death count is 21,800, so it's slowing to about 500 per day. Maybe Macron will liberate us soon.

In the meantime, I'm content to become better acquainted with my neighborhood. I peruse streets within my perimeter stopping to notice the windowed walls of former artists' studios and to admire the astonishing variety of designs of wrought iron window grates and balconies. Legions of artists must have been busy in the decades around 1900 when these buildings were constructed, drawing a dizzying array of patterns: chevrons, Greek keys, arabesques, hearts, plant tendrils, arrows, bells, tulips, quatrefoils, fish scales, monograms. I have yet to recognize grate designs repeated regardless of where I wander.

I love the outdoor museum of sculpture Paris's building facades offer. Many display pairs of vigilant stone figures either flanking or hovering above doorways: women with updos and tendrils blowing in an imaginary wind who wear puffy-sleeved blouses with low-cut bodices, their chubby, dimple-elbowed arms carrying baskets of fruit (the rue Notre-Dame-des-Champs); on the rue Auguste Comte, a contrasting pair of female figures, one in classical *contrapposto*, clad in gauzy, breeze-blown drapery, right hand limply touching her breast, left hand maladroitly tipping a vase of water that would topple to the ground were it not carved directly into the building. This floozie's eyes roll back, her inane smile and loose tendrils of hair reminiscent of the insane Ophelia. At her feet, smoke billows from a bowl, hopefully with an intoxicating vapor that explains her strange comportment. Perched atop the opposite volute, her nude sister balances on one foot, apparently in the midst of a bacchic dance, with hair and drapery fluttering behind her and a goblet on the verge of dropping from her limp hand. The low relief grape vine sprouting from the ground confirms that this naked frolicker has imbibed excessively.

My favorite ornamental façade is at 7 rue Auguste Comte. It has an African theme on the ground level, with elephants wearing tassled headdresses, their trunks curled around cannonballs, with ears held by chubby, curly-haired putti. They're paired with lions donning impressively varied expressions that collaborate to support the protruding upper stories. Above them, the heads of children perform the easier task of carrying the volutes that hold stone balconies, with their delicate, lacey iron balustrades.

67 boulevard Raspail displays two inspiring relief sculptures of nude partial families flanking its entry: on one side a father, child, and baby with the inscription "Good Luck" below, hopefully not in a how-will-dad-manage-to-raise-his-children-without-mom kind of way. Dad pauses in his labor, his oversized right hand resting against his groin and grasping what appears to be an axe or hoe, his extended index finger with its pronounced nail evoking—intentionally or not—a phallus. He turns to look back at his chubby infant, lifted-up by the older child, as dad cradles baby's head in his enormous left hand. A mastiff, muzzle protruding from the building surface, brings up the rear.

On the opposite side, there's another nude trio followed by a loyal mastiff also inscribed "Good Luck," perhaps expressing skepticism about a mother raising two boys without a father. Here, two young boys with physiques evocative of Egyptian *kouroi* walk hand in hand, solicitously regarded by a maternal figure standing behind them. The younger of the two gazes lovingly up at her while his brother reaches back with his free hand to hold hers. Down the block, one finds more familial relief sculpture: a mother bird dives toward her nest perched in a low-relief oak tree to feed greedy, open-beaked hatchlings. I often pass the magnificent Hotel Lutetia, built in 1910 at the corner of the boulevard Raspail and the rue de Sevres, a stunning example of the transition from the florid splendor of Art Nouveau to the geometric elegance of Art Deco, with interiors more exquisite than its exteriors. Now, though, I content myself with admiring Lutetia's creamy limestone façade, punctuated by bowed windows and ornamental sculpture featuring fruit, garlands, and energetic putti, a balance of exuberance and order that epitomizes Paris itself.

People continue to applaud essential workers nightly at 8 p.m., and one finds uplifting signs of solidarity everywhere: in shop and restaurant windows, on bus stops, and on the electronic publicity boards planted on major streets. There's even a hashtag 'one applauds'. The messages are all supportive and encouraging: "Thank you for your courage, solidarity, humility, humanity, empathy, strength, and selflessness," for example. And there are instructive ones posted by the City of Paris: "Coronavirus: Master these good practices to limit propagation. Wash your hands often. Avoid shaking hands and kissing. Avoid leaving your home unnecessarily. Aerate your home. Cough and sneeze into your elbow. Use disposable handkerchiefs and only once." The emptiness of the streets is astonishing. At what point in history could one stand during the daytime in carefree safety for several minutes in the middle of the Rennes-Saint-Germain intersection, one of the busiest on the Left Bank?

Tuesday 28 April

This evening, I had planned to enjoy Anna Netrebko singing *Adriana Lecouvreur* at Opera Bastille, another determining factor in my initial decision to spend April in Paris. It would have been my first time in Paris's 'new' opera house, and now I can't imagine when that might happen. Right now, the thought of sitting in a crowded, enclosed space with a chorus of singers projecting droplets toward a vulnerable audience seems unwise. I was supposed to return to Stockholm this Friday, but Scandinavian Airlines cancelled that flight as well as my May 4th flight from Stockholm to Warsaw, where I should have given four lectures on Symbolist art in Scandinavia at the university during May. I now have vouchers for future travel. Had I known I'd be stranded in Paris with no possibility of socializing, I would have packed differently. My black leather skirt and black Bally dress shoes are superfluous; I'd gladly trade them for an extra pair of yoga pants because that's pretty much all I wear. My black cashmere sweater (usually more practical in Paris) wearing thinner by the day substitutes for the anorak I couldn't imagine having needed when I packed. Luckily, there's a branch of the cashmere shop Eric Bompard on the rue Vavin, so I can replace it if Paris shops ever reopen.

The pandemic has also temporarily quashed plans to sell my rental condo in Purgatory. The current renter would have stayed on if he could, but when I told him I was selling, he immediately found a new home. Now that the real estate market has collapsed, it seems prudent to find another renter for two years until the pandemic blows over. Luckily, a new grad student in my department is eager to move in. I informed the current renter that he can stay on through July paying just utilities, an offer to which he happily agreed. I also proposed a similar arrangement to my landlord in Paris, a retired American professor who usually spends summers here but can't, due to travel restrictions. She kindly agreed that I'll pay €600 to cover utilities for the four months—May-August—when I have no income. Phew. Another problem solved.

Since March 17th, whenever I leave home, I carry an *attestation* that explains the purpose of my departure. Mine is usually "to accomplish purchases of first necessity in authorized establishments." I use the same handwritten one each time changing only the time and date, although I have heard that's not always acceptable if you're stopped by the police. I've never seen anyone stopped. Not even cars. In fact, police rarely appear in my neighborhood, perhaps because it's now so depopulated, perhaps because it's so bourgeois, sort of like Manhattan's near West Side. I don't always wear gloves as I did at the outset, but I do always carry hand sanitizer and wash my hands immediately upon returning home, as Mother trained me.

This evening, Trocadéro Man called to have what I assume is a 'relationship over' conversation; he asserted that we became bored with one another. Well, I was never bored by him, and he's the first person ever to have found me boring. People have found me many things they don't like—aggressive, impatient, distracted, catty—but never boring. He said he'd like to remain friends and that he would call when *confinement* ends, but I'm not holding my breath. I'll miss his mother, who taught me to make seven-vegetable soup, helped me decide on the cover image for my latest book, kissed me on the forehead, *tutoye*red me, and treated me like a member of the family. I even had my own sterling silver napkin ring.

We talked for an hour during which I explained my puzzlement by his decelerating communication following our October rendezvous in Venice and his evident lack of interest in joining me at his electricity-free chalet in the Quebec wilderness, where I spent a pleasant week of solitude at New Year's. I think I more hoped than expected that he'd join me there, eager to relive the magical time we had in November 2018.

Then, after driving five hours from Montreal, we were transported with all necessary provisions for five glorious days by a snow-mobile caravan piloted by the locals who looked after the chalet in exchange for using it as a refuge, mainly during hunting season. With its toasty interior, comfortable furniture, and cooking and bathing facilities, the chalet is a far more desirable hunting post than the typical tiny, exposed stands without amenities reached by ladders and stuck in desolate fields. Although the temperature dropped far below freezing, the wood stove kept the spacious two-story chalet—perched on a hill overlooking the snow-bedecked lake—cozy warm.

We woke to clouds of breath suspended in the chilly morning air and dressed under the covers, where we kept warm for the night our fleece long underwear, all the indoor clothing required during snowy winters. I busied myself preparing steaming bowls of oatmeal while Trocadéro Man restarted the fire we were too soundly sleeping to replenish during the night. We spent the very short yet bright sunny days exploring the woods, looking for animal tracks, making snow angels, watching the wind blow snow off tree branches, and shoveling snow off porch and steps.

Sated by an early dinner, we sunk into the sofa, mesmerized by the fire flickering and crackling in the stove. We humidified the cabin by pouring water on top of it, observing the beads race toward the edges of the stove before evaporating. We played chess by the dim light of gas lamps, studied routes for his upcoming single-engine flights, read poetry aloud, and he sang me songs. Trocadéro Man has a melodious voice and loves to sing. One of his singular charms—and one of the things I miss the most—is his sere-nading me with *chansons* or reciting poetry from memory as we walk evenings, pinkies locked, on the silent Paris streets. Before turning in for the night, we'd fill the stove with wood, wedging in branches when there was no more room for chopped chunks and then stand on the porch in the limpid, arctic night air gazing together at a ceiling of stars so densely packed that one could imagine that every star in the universe was visible.

My typically active, social, somewhat peripatetic life has, under the exigencies of the pandemic moment, turned inward to memories, reflections, and imaginings, a direction that feels natural and pleasurable. It leads me to examine how significant moments, those indelibly imprinted, could so assertively yet falsely portend a future. It must be a matter of alignment, and I don't yet feel confident about discerning when my interior voice accurately assesses a situation and when it's contaminated by baggage from my past.

Chapter 4
May: Déconfinement and Shifting Direction

Saturday 3 May

Today, like a kind of reverse prisoner, I watched from outside the three-meter-high iron fence surrounding le Luco grounds workers carefully pruning ornamental roses and spreading humus that smelled of growth and springtime. The park is resplendent with flowers on bushes, lawns, and gardens in all imaginable nuances of red, yellow, violet, and white. Roses unfurl. If I could have any job right now it would be a groundskeeper in a Paris park, access to which is currently forbidden to all but their suddenly enviable employees. I'm tiring of my one-kilometer travel limit and long to stroll the quays of the Seine.

Are the chestnut trees flowering or has that phase passed? I survey my limited domain daily since the weather turned beautiful: sunny, cloud-speckled skies and sweet-smelling air beckon. The small plaza between le Luco and Esplanade Gaston-Monnerville functions as a common yard for the neighborhood, accommodating playing children and nannies, personal trainers and clients, and athletes performing fitness rituals. Cockatoo Lady appears mornings with her feathered companion.

There are now 24,500 total COVID-19 deaths in France, and the U.S. is now clocking 1,500-2,000 deaths per day. French news provides a superfluity of data regarding the pandemic: details of its status in Paris and the various regions of France, the debate about whether Hydroxychloroquine can ameliorate or cure COVID-19, as Dr. Raoult of Marseilles confidently asserts. Raoult, appearing on all channels with his unkempt, shoulder-length, white hippie hair, could easily be taken for a typical Parisian *clochard*: a well-behaved, often intellectual, homeless person, a kind of street philosopher. The main difference is that Raoult thrives on attention whereas *clochards* do not.

Although no one enjoys COVID-19 restrictions, no Europeans —except Swedes and perhaps Brits—accuse their governments of reckless or non-existent protocols. The lack of transparency and the conflicting precautionary advice afflicting the U.S. condemns its citizens to states of confusion, stress, even panic. I feel safe in Paris. Few people resist mask wearing in France, where refusal to comply merits fines of €135 for a first offense, €400 for a second. The penalty escalates to €3,700 for a third, and six months of jailtime for a fourth, a measure that underscores the importance of compliance. In the land of 'no shirt, no shoes, no service' I don't understand American citizens' resistance to masks, which have a practical, protective purpose. I often wish I could wander about topless in the summer heat but that's illegal there, even though it never leads directly to the death of fellow citizens. Distraction, perhaps. Europeans are incredulous to see the U.S.—the mastermind of many modern military invasions—with no coherent pandemic management plan.

Americans often seem seized by irrational fears and unaware of the latest scientific findings, discussed *ad infinitum* by European experts and journalists. Many remain frightened and isolated at home, ordering groceries online for delivery and avoiding interactions with family and friends. At the same time, Europeans and Canadians, respecting government-advised precautions, pursue many of their usual daily activities with few worries about contagion. And with supply chain management a crucial part of military operations, why is the U.S. government unable to guarantee the efficacy of supply chains at home? And why the rush on toilet paper?

There are a host of substitutes. I remember thinking *how sensible* when I saw a pile of newsprint beside toilets in rural Serbia while touring there in the late 1980s with Zlatne Uste Brass Band during my brief flirtation with life as a folk musician. Nothing goes to waste on a Serbian farm.

Saturday 9 May

The other day, I surfed the Internet in search of agents for *Denmark and the Invention of Modern Happiness* because I would like to market it to a broader public rather than to the academic world to which my books are generally addressed. It tells the fascinating story of how interclass solidarity and the principles of social democracy—a movement established more than a century later—emerged and first thrived in eighteenth-century Denmark. The legacy of this history forms the foundation of modern day Scandinavian *hygge*: the ability to enjoy a relatively carefree life blessed by benefits of which most Americans can only dream. These include: a minimum of five-weeks' vacation, relative socio-economic equality, free healthcare and education at all levels, excellent infrastructure and public trans-portation, child subsidies for all, a year or more of parental leave, subsidized minimum housing standards, a salubrious work-life balance, and ongoing efforts to impede environmental deterioration.

While agent-browsing, I discovered many interested in women topics—particularly lesbian and historical fiction—which got me thinking. I had tried earlier in the week to resume writing the first in a series of novels about episodes in the lives of women artists, a subject I teach regularly. Begun a decade ago while living in Germany, it concerns the passionate romance between German painter Gabriele Münter and her Russian teacher-lover Vassily Kandinsky. Imagining Bavaria circa 1900 while in Paris was diffi-cult. Frustrated, I decided to write a novel based on the life of a French woman artist who lived in Paris. I somewhat randomly settled on a decade in the life of Rosa Bonheur and her partner Nathalie Micas.

Bonheur, who specialized in painting animals, became the nineteenth century's most critically and financially successful woman painter. My story begins in 1848, the year of Europe-wide revolutions and the year the new French government awarded Bonheur the prestigious commission that launched her career. It was also when France became the first nation to enact universal male suffrage, although—ironically considering Bonheur's success—Frenchwomen didn't get the right to vote until 1944. 1848 was also the year France's short-lived Second Republic was established, with Napoléon Bonaparte's nephew Napoléon III as president. Three years later, hoping to realize the dream of his uncle, he declared himself emperor, thereby inaugurating the Second Empire. Under Napoléon III's leadership, Paris transformed into its now familiar constellation of balconied seven-story buildings and broad boulevards.

Although I'm unsure where Bonheur lived, in my story she and her childhood best friend and life-long companion, Nathalie, inhabit my neighborhood. I can now fill the pages with descriptive details because I can easily imagine daily life during that era. For a while in the 1920s, Hemingway lived on the nearby property of a sawmill on Notre-Dame-des-Champs where a Deco apartment building now stands. Back then, horse-drawn carts delivered felled trees, and the high-pitched whir of saw blades cleaving planks made this a noisy neighborhood, as it certainly was in Bonheur's day. One rarely thinks about the extent to which small industries once dotted the streets of Paris: mills, factories, slaughterhouses, stables, and workshops. This era lasted until the 1970s in the Nineteenth and Twentieth Arrondissements when forests of too-tall residential buildings replaced them.

I have always loved writing fiction, although I have never finished anything. My first novel, *Mystry at Oak Hall Manor*, written when I was seven (before my spelling had improved), remains incomplete at four, suspense-filled, hand-written chapters. Interestingly, it unfolds in Paris. We'll see how far I get with Rosa and Nathalie. I appreciate, at any rate, the universe blessing me with this unexpected time to delve into something I have always wanted to do but for which I have never made the time.

Yesterday was Victory in Europe Day, the day in 1945 Germany surrendered to the Allies. A parade normally processes up the Champs-Élysées from the place de la Concorde to the Arc de Triomphe, where the eternal flame marking the Tomb of the Unknown Soldier flickers. Today was different. No public. Just several prominent officials, including Mayor Anne Hildago, Prime Minister Édouard Philippe, President Macron, and an honor guard. Distancing but no masks. And no traffic in a location that is usually a dangerous vehicular whirlpool. Instead of the show of power and security with which most heads of state travel, Macron arrived in a four-door hatchback driven by a chauffeur, in accordance with head-of-state protocol. Two military representatives, one male, one female, together laid a wreath of red, white, and blue flowers on the tomb. Macron, standing alone, brow furrowed, bowed his head and led a minute of silent remembrance in the strangely vacant plaza. Afterward, a small military band and choir performed "The Marseillaise." It was a restrained, dignified, and moving event. As a finale, nine military planes flew overhead trailing red, white, and blue, creating a vaporous French flag in the cloudless spring sky.

I had a pleasant conversation with Jean from the French dating site—the usual getting-to-know-you chit chat—and discussed meeting following *confinement* liberation, which occurs on Monday. Soon, I'll be able to walk to the Eiffel Tower, the Seine, and the Marais! Parks, shops, and museums will open! Spring is in the air, and I'm eager to bask in the sights, sounds, and smells of a tourist-free Paris. Tomorrow, I've scheduled a Zoom date with a promising American fellow from New York with whom I have lots in common: tennis, travel, music from opera to bluegrass, and swing dancing.

The French COVID-19 death toll now stands at 26,500, and I've stopped taking my temperature; six weeks of twice daily measurements should provide a sufficient baseline should that information become necessary.

Monday 11 May

Confinement Liberation Day! With the wariness of a housecat contemplating the breech of its domestic threshold, I considered my ambling options. Enticing destinations forbidden for the past two months swirled through my mind: artsy Montmartre and the Oz-like domes of Sacré-Cœur, the Latin Quarter, whose pristine medieval buildings lean against one another like drunks at closing time. Or perhaps the Marais with its inviting gauntlet of falafel joints on the rue des Rosiers; food thoughts are ever-present when I'm in Paris, like the subconscious awareness of impending danger when roaming sketchy, urban American neighborhoods. Notre-Dame? The Eiffel Tower? I felt the same confusion as I do at bagel shops when trying to settle on a schmear for my double-toasted sesame bagel. Two destinations harkened most insistently: the Seine and the Eiffel Tower. The best time for the Tower is during its spectacular hourly evening twinkle. Decision made.

I changed out of my pandemic uniform—black yoga pants and my now shabby black cashmere sweater—into beige linen trousers and a blue blazer. I draped my red cashmere pashmina patriotically around my neck and slipped into my comfy Paul Green walking shoes. Dressed like a human French flag, I crossed the threshold into the sunlight and zig-zagged through the progressively narrower and more ancient *rues* of the Sixth Arrondissement toward the Seine, the aorta of Paris, with the reflexive compulsion of a squirrel drawn to its clandestine nut stash.

After crossing the rue de l'Université, I detoured onto the rue de Beaune, a short cobblestone street lined with colorful wood facades in one of Paris's posh antique districts. Charming lanes, survivors of turbulent centuries, offer a comforting sense of permanence. I paused before the window of a small cane shop, wondering what previous merchants had occupied the space—dressmakers or milliners, jewelers or watchmakers, bookbinders or stationers, upholsterers or cabinetmakers? My eyes darted from one curious svelte masterpiece to the next. Canes of African blackwood, bakelite, bubinga, cocobolo, ebony, grenadilla, ivory, and mahogany with handles of silver, gold, blown glass, Rhinoceros horn, jade, amethyst, and rock crystal, carved, polished, or with decorative inlays were stuffed into umbrella stands and hung from the walls. They were crowned with an imaginative array of handles: parrot and elephant heads, nude women, vigilant lions and bulldogs, graceful, long-necked horses and giraffes, even heads of little girls wearing hats. Multi-purpose canes included tips with daggers, handles with smoking pipes or pill boxes, and hollow ones for transporting secret documents. Canes for women and for men. For the opera, for walking, and for concealing epees for duels.

Although I'd prefer to believe that I wandered there by coincidence, I acknowledge that memories beckoned. This was one of many places that now—but hopefully not forever—evoke memories of Trocadéro Man. The former, now-deceased proprietor was a beloved family friend. We strolled to the shop one warm June evening two years earlier, pinkies hooked, after dining nearby at the venerable La Procope. We slurped oysters and chewed on mysterious shelled delicacies that tasted salt and had the consistency of sneaker soles. Benjamin Franklin had eaten there and I had always wanted to. Trocadéro Man was a seductive dream fulfiller. Afterward, his *moto* whisked us past Saint-Cloud, to a family property near Versailles for one of many unforgettable nights. The memory felt more wistful than painful. I saw myself smile in the window reflection and continued toward the Seine.

Tuesday 12 May

Today, I wandered over to le Luco. I noticed that the little triangular plaza at the intersection of the rues Vavin and Notre-Dame-des-Champs hosted—for the first time in two months—people reading books and newspapers, drinking coffee, eating lunch, and chatting as they sat on benches surrounding one of Paris's signature 'caryatid' fountains. These 'Wallace fountains' began appearing in the 1870s, a private initiative of Englishman Sir Richard Wallace, a philanthropist who decided Paris neighborhoods needed accessible sources of potable water. He also collected art, now on view in his former London residence, Hertford House.

My conversations with Mark in New York have been great: he's easy to talk to, friendly, and we share many interests. We talked for two hours each on Sunday, Monday, and Tuesday and never ran out of topics. He, too, loves Paris and used to work for a French publisher. And like me, he can envision living here.

Today's sunny skies and brisk air inspired a ten-mile walk. I tingled with excitement, as if anticipating a long-awaited meeting with a dear friend. A tangle of possible routes presented themselves, but more than anything I wanted to see the progress on Notre-Dame and to read the panels explaining the conservation and restoration process displayed along the cathedral's north side. I felt the thrill of an escapee, acutely sensitive to my surroundings: the perfume of raspberries filling my nostrils as I walked past fruit sellers, timbres of voices, the breeze against my face. When out and about, my sensory awareness has become sufficiently intense that it pushes all thoughts from my mind. Walking Paris has become a meditative experience.

I strolled down the rue Vavin stopping to take a few deep breaths in front of the *fleuriste*, whose magnificent blooms spill out to the curb. I followed the perimeter of le Luco to the rue Vaugirard and over to the stately Saint-Sulpice, whose Baroque twin towers echo those of Notre-Dame. I turned down rue Monsieur-le-Prince, then followed the rue de Bac to the Seine and encountered few people, just the odd dog-walker or retiree with a baguette under their arm. As I strolled the Seine's quays, there was no need to pay attention to other pedestrians because there weren't any. Place Saint-Michel was empty save for several entitled pigeons strutting about. Notre-Dame appeared little changed since pre-*confinement*, although significant progress has evidently been made on its interior. I read the long row of illustrated panels that explain the salvage and restoration process. Fortunately, the magnificent organ, with its palpably vibrating low register, survived virtually unscathed.

Afterward, I passed Sainte-Chapelle, open but with no line. It was sunny; I should have gone in. Once on the Right Bank, I walked to the Louvre. A few random souls circulated in the large plaza shared by I.M. Pei's glass pyramid and Giancarlo Bernini's equestrian statue of Louis XIV. The famous Italian sculptor began it during his stay in Paris during the 1660s, when Louis XIV had hired him to redesign the Louvre façade. The king detested the statue when it arrived from Rome in the 1680s and hid it in a corner of the Versailles gardens. Here, it looks strangely misplaced, an afterthought.

From there, I strolled to the Palais-Royale, then back through the Tuileries Gardens, across the almost traffic-free place de la Concorde, and through the park that runs along the Seine to Trocadéro, now overgrown and unmown. Wild red roses blossomed amidst poorly maintained park benches in desperate need of repainting. On the spacious Trocadéro plaza, I enjoyed in solitude the most spectacular view of the Eiffel Tower. I stood there alone save for the figural sculptures that—in COVID-19-solidarity—sported masks.

I paused for a moment to take it in. No Africans selling bottled water or Eiffel Tower trinkets. No shorts-and-white-sneakers-wearing American tourists. Not a soul. Just a pup tent erected by a shrewd homeless man in the best imaginable spot in Paris: at the far edge of the plaza, exactly centered, with an unimpeded view of the Tower. He must have spent *confinement* nights lying in his sleeping bag, gazing at the illuminated Tower of Three Hundred Meters, as it initially was called, thanking his good fortune for remaining undisturbed in such a plum spot. I would be disingenuous were I not to admit that part of my motivation for going there was its evocation of memories of champagne and macadamia nuts on Trocadéro Man's penthouse terrace as we watched the hourly twinkle of the Eiffel Tower from upholstered chaises. I walked through Trocadéro Park down to the Seine and to the Eiffel Tower, best enjoyed from a distance.

After crossing pont d'Iéna, I headed east across Invalides and past the ostentatious *palais* formerly inhabited by Trocadéro Man's great grandparents. In the evening, I returned to the Eiffel Tower, zigzagging through the side streets of the Sixth and Seventh

Arrondissements. How fragrant they were! How little traffic, pedestrian or vehicular, there was! I began noticing jasmine vines everywhere.

I've missed the smell of jasmine since abandoning my idyllic red cottage in the lake-dense forests surrounding Tolg, Sweden. It wasn't easy to relinquish the wall of lilacs surrounding the house on three sides or the huge, fragrant, jasmine bush beside the kitchen window. I loved standing beside it, pulling its fragrance into my lungs with an avidity generally reserved for prescribed therapeutic activities; it functioned as a gigantic floral vaporizer. I had never seen jasmine vines before, and it turns out they are everywhere in Paris, hugging iron garden fences and window grates, framing windows and doorways. The cool, evening air releases their intoxicating perfume.

Museums have opened, but large ones require reservations, so I went online and booked visits to the Louvre and Musée d'Orsay. I'm also determined to visit a smaller museum a week, ones I've never visited—like Cernuschi—or at least not for a long time—like Gustave Moreau.

Wednesday 13 May

Finally! I can legally return to place Monge, where vendors from the surrounding countryside gather to sell their wares on Wednesday, Friday, and Sunday mornings. I stuffed shopping bags into my pocketbook, slipped on a lightweight jacket, and stepped out into the sunshine. I walked down the rue Vavin, around le Luco, past the cockatoo to the rue Auguste Comte. I crossed the not-so-busy boulevard Saint-Michel and passed the Institut Océanographique, where Trocadéro Man and I once attended a preview of *700 Sharks in the Night*. With wander restrictions lifted, I find myself stumbling upon Trocadéro-Man memories strewn throughout the city like *madeleines de Proust*. They add yet another layer of historical complexity to my experience of Paris. Next door is the rue d'Ulm laboratory where Louis Pasteur developed the rabies vaccine.

My quickening pace reflected my eagerness to get to 'my' cheese stand, where I greeted Cheese Man and ordered slices of aged cow's-milk Gouda and truffled Brie for the first time in two months. It was nice to see him and *Maman* again. He offered me a sliver of something delicious, although I have no idea what, and I bought a slice of that, too. As Cheese Man packed my purchases, he gifted me a round of fresh sheep's milk cheese. I bought vegetables from the organic stand next door and fresh cilantro, red lettuce, and kale from Grumpy Greens Man, who sells wonderful greens and a small assortment of garden vegetables across the way. There's nothing better than the dirt-on-the-roots freshness of produce at open-air markets and the pride of vendors in their artisanal agricultural methods.

Next, off to Mococha. I'd been dreaming of it for two months, and my mouth watered as I approached. Madame Chocolat seemed glad to see me.

"Ah, bonjour! It was a long imprisonment."

"Yes," I agreed, "it was almost intolerable," a sentiment I knew reflected the mindset of most Parisians. The exotic perfumes of Vietnamese cinnamon, Provençal lavender, Honduran coffee, and Ghanian chocolate nearly sent me swooning. Together, we selected the week's assortment, which included a few new items her *chocolatiers* had introduced since my last visit. As I savored my parting *douceur*, I headed downhill to La Fontaine aux Vins. There, after reading the labels of the wines on display in crates outside the shop, I bought two bottles of Bordeaux selected by Monsieur, a Côtes de Bourg and a Côtes de Blaye from vineyards on the banks of the Gironde. He wrapped them in white tissue paper as I paid and thanked Madame.

"No," she insisted, "it is I who should thank *you* for the pleasure of serving you at our little shop!"

Sadly, most businesses remain boarded up or have closed permanently, reminders of the ongoing, yet hopefully abating, pandemic. Many restaurants and cafés have adjusted to the no-inside-service mandate of *déconfinement* by blocking entrances with café tables equipped with bottles of sanitizer and sometimes napkins, condiments, and free masks. Menus are posted out front, usually on blackboards since proprietors are experimenting cautiously with new conditions.

On the way home, I noticed masks on the statues of Louis-Nicholas Vauquelin, an eighteenth-century pharmacist and discoverer of the elements chromium and beryllium, and Antoine-Augustin Parmentier, a pharmacist-contemporary who promoted the benefits of the potato, at that time a recent introduction in France. They stand in the courtyard of the Académie Nationale de Pharmacie across from the Esplanade Gaston-Monnerville. The sky-blue medical masks reminded me that however normal one yearns to feel, the world ship has yet to right itself.

Friday 15 May

This evening, I wandered along the Left Bank quays from the place Saint-Michel to the Park of Ugly Sculpture, at the easternmost edge of the Fifth Arrondissement. Officially the Musée de la sculpture en plein air (Museum of Outdoor Sculpture), Google Maps describes it as a "garden with striking modern sculptures." They're being diplomatic. The sculptures are recent and hideous. By the time I reached the area containing small, Seine-side performance terraces, the sun had set. Salsa and tango groups reveled in their newfound freedom, captivated by the music like cobras by a *pungi*. Social distancing was practiced half-heartedly, with alcohol consumption shortening the acceptable threshold of separation. The reflection of lights from buildings along the river shimmered in the still water. Boat traffic has not recommenced.

Most evenings, I have spent two hours talking to Mark. I feel almost as if we're already a relaxed and contented couple. His only wife died five years ago, shortly after which he began dating the longtime friend in his building who consoled him in his grief. He had wanted a true couple relationship, but she preferred separate apartments and semi-independent lives, so a year ago, he ended it. That all sounds fine, and he plays tennis, something I have missed in recent years. Perhaps, if Mark and I live in Paris we'll be playing in le Luco before long. Still, it's premature to have my racket restrung.

I also talked to Inge and Jürgen, who continue, good humoredly, to badger me about visiting. It's almost as though they don't realize there's a pandemic. I'm not even sure if, as a Swede or an American, I would have to quarantine, nor if it would be possible to cross the *Bundesland* border into the state of Saxony, where they live. Rules change from day to day. As Hanna says, plans are now just wishes. If I could go, it's impossible to predict if I could then return to France since borders are tightening. Staying put seems the safest strategy. The pace of COVID-19 deaths in France has slowed to fewer than 500 per day, and the total death count hovers around 27,500.

Sunday 17 May

Today is Norwegian Independence Day. Usually in Oslo there's a parade and lots of festivities; I wonder what kind of celebrations Norwegian officials allow this year. I'm guessing few, if any, because that government errs on the side of caution, currently enforcing fourteen-day quarantines for anyone entering the country. The border with Sweden is closed.

This morning, I visited the renowned organic-only, open-air Sunday *marché* at the intersection of the boulevard Raspail and the rue de Rennes. All vendors wore masks but only some shoppers. Plastic sheets hanging from cross bars protected most stands, while other vendors simply wound plastic wrap around poles at either end of their concessions. Some permitted customers to select produce themselves, but many kept to the more traditional practice of requiring customers to state—or point to—what they want and relying on the judgment of vendors to choose.

Although Americans often find this practice annoying and a perceived infringement of their shopping liberty, there are good reasons for it. In Europe, food vendors consider themselves experts in the products they sell; choosing your own without consulting them might be considered an affront. You generally get the very best quality when asking the vendor's advice, informing them when the items will be eaten and how you plan to prepare them. It's the *only* way to insure the optimal culinary experience. You can be very specific—three peaches for today, three for four days from now—and they will select different degrees of ripeness or varieties depending on whether they will be consumed raw or cooked and in combination with what.

I learned from my mother and grandmother about the best varieties of apples and potatoes for particular uses: red or new potatoes for salad, Maine for mashed, and Idaho for baked; with apples, Ida Red, Delicious, and Macintosh for eating and Granny Smith, Cortland, and Jonagold for baking. In France, one finds an equally broad array of many other fruits and vegetables for which the advice of experts is indispensable. Happily, it's asparagus and strawberry season. I bought two of the four available varieties of strawberries—Gariguette and Mara des Bois—as well as white and green asparagus, which in Germany is divided into smaller categories that include thickness and local origin, at varying prices.

I had delightful evening chats with Mark, Hanna, and several friends. I can't wait to meet Mark, who seems a perfect match, from his Irish Catholic upbringing, flower-power teenage years, and small liberal arts college education, to his love of swing dancing, bicycling, tennis, and foreign lands. He seems authentic and honest; hopefully my instincts don't lead me astray.

Tuesday 19 May

Paris restauranteurs have busily been obtaining permits to expand their outdoor seating to the streets. In every arrondissement, temporary terraces the width of parking spaces and the length of their facades are popping up like rain lilies. Lucky establishments enjoy locations with spacious sidewalks and parking lanes. My heart goes out to tiny mom-and-pop establishments with sidewalks the width of a curb and no available street space. They remain closed. Major Left Bank restaurants and cafés are now open: Deux Magots, de Flore, and Lipp on the boulevard Saint-Germain, and Dôme, Select, Cupole, and Rotonde near me on the boulevard Montparnasse.

I arrived at the Louvre at 11:00 a.m. today. The pyramid plaza was vacant. No crowd, no crowd-control ropes, no guards directing visitor traffic; I wondered if the museum were open. I flashed my International Council of Museums get-in-free card (as a child, Hanna dubbed it the 'magic museum card'), after which my feet were magnetically drawn to the Denon wing to visit the late-eighteenth- and early nineteenth-century paintings about which I teach and write.

The padded benches in the long maroon gallery inhabited by my favorite painting there—Théodore Géricault's *Raft of the Medusa* —were empty, as was the gallery itself. I stood before this painting, which I love not so much for its beauty (it isn't pretty) but for its emotional intensity. The artist worked on it like a maniac for almost two years, investing the totality of his mental and physical energy, a compulsion that deteriorated his health to the point of enfeeblement: Géricault died at age thirty-three in 1824. I have always admired his passion, dedication, and daring to paint an enormous paean to a humiliating government scandal; the first monumental, government-critical painting in the history of art.

Géricault represented the aftermath of a shipwreck a few miles off the coast of Senegal, a colony awarded to France at the 1815 Congress of Vienna, the meeting that ended the Napoleonic era and reinstalled the Bourbon dynasty onto the French throne. It also marked the beginning of colonialism in Africa: the Congress distributed chunks of the continent to participating European nations.

King Louis XVIII, younger brother of the beheaded Louis XVI, leveraged his position to bestow political favors and sent eager new landowners and a governor to Senegal in 1817. They traveled on three ships, one of which was captained by a political appointee with no maritime experience. His ship ran aground on a sandbar several miles off the coast. Rather than staying on board as custom dictated, he and the richest passengers commandeered the few lifeboats, abandoning 150 passengers, including the ship's engineer and doctor. We know what happened because the doctor kept a diary. Under the engineer's guidance, they constructed a huge raft with a sail and railing for the remaining passengers and some supplies. The weight caused the raft to sink about one meter, submerging all to their waists in sea water, an untenable situation.

Violence broke out almost immediately: soldiers had guns and civilians had knives. Each morning, fewer passengers remained due to accident, cannibalism, dehydration, or murder. By the time help arrived three weeks later, fourteen passengers remained, and of those, seven survived. Anti-royalist newspapers publicized the scandal, a completely avoidable tragedy. These reports galvanized Géricault. He submitted his painting as 'history'—the most prestigious category—to the annual, government-sponsored 'Salon' exhibition held at the Louvre. Traditionally, history subjects represented past events (actual, biblical, mythological, even episodes from literature) or glorifications of current events, such as David's 1800 portrait of Napoléon crossing the Alps on a white steed. But this was the first time an artist dared to indict the government in monumental form.

Géricault's audacious decision led to obsessive painting day and night, during which he produced little salable work and spent a fortune on the materials required to cover 380 square feet of canvas with oil paint. It also signaled the rebellious moment of artists' liberation from subservience to church and state patronage and the debut of openly oppositional, politically engaged art in France. It expressed fidelity to the egalitarian values championed by French revolutionaries.

You get the best impression of the painting's original appearance in color photographs taken before World War Two. Since the painting left Géricault's studio, it has darkened steadily, an inevitable process that chemists and conservators are powerless to retard, much less halt. Like many nineteenth-century artists, Géricault experimented avidly. One of the most popular materials at the time was bitumen, the black, liquid tar that oozes from asphalt in the heat of summer. Adding this to oil pigment thickens the paint, gives it texture, and helps it to dry faster. Artists could not have imagined it meant the gradual erasure of their pictures. But it did.

This bold masterpiece, not the *Mona Lisa*, was the first painting I showed my daughter on her debut visit to the Louvre in 1998.

When I initially saw Leonardo's famous portrait in 1974, it hung beside the other, more interesting, Leonardos in the Louvre, now downgraded to the long gallery one traverses to see the superstar. I've never understood why in recent decades the *Mona Lisa* has risen to star status, protected by plexiglass and the central attraction of a gallery of velvet ropes and snaking lines of admirers waiting up to an hour for the privilege of a closer, but by no means close, view. Today, three people stood in front of it, the rope barriers, superfluous. The total French death count from COVID-19 has reached 28,000; the U.S. has breached the 100,000-mark.

Sunday 24 May

The weather has been glorious, and I have spent most of the week exploring surrounding neighborhoods. Each day is a dilemma: I feel like someone who won the supermarket sweepstakes and has ten minutes to amass maximum value. After completing must-do tasks —assessing articles for ARTS and responding to e-mails—I'm torn between writing and taking advantage of what feels like a once-in-a-lifetime opportunity to revel in a Paris without tourists. But writing I can do anytime and enjoying Paris I can't. So, onto the streets!

In the retail areas of Paris, eager shoppers deprived of two months of spring shopping stand patiently absorbed in books or cell phones as they await entry into their favorite boutiques. Attendants, usually uniformed, admit one person for every one that exits, even at department stores like Bon Marché. Larger and upscale stores employ a dedicated, white-gloved helper to squirt sanitizer into the palms of arriving shoppers.

This formality reminds me of the days when Lord & Taylor on Fifth Avenue unlocked its doors at 9:30 a.m., thirty minutes before opening, and invited customers into the space between the front doors and the makeup counters. When I was in graduate school, I would often stop by on the mornings I headed to the nearby New York Public Library on 42nd Street. Folding chairs provided seating just inside Lord & Taylor's entry, and uniformed maids donning black or pink dresses with white collars and scalloped aprons served cookies and hot tea to all, almost exclusively female, comers: blue-haired matrons, presentable homeless, Long Island housewives, me. Such gestures made New York a wonderful place to live. That tradition ended—if not earlier—the day Lord & Taylor's closed permanently in January 2019. I wonder what happened to their marvelous, mechanical, Christmas window displays. They were the best in New York, transporting one back to Old-fashioned Land, an era when ladies wore fur muffs and men ice-skated in silk top hats.

On Friday, I headed to Galeries Lafayette near the Opéra Garnier to buy a black t-shirt. The weather was getting warm, and my summer clothes were either in Purgatory or Stockholm. I didn't have to wait but did receive a sanitizer squirt from a uniformed and gloved attendant. In conformity with new hygienic measures, dressing rooms were blocked, and signs informed shoppers they could return anything that doesn't fit.

Today, after shopping at the Raspail-Rennes marché, I decided to peruse the First Arrondissement, normally swarming with tourists and workers and so saturated with traffic noise and exhaust fumes even on weekends that I usually avoid it. I walked down the rue Bonaparte, past the Hotel Bonaparte, where I sometimes stayed in the 1980s, past Pierre Hermé, where Hanna and I often bought croissants (she, always an Isfahan, their signature, sweet, rosewater flavor) when I visited during her junior college year. We devoured them beside the fountain in the adjacent place Saint-Sulpice.

I crossed the pont Royal and traversed the gravel plain where the Tuileries Palace stood until it was destroyed by local insurgents during the short-lived Paris Commune in 1871. When I reached the rue de Rivoli, I found this grand thoroughfare empty except for cyclists. That's been one of the benefits of the pandemic: Mayor Hildago, determined to make Paris a friendlier, greener city, has increased the number of dedicated bike lanes. They now stretch the entire lengths of the boulevards Raspail and Saint-Michel and along the Left Bank quays from the Park of Ugly Sculpture to the Eiffel Tower.

Bike sales are booming in post-*confinement* Paris. But still, the rue de Rivoli vacant? Even on Sundays, its commercial establishments and hotels are normally bustling, the loggias obstacle courses of souvenir stands hawking berets, placemats, and mugs. Now, everything is closed, including the insanely popular original location of the tearoom Angelina, usually discernible by its long line of tourists waiting to sip its thick hot chocolate or to sample a Mont Blanc, its renowned (and grotesquely sweet) meringue pastry. At place des Pyramides, I circumambulated Emmanuel Frémiet's gilded, equestrian statue of Joan of Arc for the first time ever without fear of being hit by a car.

Only a few entrances to the Palais-Royale were open. Built in the seventeenth century for the powerful Cardinal Richelieu, Louis XIII and Anne of Austria resided there before decamping to Versailles. Now it's the home of exclusive shops like Stella McCartney and Marc Jacobs as well as to Paris's most venerable, Michelin-starred restaurant, Le Grand Véfour, established in 1784. The Palais loggias appear dramatic in the morning light, lessons in one-point perspective. Square-bayed ceilings stretch into the distance, the floors beneath marked by a repetitive pattern of sunlit arches punctuated by the shadows of spiky iron gates.

Only in the First Arrondissement does one find homeless storing their worldly possessions in the sturdy, prestigious bags of nearby shops: Celine, Dior, Longchamps. Like homeless elsewhere in Paris, those of the First Arrondissement are generally tidy and considerate. Unlike their colleagues in New York or Stockholm, they seem to have either purposefully chosen this off-grid lifestyle or to retain their dignity despite having fallen on hard times (neither alcohol nor drugs seem to be an issue). Some sleep in tents, others form pods under broad overhangs. They rarely beg and spend their time organizing scrapbooks, reading, and sharing meals. In no other city will you see so many homeless absorbed in reading. And it's an impressive range of literature: Descartes, Foucault, Zola, Hemingway, Shakespeare, Heller, Le Goff, and, as with all Frenchmen, Goncourt Prize-winning novels.

I wandered the fashionable rue Saint Honoré, comparing COVID-19 instructions posted to shoppers and studying window displays with the relish others reserve for museum installations. I especially like the hat shops. Such creativity! Some hats resemble Alexander Calder sculptures, while others are so small and delicately molded that one wonders what tricks must be mastered to fasten them to the wearer's head. All *chapelleries* have hopped on the mask bandwagon, fashioning custom masks twinned to millinery confections. My favorite milliner is Veronica Marucci, a true *artiste de chapeaux*. If ever I am invited to Ascot, she will design my hat.

On my way back, I stopped by Saint-Germain-l'Auxerrois, the splendid, thirteenth-century parish church for Louvre residents, where triplet groups of dignified jamb figures guard the entrance. They perch atop unfortunate sinners, including bird and serpent hybrids. One wears a crown. What detested monarch might he represent? One sufficiently despicable that medieval sculptors created his stone effigy for all eternity to ponder.

Tuesday 26 May

I'm beginning to realize that I'll likely teach my two courses remotely in the fall. A lot to learn in preparation, but I won't worry about it until August. Yesterday and this evening, I made my now customary stroll to the first twinkling of the Eiffel Tower, at 10 p.m. On my way, at the northeast corner of the boulevard Montparnasse and rue de Rennes, across from Tour Montparnasse and beside the newsstand, I noticed an elderly man seated at a card table absorbed in his jigsaw puzzle. His recently completed puzzle—a English style cottage set in a floral garden—was mounted on cardboard and leaned against the newsstand. *So* much to wonder about. Does he live in a tiny apartment with depressing views of walls, and this is his way of extending his domestic space? Is he escaping a tiresome wife for a few precious hours? What did he do before he retired? Why does he choose such a busy spot? Has he been doing this for years? Does he outdoor puzzle in all seasons?

With much reduced traffic, the corner is neither hectic nor permeated by exhaust fumes. But maybe Puzzle Man isn't there habitually, and maybe public puzzling is only a pandemic occupation. Were I braver and more confident in my French, I would ask him for an interview. At the Champ-de-Mars, lawns were roped off but those of Les Invalides a few blocks further east were not, and they were choc-a-bloc with picnickers avidly exercising their newly found freedom. You would never suspect that a pandemic rampaged to see them chattering cheerily at close and unmasked proximity.

I've invested in diapers. Yes, diapers. It took me a while to work up the courage to ask at the local pharmacy, but I finally did. With restaurants and cafés closed, there are no bathrooms available, except, of course, the public ones stationed at convenient intervals on streets and even at the Champ-de-Mars. But wild horses couldn't drag me into one. I've spent enough time using outhouses in Sweden (summer cabins there often remain unmodernized) and 'Turkish' toilets in the Balkans (and in Parisian cafés in the 1980s). Despite assurances of sanitizing following each use, I still prefer to refrain. So, diapers it is. I have always wondered about them, thinking they might offer convenience on long airplane flights. Yesterday, I put them to the test. I had to pee desperately on my return from the Eiffel Tower, so I paused along the toney rue de Grenelle pretending to look—well I did, actually—at a shop window. In process, I wondered, *how much liquid can these things hold?* And while I am not exactly sure, enough, as it turns out. What a relief. Even when unused, the unbreathability of diapers heats me up as do masks, but under the circumstances they are tolerable inconveniences.

La Coupole, Montparnasse's most iconic brasserie, has been closed since March. It installed plexiglass barriers along the perimeter of its terrace overhang, and a contingent of homeless moved in at the beginning of *confinement*. They're tidy and well-orga- nized, each with a similarly sized plot for their mattress and worldly possessions. Sometimes, they dine together, other times, play cards. They don't seem unfortunate or sad, but still, it's not exactly glamping.

I've been impressed by the large number of homeless on the streets of Paris, especially in the nicer neighborhoods (except for the snobbish Sixteenth Arrondissement, populated only by day-begging Roma) and by the fact that they're accompanied by little filth or fear.

When the homeless leave their encampments—whether in a doorway, under an overhang, or in a tent—their neatly stored possessions remain undisturbed. A tacit respect for domestic space reigns, even if it's public and technically illegal. On the boulevard des Invalides, one fellow has pitched a tent on the sidewalk beside the fence surrounding the Army Museum. It has a covered entry, a mat on which to leave shoes before entering, and a ten-foot-tall potted palm, giving his residence an air of permanence and respectability. I wish I had the courage to interview these people because I am very curious about their life stories and the circumstances that led to this lifestyle.

Tonight, I talked to Mark, who confessed "I think I'm falling in love with you." No one has ever said that to me before that I remember; these wonderfully romantic words make my heart flutter.

Wednesday 27 May

This morning, I returned to Marché Monge and the rue Mouffetard for Gouda, truffle Brie, wine, and chocolate. In the afternoon, a prospective fall renter of 'my' apartment stopped by. Caroline is a professor of Ecology from St. Louis who also contemplates a future in Paris. We began with masks. I showed her around, and because we had such nice a time chatting and she had already recovered from COVID-19, we demasked, and I offered her a cup of tea while we got acquainted. Although I have not missed human contact, it was nice to encounter a kindred spirit.

After dinner, it was on with diapers and off to the Eiffel Tower for the 10 p.m. twinkle. There are a limited number of routes, and I enjoy them all, although I always wind up at the lawns of Les Invalides, where I catch my first glimpse of Eiffel's originally temporary monument. Each walk brings new discoveries, including the impressive Grenelle Four Seasons Fountain beside the Maillol Museum entrance, which I first noticed on my way home one evening in its illuminated splendor. I remembered that an engraving of it was featured on the oversized Christmas cards of thick hand-made paper that Mme. Vierny sent me annually for a decade or so beginning in the early 1980s.

Mme. Vierny was Maillol's last model. She began her career as a teenager in the Mediterranean town of Banyuls-sur-Mer, where Maillol lived near the Spanish border; she became his heir when the artist died in 1944. Mme. Vierny was small and stocky with jet black hair and the aggressive self-assurance of a parvenue. I met her while in graduate school and writing a paper—later my first publication—on Aristide Maillol's monument to Auguste Blanqui, a kind of nineteenth-century Bernie Sanders who spent more than half his life in prison. I admired his passion and commitment to the cause of egalitarian rights for all.

Our first meeting occurred at the Hotel Westbury, at Madison Avenue and 69th Street, where she stayed when visiting New York. We had tea in her suite. The second meeting was in Paris. I went to her home, inherited from Maillol and designed by Charles Garnier, architect of the Paris Opèra (now Opèra Garnier), as his personal residence. Majestic but not enormous, one of its property boundaries is defined by the Four Seasons Fountain (thus I *must* have seen it before even if I don't remember), built in the mid-eighteenth century, and on the other, a two-story wooden portal. Mme. Vierny's maid escorted me to a small *salon*. The room where we sat had a relaxed elegance that somehow did not seem the proper setting for her Capuchin monkey, Rocky (she adored Sylvester Stallone), that hopped all over the room like an imp on speed.

The maid arrived with a silver tray holding a coffee service and a plate of madeleines. She returned a few minutes later with another silver tray, this time bearing three small Maillol sculptures. Nude females, as one would expect. I assumed Mme. Vierny had selected them because they related to my project: the *Blanqui Monument*, also called *Action in Chains*, a robust striding woman with wrists shackled behind her back. It's installed on a central square of Blanqui's tiny, ancestral village of Puget-Thèniers in the Alps Maritimes north of Nice.

That might have been part of her point, but what impressed me was her command:

"Pick it up!"

I did.

"*Feel* it!"

I ran my hand over the surface.

"Do you know why I'm telling you to do that?" she asked.

"No," I replied sheepishly.

"Because Maillol turned from painting and textile design to sculpture when his eyesight began to fail in the 1890s, and he was no longer able to perceive nuances of color and texture. He made sculpture by touch. He studied the contours of the model's body with his hands and then replicated them in clay."

I may have shuddered, imagining an elderly man running his hands over a young woman's body. But then I thought, *What's the matter with me! That makes sense.* I wondered if he were the first sculptor to adopt that strategy. My thoughts strayed to Michelangelo and Rodin. I'd never read about this situation in any Maillol scholarship (and I'd read it all and also spoken to Maillol scholars), and it reinforced the importance of meeting (when possible) those with firsthand knowledge of artists. This bit of information provided crucial insight into understanding Maillol. In fact, we all possess essential facets to our character that remain unknown unless the right person reveals them to the world through an anecdote, don't we?

Despite parks remaining closed and the lawns of the Champ-de-Mars roped off, scofflaws abound. Tonight, several clusters of brazen young people violated regulations, picnicking maskless on the great lawn in front of the Eiffel Tower and sharing wine and food in a way that seemed risky under the circumstances. Joggers and dogwalkers congested the paths, and a small group of old folks practiced tai chi. The twinkling lasts five minutes, after which I return. If I'm striving for efficiency, I take Grenelle to Raspail to Notre-Dame-des-Champs. Otherwise, I thread my way home on smaller streets. The rue du Cherche-Midi has the most interesting windows and Bon Marché has magnificent Art Nouveau tilework on the interiors of its portals.

Illegal bars and cafés have popped up everywhere, initiatives of impatient proprietors. Service is outdoor only with limited offerings and standing only, but that hinders neither establishments nor customers. Socializing in Paris occurs mainly in public spaces and inhabitants are eager to resume their habits. Still, many—the unmasked and undistanced—throw caution to the wind in their eagerness to return to an unwarranted sense of normalcy. The world is still far from normal.

Saturday 30 May

George Floyd's murder in Minneapolis by a police officer who knelt on the African American's neck until he suffocated shocked an incredulous France. It prompted intensive coverage on all networks, along with special reports about the history of racism, police brutality, and the infiltration of right-wing extremists into American police forces. French experts on American culture have suggested that part of its problem lies with poorly screened and trained police. Inquisitive journalists were appalled to hear that American police officers receive as little as ten weeks of training. In contrast, everywhere in Europe police education takes a minimum of two years of full-time study, with a curriculum that includes law, human rights, international and media relations, crisis management, and psychology.

The George Floyd tragedy has struck a nerve in France, evoking an unresolved 2016 incident in which Adama Traoré, a black Frenchman, died of asphyxiation while in police custody. His articulate and outraged sister Assa, wearing a "No Justice, No Peace" t-shirt, has galvanized a Black Lives Matter movement in France. In recent days, protests attracting thousands of participants have been held in place de la Republique—the main arena for protesting in Paris—and more and bigger ones are planned. Even though held outdoors, French officials express concern about such events worsening the COVID-19 crisis.

Today, parks reopened. Le Luco, its verdant lawns untrammeled for three months, teemed with visitors desperate for nature. Older folks played *pétanque*, younger folks played tennis, the team of ponies gave rides, people read and sunned, children sailed boats in the big basin, and joggers—many, many joggers—trotted elbow-to-elbow on the gravel path along the park's inner perimeter. And good luck finding a chair to sit on. Or a bench. As soon as someone shifted their weight, replacements eagerly edged closer, like awaiting diners in a no-reservation restaurant. I prefer to go there when competition is minimal, especially with the pandemic raging, so I returned home to work. The longer I'm in Paris, the more I love it, but I wonder if I would feel the same were hotels filled to capacity and pickpockets cruising the Champ-de-Mars. The Paris I love might just be the Paris of this unprecedented moment in time.

Sunday May 31

When I awoke this morning, I thought I should take the opportunity to visit somewhere crowded with tourists in normal times and decided on one of my favorite Sunday outings, Montmartre. I took the 68 Bus from the boulevard Raspail to place Blanche, where Manet once hung out, and followed the steep rue Lepic, named, I imagine, after the family of the dour viscount painted by Degas crossing place de la Concorde with his equally non-plussed dog and daughters. Few souls occupied the usually crowded steps of Sacré-Cœur or the plaza in front of it. I walked over to place Tertre, normally jammed with pleasure seekers—like an amusement park on a Friday evening. I counted a half-dozen people, mainly locals, casually chatting.

Until recently, artists dominated the square, their easels lined up in tidy rows, displaying and painting colorful images of the city's attractions: Sacré-Cœur, Notre-Dame, the Eiffel Tower, the Arc de Triomphe. They worked in sizes large and small, in watercolor and oil, and in every imaginable style for sale to tourists desirous of an authentic work of art that doubles as a souvenir. By some regrettable legal trick, restaurants around the square—all currently closed —have colonized this space, exiling artists to the periphery, a kind of frame of art and artists around a center of diners and drinkers. It has always been artists who attract tourists to this square, not restaurants (most of which are mediocre at best), and I find their marginalization heart-breaking. Surviving as an artist is sufficiently challenging if you are skilled at making quick portraits in pastel or charcoal. These greedy restaurants already had space, indoors and out. Even under a socialist mayor, capitalism trumps culture.

I found myself on a back street I apparently had missed during numerous previous visits, and stumbled on Musée Montmartre, a lovely surprise. It occupies the former residence of Suzanne Valadon, an Impressionist model turned modernist artist, whose son, Maurice Utrillo, was the father of Montmartre tourist painting. Her studio and living quarters are so well preserved that one feels transported back a century, and the garden generates a relaxed, rural atmosphere. At the back of the garden—hospitably furnished with tables and chairs inside a fragrant perimeter of flowering bushes—hangs the swing that inspired Renoir's eponymous painting. Beyond lies a second garden along with one of Paris's few apiaries (le Luco also has one) and a small vineyard. Atypically, I returned home once satisfied by my adventure instead of once desperate to escape jostling crowds. This Paris-without-tourists invites reverie and picturing the past to a far greater extent than during normal times. Human absence renders the city's sensorial world more vivid and delicious.

Chapter 5
June: Big Decisions and Widening Horizons

Tuesday 2 June

Today, restaurants and cafés reopened with terrace-only service. Since the government announced this impatiently awaited news two weeks ago, there has been a flurry of activity in the twenty arrondissements of Paris. Enterprising proprietors with available street space have constructed a wide array of temporary dining terraces. Pallets are the favored construction material. On the rue de la Grande-Chaumière, the restaurant Esttia has built two parking-space-width dining areas on either side of my building entrance. They conform to the preferred model: upright pallets create a rustic balustrade around tables-for-four on a 'floor' of pallets overlain with green Astroturf; planters—here, sprouting yellow, white, and violet pansies—hang along the exterior perimeter. Seating capacity is probably only a smidgen less than indoors. Regulars have lost no time in finding their way back, and by the time I returned from a brief shopping expedition around noon, guests occupied five of the eight tables, conversing cheerfully as they considered menu options.

A few blocks north, on the rue de Fleurus, where Gertrude Stein once lived, the café/bakery Bread&Roses has bracketed its pallet-and-Astroturf terrace with cedarwood planters filled with delphiniums and placed large white umbrellas over each table. Down the street, Bistro la Gorgée took a more spartan, industrial-chic approach by painting bright green its linkable metal barriers that separate tables from traffic and bracketing its space with rectangular grey steel planters filled with beach stones and minia-ture trees. Two large white canopies roof the tables.

Less ambitious establishments, already suffering financially despite government assistance, have installed tables on the street with a few potted plants to ward off vehicles. Like most restaurants with adjacent squares or broad sidewalks, Le Vent d'Amour ('the wind of love'), on the corner of the quai de la Tournelle and the eponymous bridge, has colonized the triangular pedestrian space beside the bridge, setting up a half-dozen tables with festive, red-checkered tablecloths. Although not private, diners do have spectac-ular views of Notre-Dame and Île Saint-Louis, while harried servers dodge traffic to deliver food and drink.

This is a moment of creativity, challenge, and entrepreneurship not only in how Paris looks: pleasantly uncrowded, a surge of new dining terraces, an explosion in graffiti that perhaps reflects *confine-ment* frustration, and a sudden emergence of bicycle traffic. Bicycle sales boom, inspired by a reluctance to ride potentially disease-ridden public transportation traveled by fellow passengers who find it acceptable to wear their mask below their noses and sometimes further down, as a kind of ineffective chin support. Weight gain, two months of limited exercise, and fresh air opportunities undoubtedly also inspire. The augmentation of bike lanes facilitates bike riding, with the result that the streets of Paris are beginning to resemble those of Amsterdam and Berlin. At rush hour, cyclists crowd together at red lights, jockeying for advantageous take-off positions like marathon runners at the starting line.

These new developments remind me that Paris, a city I love in part because of its fierce preservation of tradition and history—in architecture, artisanal occupations, horticulture, dance, and music—is really a living organism undergoing a steady process of transfor-mation, even if its changes occur so incrementally that they often escape notice. I now observe many more details about the city, its inhabitants, and its habits, than on prior visits because the distractions and veneer of hectic contemporaneity that usually overlay one's experience have been eradicated by the pandemic. COVID-19 has disrobed Paris, rendering it naked, raw, authentic, and endearing; solitude enables me to revel in it with sharpened senses. Denmark might have invented modern happiness over the course of the eighteenth and nineteenth centuries, but the pandemic—with its fear-inducing urgency tempered by a strangely elastic experience of time and a more profound connection to place—has induced in me a satisfying sense of modern happiness.

Thursday 4 June

With cafés and restaurants now open, I can finally visit my favorite Chinese noodle shop, appropriately named Happy Nouilles, on the rue Beaubourg. It's an authentically shabby noodles joint whose hand-pulled noodles are unsurpassed anywhere, including in Shanghai. I like to sit outside, where I can watch through the window the well-muscled noodle-puller tossing, stretching, folding, as he transforms lumps of raw dough into uniform lengths of savory goodness.

As I passed the Centre Pompidou, banners hanging from its signature, multi-colored exterior scaffolding announced the extension until fall of the exhibition "Christo et Jeanne-Claude Paris!" The show, planned years in advance, is now a poignant tribute to the extraordinary artist-couple, whose wrap and installation projects —the giant yellow and blue *Umbrellas* in Japan and California, the orange *Gates* in New York's Central Park, the hot pink *Surrounded Islands* in azure Biscayne Bay, the silver *Reichstag Wrapped* in Berlin, and my favorite (perhaps because it's the only one I've seen in person), the *Pont Neuf Wrapped*—have enriched the lives of the millions who have witnessed them.

Curators organized the exhibition in anticipation of the couple's upcoming project, the wrapping of the Arc de Triomphe, initially scheduled for April 2020. When Christo heard that birds nest there in springtime, he moved the project to September, by which time the baby birds should have left their nests. When the pandemic struck, he postponed the project for a year, until September 2021.

I witnessed the installation of the *Pont Neuf Wrapped* with my mother in September 1985. Before I left to conduct dissertation research in Göteborg, Sweden, we spent three glorious weeks on a mother-daughter odyssey that included the Côte d'Azur, Provence, and Paris. Daddy stayed home with his garden. Christo is my favorite contemporary artist because his projects are altruistic: they infuse viewer-participants with joy through aesthetic pleasure. Unlike many works of art, theirs are free and accessible to all. There isn't a single witness whose life is not at least momentarily transformed by these projects, which embody delight in the magic of life. A team for decades, Christo was the creative and Jeanne-Claude (who died in 2009), the manager. While inspired to create these works for their personal gratification, they—like any conscientious host and hostess—wanted to share the joy, an unavoidable consequence because their temporary, usually three-week-long, projects always occur in public places.

Since the pair was stubbornly determined to realize their projects with absolute autonomy, they financed them themselves, too. No fund-raising or rich donors, although wealthy art aficionados would have wrestled for the privilege. The Christos raised money through the sale of drawings, prints, collages, and plans that Christo made as part of his creative process in addition to utilizing their impressive art collection as collateral. One-of-a-kind drawings by the artist's hand, priced according to size, were sold to museums and collectors. Once the Christos, as they are called, raised sufficient funds for a project and obtained the necessary permissions, the physical work began. Engineers design and test fabrics and anchoring materials to ensure they are safe and environmentally friendly (all materials are recycled), and relevant teams of experts are hired: sometimes scuba divers, often mountain climbers.

A secondary, yet essential, aspect of Christo projects is 'getting to yes'. Because their installations occupy public spaces, many permissions must be obtained: landowners both public and private, governments municipal and national. For instance, when they envisioned the *Wrapped Reichstag* in 1971, Berlin was a divided city and the Reichstag, a bombed-out shell located in the British Sector adjacent to the Russian Sector with its treacherous No Man's Land, a spot where dozens died trying to escape the Communist East. Christo and Jeanne-Claude required permission from the East German government to temporarily install equipment necessary to realize the project, permission they never received. When Germany reunited in 1990, permissions were eagerly granted and the project, executed in September 1995, became a symbol of German reunification.

The *Pont Neuf* project required permission from individual property owners in view of the bridge, the mayors of the arrondissements it spanned, and city, state, and national governments, any of which could have killed the project by withholding consent. The mere obtaining of authorization constituted a daunting, if eventually successful, task. The wrap of the bridge, sidewalks, and lampposts in a neutral clay color that shimmered differently in natural daylight and artificial evening light, took three weeks to install and lasted almost three weeks once completed. The street itself remained uncovered, since Christo and Jeanne-Claude abided by an ecological 'do no harm' philosophy that mandated that the spaces they temporarily occupied continued normal usage.

During our several stints in Paris planned specifically to observe various stages of the installation, Mother and I frequently strolled from our nearby hotel on the rue Jacob to watch the progress: mountaineers rappelling down the sides of the bridge, scuba divers anchoring fabric underwater with ropes. We weren't alone. At first, many considered it a construction site, but as lampposts were wrapped and fabric unfurled onto the sidewalks, it become clear that something else was under way. Increasing numbers of spectators flocked to inspect the day's progress, especially in the early evening. Observers marveled and chatted with strangers. The project worked its social magic. This, in fact, is the most inspiring aspect of Christo projects: you find yourself newly sensitized to the beauty of your ever-changing environment and moved to appreciate it with childlike awe. And to share it with others. It almost works the effect of a few drinks, inducing a pleasantly intoxicated state in which you suddenly feel comfortable striking up conversations with strangers.

After our sojourn in the south, Mother and I returned to Paris for the final installation stages and the 'opening'. Art openings are often exclusive events where diamonds sparkle and champagne flows. But not a Christo and Jeanne-Claude opening. They made works in public spaces for the public, and the public attended. No black-tie previews for the rich and well-connected, but gladly many curious journalists hovering about. Establishing a press office is one of their first orders of business. Friends who worked with Christo tipped me off that on opening day, the satirical weekly *Le Canard enchaîné* ('the chained duck') would include a centerfold of Christo's rendering of the completed project; I bought several as gifts, which Christo kindly autographed.

While this moment, this opening, was exhilarating, the expanse of time before and after constituted the true achievement of the wrap. People shopping or heading to and from work walked on the fabric and found themselves, literally, part of the artwork. Art and life merged in an effortless, inspiriting way that enhanced rather than interrupted the flow of life. Confrontation with this absurd, gratuitous gesture invited a response of pure pleasure. Everyone who has experienced a Christo project has participated in some way and remembers it fondly. What other works of contemporary art exert that impact? Christo's projects are efforts of unmitigated good. They generate a wrinkle in the universe that provides a glimpse into how the world could be—one of beauty, bliss, plenitude, and creativity. Although, sadly, the artist won't witness the *Arc de Triomphe* wrap next year, it seems fitting that this gentle soul died peacefully in his sleep a few days ago after spending a productive day working in his Soho, New York studio.

Friday 5 June

Paris in particular, and France in general, must have more miniature breed dogs per capita than anywhere else on the planet. Who thought there could be so many Cavalier King Charles spaniels, Malteses, or Yorkies? In the 1970s and '80s, there were legions of long-haired Dachshunds and German Shepherds, but no longer. I wonder if there exists a sociological study to explain the waning and waxing of dog-breed popularity? If the partner thing doesn't materialize for me, I'll get a dog. A small, portable one. I'm leaning toward a Havanese, although my heart yearns for a Bernese or a Newfie, the magnificent giant I grew up with. A dog would ensure my getting outdoors regularly and satisfy to some degree my need for affection. But first, I need to settle on a permanent home location. I'm progressing on the Bonheur novel, immersing myself in the daily life of Rosa and Nathalie and Nathalie's mom, who lived with them. I record their conversations and accompany them on outings. Occasionally, they move faster than I can write. They, too, frequent le Luco.

Although much of the week was glorious—warm and sunny— today was rainy. Caroline, the professor who looked at the apartment recently and with whom I have picnicked several times in le Luco, invited me to tag along to the Banksy exhibition at Espace Lafayette-Druot in the Ninth Arrondissement with her and her friend Bruno. Banksy's insights are raw and pertinent—the perfect show at this tragic and absurd moment: a dog begs for a bone from its master, the bone being the dog's own tibia amputated by his bourgeois master, who holds a bloody saw in his other hand. A rat wearing a peace sign necklace holds a protest placard that advises 'get out while you can'. *Should I*, I wondered? After all, repatriation remains an option. Were my two citizenships not in countries either flailing in a state of utter chaos by the pandemic and partisan politics (U.S.) or mismanaging the COVID-19 crisis in a cruel and senseless manner (Sweden), I may have taken Rat's advice.

But I can't predict how events will unfold, where or when things will improve, what travel options will be available. Furthermore, Dr. Fauci advises against travel, and I trust him. Since there is talk of border closings and quarantines, it seems sensible to stay put. I'm also afraid to travel because one can't know if fellow passengers are asymptomatic yet communicable, if they will respect recommended hygienic precautions, or if hygienic precautions will be enforced. Inge and Jürgen in Hainewalde and Robert and Marita in Potsdam have invited me multiple times to shelter with them, but unanswerable questions hold me back: How to get there safely? Would I be able to return to France, my location of preference for the moment?

After viewing the exhibition, Bruno returned home to his ailing wife (not COVID-19) in the Seventh Arrondissement, and Caroline, currently living in the Sixteenth, and I decided to dine together. In normal times, finding a table in that busy commercial neighborhood at 7 p.m. on a Friday evening is daunting. And this was the first Friday after *déconfinement* that restaurants were open, with outdoor seating the only permissible option. To make matters worse, it was sheeting rain, thereby limiting desirable seating to adequately sheltered spots. After two months of being cooped up and isolated, Parisians avidly flocked to cafés and restaurants. Customers sat huddled together at every establishment we passed, and many restaurants had positioned tables too close together for comfort. Diners and drinkers seemed unperturbed if a bit damp. I felt wary even if Caroline now feels invincible, fortified as she is with antibodies since recovering from COVID-19 in March.

We eventually found a restaurant on the rue Montmartre with no vacancy at its outdoor tables but which had a wall of large open windows, rendering the interior as well-ventilated as the terrace. The interior offered total protection from the steady rain and was safer from a hygienic perspective since no one was there and spacing was better. I asked a waiter if we could sit inside. The waiter asked the manager. The manager said 'sure', so we were seated indoors illegally. We felt the thrill of being outlaws.

Passersby noticed us. They, too, requested indoor seating. By the time we finished our salads and paid the check, every indoor table was occupied. It still felt far safer than restaurants that put up close-sided plastic tents with no ventilation that—because they were technically outdoors—could legally fill their tables. I'm beginning to realize that common sense isn't all that common. Caroline and I parted ways— she, heading west, I, south. I opened my umbrella and walked down the rue du Louvre, past the old-fashioned neon sign advertising Agence Duluc Détective. A fixture for decades, it evokes images of trench-coated detectives stealthily shadowing their marks; it made a cameo appearance in Woody Allen's *Midnight in Paris*. I passed the Louvre's main façade and envisioned gold-encrusted carriages pulled by teams of matching prancing horses kicking up dust as they entered the central portal of the royal palace.

Thursday 11 June

Today, I walked to the Marais, a charming, partly Jewish, neighborhood, whose four- and five-story buildings date to the sixteenth and seventeenth centuries. A yen for falafel motivated me. I went where the crowds go, L'As du Fallafel on the rue des Rosiers because I like their fresh-squeezed mint lemonade. Their falafel and hummus are also terrific but not necessarily better than Chez Hanna, Miznon, or King Falafel Palace nearby. I bypassed the long line of people waiting behind crowd control ropes for falafel wraps and was seated immediately. Restaurant regulations have shifted dramatically during the past week since government officials realized that trying to prevent Parisians from indoor dining would result in riots. They acquiesced to distancing and hygienic requirements although not all establishments respect them. L'As personnel initially seated customers at alternate tables, but as more diners arrived the in-between tables filled as well. Some restaurants have removed tables or inserted plastic partitions in compliance with hygienic regulations, but that was not the case at L'As.

Fortified and content, I wandered over to place des Vosges, the Marais's central park, and spent an hour sitting on a bench writing. And daydreaming. I remembered from reading one of the most engaging books ever written about Paris, *How Paris Became Paris. The Invention of the Modern City* by Joan DeJean, that this verdant oasis, the very first purpose-built public square in France surrounded by buildings, was originally paved and called place Royale. Official public celebrations for up to fifty thousand occurred here, beginning with the 1612 announcement of two royal engagements.

It was also Europe's first urban planning project financed by private investment. The fact that King Henri IV offered tax incentives and titles of nobility to the Lyon silk manufacturers who first settled here probably helped. The red brick and limestone facades appear harmoniously unified, but interiors exhibit tremendous variety. The first inhabitants were parvenus—self-made, rags-to-riches men—a new phenomenon at the time. By mid-century, most had profited from steeply rising real estate prices and sold their properties to aristocrats, the wealthiest of whom built lavish mansions nearby. Many of these have since become museums, archives, institutes, and headquarters. Paris has a long history of transforming private residences like the Louvre into public and commercial spaces.

Tuesday 16 June

Mark has been calling me *cherie* and *mon amour*, appellations that makes me melt inside and trigger a tingle of happiness. The power of words. We have now decided to meet. But where? While there is talk of drug companies developing vaccines, that reality seems farther than the horizon. Since June 1st, France has been off limits to Americans, and I immediately thought of Sweden as a replacement, somewhere near my beloved Tolg. I yearn for nature, so I suggested a cottage on a lake in the south of Sweden, an idea he liked. Mark is eager to discover 'my' Sweden, and I investigated rentals for a few weeks in July hoping he can travel there. I found several secluded cabins on or near lakes.

The search catapulted my thoughts back to halcyon summer days exploring the peripheries of the two lakes situated on either side of the canal where I keep my boat (I still have it) hauled up onto the grass and tied to a tree. In one direction lies Lake Asa, less interesting once there (although Herman Göring reputedly once landed there in a seaplane with his Swedish wife). The way there, however, through the mysterious 'Troll Forest'—as Hanna and I christened it—is magical. It's a quiet and dark passage with arthritic tree roots arching into the water and forming little mossy caves in which one can imagine Water Rat from *The Wind in the Willows* dwelling. I used to go there during light rains when I had a hankering to row because it's sheltered by a leafy awning of trees. Afterward, I would sit there, smoking a joint and listening to the gentle tapping of raindrops on leaves and the occasional whooshing sound of flying geese, for whom the canal served—as for me—as a kind of highway linking the two lakes.

My happy place though is Lake Tolg, much more fun to explore, with its irregular coastline punctuated by red-painted farmhouses perched on hills, fields of foraging cows and goats, forests and islands to explore. I would often row out to the middle of the lake, drop anchor, make my seat into a comfortable cot with a towel mattress and shoe pillow, and lie, rocking gently from side to side watching the clouds. The sky there is frequently filled with Simpson Clouds. I also enjoyed stretching out with a book on the mossy forest floor, soft and inviting as an eiderdown mattress, until words blurred on the page, my eyes fluttered closed, and I fell asleep.

I love the berry-rich forests of southern Sweden because they recall childhood memories of summers spent exploring the coastal forests of Maine, where my family spent several weeks each summer. There, I whiled away hours chipping tiny garnets in the granite quarry, my first get-rich-quick scheme after my father gave up on my appreciating sketching the way he did. Mother promoted berry picking by baking a pie when I had gathered sufficient wild blueberries or strawberries. I could pick enough blueberries in three or four hours, but wild strawberries took twice that amount of time and eating while picking constituted a greater danger, so strawberry pies were a rarity.

Having someone besides Hanna with whom to share the extraordinary forests of southern Sweden feels important. I found several good cabin candidates, but suddenly Sweden—the pandemic-be-damned country—has also closed to Americans. Iceland remains possible. Halfway between Europe and the U.S. and still open, it offers a reasonable alternative. I'll miss verdant nature; Iceland's terrain is harsh, windswept, treeless. But the thought of honeymooning with Mark makes me quiver with anticipation. If our expectations are met—and I feel sure they will be—we've agreed that I'll move to New York shortly afterward. Perhaps a crazy decision in pandemic times, but most of my friends are there, and I find the thought of settling down compelling.

We've bought tickets and are eager for ten days of togetherness. Mark's making travel arrangements because he has dreamed of going there and has sights he hopes to see. I just want to be with him, lindy hopping to recorded music on a terrace in the shadow of an Icelandic volcano. Who would have thought I would luck into finding my soulmate this easily? The Law of Attraction meditation I listen to on Sunday mornings must be working. The universe is sending me what I deserve.

Friday 19 June

I spent much of the week editing articles on the less-than-riveting subject of art history's institutional history in Sweden. I can't imagine who besides the authors will read these pedantic, trivia-filled essays, but with no summer income, I'm grateful for the gig. Mostly, I worked in le Luco, now back to its old self, with neighbor-hood residents occupying its sturdy green metal chairs, some of which have reclined backs perfect for sunning or napping. I like walking past the spot on the east terrace where van Gogh painted one of his few Impressionist-style paintings: a view of the basin, fountain, and palace on a sunny spring day a few years before the Eiffel Tower poked up from the horizon above the palace's *orangerie*.

My favorite spot to sit, however, is on the west terrace under shady trees beside the sculpture of Anne of Austria, powerful mother of Louis XIV. From there, I enjoy a sweeping vista of Luxembourg Palace, flower beds, the basin and fountain, the east terrace, and am near enough to the pony ride station to smell them; some people like the smell of gasoline, I relish the earthy aroma of horse manure. I occupy two straight-backed chairs, one for sitting, one for propping up my legs, which function as an *ad hoc* desk for my laptop. For variety, I sit along the pathway of grassy spots on the park's west side now and then in view of a sculpture, often my favorite, the Watteau memorial. I also like the verdant trough around the Medici Fountain, but it's currently closed for repairs, and magnificent as Jules Dalou's *Delacroix Monument* is, its location on a busy pedestrian thoroughfare discourages concentration.

Sunday 21 June

Today is *Fête de la musique*, an annual, national event. While Swedes celebrate Midsummer by hopping like 'little frogs' (as one of the songs goes) around flora-adorned maypoles singing "Here we go 'round the Mulberry Bush," on June 21 (or the nearest weekend), France unleashes a spectacular musical celebration impressively ecumenical in breadth. Every church, every music venue hosts concerts either free or with paid admission, and there are musicians —professional and amateur—in every square, on every street corner, playing everything from Bach to Django Reinhart. With scheduled events prohibited this year, *ad hoc* concerts popped up all over the city. People are suffering from live music deprivation.

In the evening, I heard faint strains of music beckoning, so out I went. At the Vavin triangle, a trio of elderly gentlemen wearing matching striped t-shirts reminiscent of the Lovin' Spoonful played bluegrass in harmonies as well-matched as their outfits. Over at le Luco, beside the tile-and-yellow brick building at the Vavin entrance, a string quartet of accomplished youngsters played Mendelssohn's Quartet in E-flat major for an appreciative crowd. Further on, near the waffle stand, a scruffy, stringy-haired Dylan wannabe crooned covers pathetically, strumming his out of tune acoustic guitar and making me wish I had lingered longer at the quartet or bluegrass groups and prompting me to hasten onward.

I exited the park. As I walked down the rue Bonaparte, I heard a brass band belting out Goran Bregović's 2000 hit "Mesečina," which moved my feet from fourth into sixth gear. By the time I found them on the rue de Seine—twelve impassioned young people playing tenor saxes, trumpets, baritones, drums, and one small fellow valiantly shouldering a sousaphone—they were playing a tune that under normal circumstances would not allow my feet to keep still, "Užičko Kolo." These musicians were not as accomplished as Zlatne Uste, the New York brass band I played with briefly in the late 1980s and with whom I toured Serbia at the invitation of the national news magazine *Ilustrovana Politika*, but their choice of music delighted.

An inquisitive *Ilustrovana Politika* reporter discovered Zlatne Uste at a Lincoln Center performance and wondered what a group of Americans—none of whom had Serbian or even Yugoslav roots—were doing playing the beloved folk music from that then-forgotten corner of Europe. The reporter contacted his editor, who was equally jazzed by the news, and they arranged a tour that included television and radio appearances and numerous performances, the highlight of which was the Woodstock/Bonnaroo-like brass-band festival in the village of Guča, a small town nestled in the lush, rolling countryside south of Belgrade. I went along for the ride the first year in the company of Hanna's father-to-be, but it was so much fun that I, a former French Horn player, decided to take up baritone and join the band. I have missed playing music during these decades of career building.

The festival highlight is a competition for the best band and the best trumpeter. Tireless, energetic Romany bands compete against ethnic Serb groups composed largely of regional farmers. ZU was the novelty guest star. As I stood on that stage in the sweltering August sun surveying an enthusiastic crowd of thirty thousand fans, I understood why the Rolling Stones never retire. I enjoy playing music with friends, but performing for an adoring field of fans that stretches as far as the eye can see is nothing short of electrifying. I doubt that riding the Kingda Ka rollercoaster could possibly be as thrilling. If one had the power to stretch time, I would have made that moment last—if not forever—certainly a lot longer. Our three tunes flashed past in what seemed like a nanosecond. Anyway, that's where I'm transported every time I hear "Užičko Kolo," which we played that day in Guča.

The young band's zeal compensated for its lack of musicality and its decibel level attracted young folks wandering the neighborhood. Surrounding bars were serving, few people were wearing masks, a growing throng was hopping up and down to the music, and I felt uneasy. Still, I didn't regret venturing out for these impromptu performances and returned home energized, occasionally *kolo*-stepping when I thought no one was watching.

Friday 26 June

Every night this week, I have headed to the Eiffel Tower for the first hourly twinkling at 10 p.m. I've also been reading a mystery set during its construction; the story of a young engineer who becomes enmeshed in labor disputes, murder, and seances while helping to design the elevators, which—like the initially temporary structure—reached higher than any others on the planet at the time. I learned that in the final year of construction the project was plagued by labor strikes, and to hurry things along Eiffel installed cafeterias on the Tower's platforms, so workers didn't waste time descending for lunch.

I chatted with Hanna, miscellaneous friends, and Mark, who has now made hotel reservations in Reykjavik for the beginning and end of our rendezvous. Although I'm a plan-in-advance kind of person, I feel no urgency to cement all details at a moment when most sane people are refraining from travel. The warm summer weather has been glorious, and the restaurants and cafés—some with whimsical names like Vegetable Slaughterhouse, The Petulant Fish, and The Smoking Dog—have revived after months of dormancy.

Not all establishments respect the one-meter rule. Cafés and restaurants frequented by older folks—venerable establishments like Rotonde and La Closerie des Lilas—do, while cafés and pizzerias frequented by younger folks often do not. In these establishments, and many line the boulevard Montparnasse, you'd never know a pandemic raged. Gregarious drinkers and diners squeeze together at tightly packed tables.

The only reveal of this abnormal moment are café tables installed on the sidewalks in front of restaurant entrances. They're equipped with pump bottles of sanitizer and clipboards on which you're supposed to write your e-mail address or phone number to enable contact tracing in the event a customer calls later to report a positive COVID-19 diagnosis. Good luck with that. In my effort to be a conscientious citizen, I installed the 'Stop COVID' phone app the minute I saw it mentioned on the news in late March. The concept was that those contaminated would register the fact, and the app would alert others of the proximity of someone infected. I've had it on continuously, and it hasn't beeped once. I may be the only person in Paris who downloaded it.

After passing Puzzle Man at Rennes-Montparnasse, one encounters another curious phenomenon on Montparnasse at the northeast corner of the rue Cherche-Midi: Paringer, a shop with floor-to-ceiling windows that wrap around the corner and furnished like a home. According to its sign, it sells chairs, beds, libraries, leather, and 'structures', and has been manufacturing items both traditional and avant-garde since 1900. The space has a casual disheveled look. And it's hard to avoid peering in. Books on shelves, oriental rugs, worn leather sofas, wooly throws, a dining table with a half-dozen chairs, a china-filled breakfront, centuries-old oil paintings on easels and walls, and lamps, candlesticks, and chandeliers confer an air of cozy domesticity. One might observe a group dining at the table in a far corner underneath the staircase or a bespeckled man reading in a chaise longue. It seems a rather public way to live one's private life—on a busy Paris streetcorner. *In what other city might one see such sights*, I wondered? Such charming eccentricities abound in Paris. After passing the Invalides lawns, stretching all the way to the Seine and jam-packed with picnickers, and standing enthralled by the five-minute twinkle of the Eiffel Tower, I returned home on a route that took me past Puzzle Man's corner around 10:50 p.m. It was dark, and he had vanished. No trace, even, of the card table. *Does he store it at the newsstand*, I wondered?

Sunday 28 June

Today, amid great controversy, local elections were held. It was one of those 'damned if you do, damned if you don't' situations. Critics of Macron's party, *Republique en marche* (REM), complained of an unconscionable disregard for public health and safety, while supporters praised scrupulous hygienic measures that permitted the democratic process to unfold according to schedule. The news showed masked and gloved poll workers, containers of sanitizing gel, helpful distancing marks on the ground, and advised bringing a writing implement, although the ones on hand were cleaned after each use. Agnès Buzyn, a medical doctor and child of Holocaust survivors who served recently as Health Minister, is running as the REM mayoral candidate, but oddsmakers favor the current mayor and Socialist Party candidate, Anne Hildago, to win.

Tuesday 30 June

What is it about the ends of months that rouse men to make relationship-ending phone calls? Trocadéro Man in April and now Mark in June. Just as I was feeling confident about having moved beyond relationship mistakes, Mark called in the morning today, which is middle-of-the-night New York time. Thus, I knew something was up, something not good, although I would never have guessed that it was to end our blossoming virtual romance. But it was. Wracked with guilt, he explained that a few hours earlier, Ex had invited him to dinner and proposed marriage, and he had accepted. Say what? *That* seems like a rather sudden change of plans. During our five-minute conversation, Mark confessed that he had broken things off with her a month—not a year—earlier, as he had told me. He evidently doesn't adhere to The Four Agreements since Number One is "be impeccable with your word." After his confession, I remained silent. What was there to say? OK, a lot, but nothing that would alter the situation and therefore nothing productive.

I would never have wasted ten or more precious hours a week pursuing a relationship with a man emotionally attached to someone else. I knew he longed for a committed relationship but found it puzzling that he took the safe path rather than daring to find out if the exhilarating life he imagined with me could become a reality. I spent most of the day in a self-doubting haze, yet paradoxically confident that I had made the best decisions given available information. Mark did restore my faith in the availability of interesting, intelligent, and promising men. And I enjoyed our virtual time together; it made me happy, and that can be enough. As the English Romantic poet William Blake wrote:

> *He who binds to himself a joy*
> *Does the winged life destroy;*
> *But he who kisses the joy as it flies,*
> *Lives in eternity's sun rise.*

I wrote Mark a letter this evening. For my sake, not his. While on my ayahuasca adventure in February, Shaman Erick suggested I write letters to those who had unintentionally caused me psycho-emotional pain, so I wrote to Trocadéro Man and my father. I explained why and how I was injured and then said I forgave them. Before embarking on my second 'journey', I ceremoniously burned them in the fire. It felt good—a conclusion to unfinished business. I wrote a letter to Mark that I didn't incinerate but sent as an email. His response, as one might guess, was 'I'm very sorry blah blah blah'. I briefly reflected on a future that will not be, knowing that I can't control what others do or think, only how I react to it. The pragmatic me realized with relief that I had probably dodged a bullet, but I can't help feeling saddened by the promise it offered.

Chapter 6
July: Sunshine and Friendships

Thursday 2 July

Mark's unanticipated announcement bothers me surprisingly little; I feel a growing sense of psycho-emotional and spiritual equilibrium. Earlier, internalizing the fact that I was powerless to control circumstances but only my response to them constituted a state as attainable as becoming a star quarterback. Before Trocadéro Man, Mark's news would have catapulted me into a fruitless cycle of rumination and regret. But no longer, thanks to meditation, tapping, breath work, hours of listening to or reading self-help gurus like Dawson Church, Deepak Chopra, Louise Hay, and Sadhguru. Personal experience has taught me that opportunities often come in the wake of disappointment, and these opportunities wouldn't have occurred had the originally desired outcome come to pass. And Paris consoles me. I need only go for a walk. Every time I step into the street, I feel revived. The creative energy, architectural beauty, and friendly smiles dissolve instantly any clouds of negativity that may have been brewing.

My university floods my inbox with announcements, few of any direct pertinence; I give them a cursory glance before discarding. But two weeks ago, one came that required attention. A 'where are you and what mode of teaching do you prefer for the fall: distance, in-person, or hybrid'? query. I revealed where I was and checked 'distance'. Excited about the pedagogical opportunity to teach remotely from Paris, I began making short video clips in front of key monuments, historic spots, and locations where artists we would study had lived and worked. My nineteenth-century art course was going to be thrilling for students stuck home with mom and dad and who had never visited anywhere more exotic than Disneyworld.

Today, however, a university official forbade me from teaching while out of the country and presented me with an ultimatum to either return or take a medical leave. Too prudent to travel, I reluctantly opted for a semi-paid 'medical' leave, unable to understand the garbled reasoning for the refusal to let me work remotely from abroad at a time when other professors I know at American universities, public and private, are doing exactly that. Caroline, for example. I immediately informed my exceptionally efficient department chair, who promptly canceled one of my classes and assigned the other to a colleague.

A few hours later, the university official wrote back rescinding the ultimatum and granting me permission to teach from abroad for the fall. By that time—I was informed by my chair—it was impossible to get my classes back (although it probably wasn't), and I had to accept the medical leave. This chain of events gave me cognitive whiplash. I had looked forward to teaching in this new manner not to mention earning my customary salary. On the bright side, this situation allows me the freedom to write for which I have yearned and the added pleasure of doing it in Paris. Since I live frugally, survival shouldn't be a problem. And the colleague who planned to share my home in Purgatory will now have it all to herself. Maybe I'll finish my book and launch a new career. A bonus five months in Paris? Who could complain?

Monday 6 July

Today, with some trepidation, I left Paris for the first time. The occasion was the celebrate spring—now celebrate summer— luncheon that Marie and Gregoire in Saint Mammès had canceled in April. I should have left earlier for Gare de Lyon, so I didn't have to take the very first bus to arrive. When the 91 pulled up, it was standing-room-only, a situation that sent my cortisol level skyward. Riders tried their best to keep to themselves, but there's only so much one can do on a crowded bus. A bead of perspiration trickled down the center of my back, tickling enroute.

I stationed myself beside a sturdily built woman whose head, with its shortly cropped hair, resembled a 1950s bathing cap. She had decided on a highly original polka-dot pattern: silver with perfectly symmetrical, nickel-sized, tatooed black dots. All that was missing was a tattooed chin strap. After pausing to marvel, I glanced around to see if my co-passengers were properly masked, and, naturally, some weren't. To compensate, I breathed shallowly and infrequently, hoping that would spare me from the assault of infected respiratory droplets. I inhaled deeply once off the bus, restoring my oxygen level before braving the train terminal.

The sparsely occupied train whisked me through the trainyards and industrial outskirts to the suburbs and suddenly to the countryside. It stopped in towns with scenic names like Quincy-sous-Sénart (located below—*sous*—the adjacent forest of Sénart) and in Fontainebleau, home of the royal palace and the immense forest. Rosa Bonheur spent her final happy decades nearby in a modest brick château enclosed by a vast brick-walled garden that is still privately owned.

Marie greeted me at the station, where I was the only one to debark. We walked the five minutes to her home, snuggled in a beautifully landscaped yard surrounded by a wall against which flowering bushes thrive. After inspecting home improvement projects inspired by *confinement* and frequently visiting grandchildren, we dined in the back garden. Joining us was Jim, Marie's English teacher from decades ago, who has since become a friend. We spoke French, and Marie showed me her most recent book, translated into English by Jim.

We compared *confinement* experiences. Jim watched lots of opera videos, Gregoire constructed a basement playroom, Marie kept a hectic schedule of international Zoom-lecturing and reading stories daily to her grandchildren. I relished my first traditional home-cooked French meal in ages. It began with *aperos* and nibbles—radishes and miniature cukes from the garden and cashews—followed by a veal roast served with potatoes and freshly picked green beans. Then, salad with bibb lettuce and *mache* from the garden and a selection of cheeses (consumed mild to pungent, and never take seconds!), and finally, dessert, a rich, gooey gluten-free chocolate cake followed by espresso. Although they all knew Fontainebleau well, when I revealed that I'd never been, it became the post-prandial destination.

The interior is a riot of exquisite visual overstimulation with sumptuous fabrics, paintings and sculptures, inlay and gilding, competing for attention. As we wandered, I eagerly surveyed its picture-dense walls to find an important painting most visitors undoubtedly hurry past: Joseph Marie Vien's 1763 *Seller of Loves*. Vien directed the French Academy in Rome, taught Jacques-Louis David, and pioneered French Neoclassicism. *Seller of Loves* is where it began. The painting is modestly sized; one can envision it hanging over a sofa. In the pastel colors of Rococo, it represents three young women in an austere Roman-style interior. Before two laconic rich ladies, a peasant girl kneels, holding in her right hand a basket containing two chubby, winged putti and in her extended left, a blue-winged third, which she dangles by its wings. The simply yet elegantly coiffed and dressed women, one seated, one standing behind her, contemplate a purchase: buy a putto and find romantic love. If only! Erotic subjects enjoyed tremendous popularity with the French ruling class in the eighteenth century, a time when aristocratic hedonism reached its zenith, an era that ended abruptly in 1789.

Vien was an astute fellow and grasped the taste of his audience and its hunger for novelty. Nothing signaled trendiness at the time more than references to treasures unearthed during excavations then in full swing at Pompeii and Herculaneum. And how to find out about them without visiting the sites in that analog era? Charles VII, King of Naples and a savvy promoter of tourism, hired artists to draw artifacts. The drawings were immediately engraved and printed in limited-edition volumes that he gifted to other European monarchs, from George III of England to Catherine the Great of Russia. Monarchs shared these treasures with artists in their employ, thereby encouraging a new style—Neoclassicism—rooted in the past and reflecting elite access to the very latest archaeological discoveries. In this painting, Vien modified a wall painting from Herculaneum published in black and white one year earlier, 1762. He adopted pastel tones and elegant furnishings in accordance with contemporary Rococo taste. The difference in social class conveyed metaphorically by the space between the aristocratic women and the peasant vendor evidenced the elite's desire to distance itself both physically and conceptually from peasants because it interpreted poverty as a sign of both stupidity and inferiority.

Afterward, we walked through the classically symmetrical Diana Garden designed by the renowned landscape architect André le Nôtre, the modest genius responsible for the gardens at Versailles and Vaux-le-Vicomte, with their intricate geometries and mechanical fountains. The sun beat down, penetrating the gap between sunglasses and brow to assault my eyes, which teared as I found myself squinting and straying into shaded spots for relief.

We stopped for a drink at an outdoor café in the adjacent village. Although undoubtedly less crowded than pre-pandemic, tourists circulated—mostly French but also Italian, English, Dutch, and German—making the most of a spectacular summer day. Touristic venues have just the right visitor density now: sufficient to assure that attractions remain open but without the lines and jostling that suck the joy out of travel. I revealed that I was writing a novel about Rosa Bonheur and happy to see the village of Fontainebleau because of its proximity to her own château, By. That revelation prompted Marie to mention that a neighbor's sister presided over the Rosa Bonheur Society and that she would try to arrange a meeting. How fortuitous! I hope that such a meeting might lead to a visit to Bonheur's château, so I can get a vivid impression of her milieu.

Jim and I traveled together back to Gare de Lyon. Throughout the afternoon, we had joked occasionally in English, and now we embraced our expat Americanness. We presented brief summaries of our lives up to that point, shared our favorite Parisian haunts, and learned we had several acquaintances in common. His significant other is an aristocrat living on the family property in Brittany, a revelation that fueled my imagination. But mostly, Jim is alone and in town. He often attends operas and concerts, especially Baroque ones, and we discussed a next meeting: lunch at his home and a stroll in nearby Parc de Sceaux, whose gardens were also designed by le Nôtre. I'm happy to have met a new attentive, gracious, kind, and interesting person as eager to befriend me as I, him.

Upon arrival in Paris in the early evening, we traversed a hallway lined with reproductions of nineteenth-century Danish paintings, advertisements for a forthcoming exhibition at the Petit Palais, "The Golden Age of Danish Painting." It reminded me of my monograph, *Denmark and the Invention of Modern Happiness*, now in suspended animation and awaiting a trip to Copenhagen. I felt a twinge of urgency to finish that book, but there is little I can do about it just now.

As of Friday, France has a new prime minister, Jean Castex. His predecessor, Édouard Philippe, a tall, handsome man with absolute composure and a reassuring manner, ran for mayor of his native Le Harvre and won. In fact, he is popular everywhere, and journalists have speculated that his ability to steal the limelight from Macron during the COVID-19 crisis may explain why the president encouraged him to run for office elsewhere. The alternative explanation posits that Philippe contemplates challenging Macron in the 2022 presidential election and therefore is establishing his distance.

Castex could not be more different in appearance and temperament. He is short and balding, with an intensity typical of working-class functionaries who harbor resentment for the privileged and that portends a fiery temper kept under careful control. A native of the Pyrénées region bordering Spain, Castex, who also speaks fluent Catalan, proudly retains his distinctive accent, a source of comment and, for some, derision. It reminds me of how Bernie Sanders adamantly retains his Brooklyn accent and folksy manner as a sign of credible authenticity.

Wednesday 8 July

Yesterday evening, I had a date with an architect who was well-educated, successful, and interested in culture—a good start that rapidly went south. He was half Vietnamese, half French, a common ethnic mix in Paris, and insisted inexplicably that he looked more Japanese. He produced a veritable dossier of information, from anecdotes to disturbingly particular racial details. Curious, I inquired why he felt this was important, a question he dismissed huffily, asserting it was simply a fact, and there wasn't a reason. *Well then*, I thought, *he needs to think a bit more deeply about this; unresolved psychological issues seem to lurk.* This topic rapidly became so annoying that I contemplated saying that although my roots are Irish, French, and Greek, people are constantly assuming I'm Finnish and then explaining why. Or some equally absurd parallel.

He proudly showed me pictures of his country house on the Normandy coast—a cement block monstrosity in Trouville, the less fashionable sibling town of Deauville—in an apparent effort to impress. It looked more to be the design of an internment camp building than of an architect's showplace home. We prolonged our agony for some reason and had a delicious dinner at Hanoi on the rue Monsieur-le-Prince. He confided that he would never eat at an Asian restaurant that served the cuisine of more than one country. While that sounded a bit snobby, I appreciated his discernment and figured there might be something to it. Pan-Asian restaurants are usually mediocre at everything except their homeland's specialties. He fell into the by now familiar French category of men fascinated by their own, relatively uneventful, lives and palpably lacking curiosity about the lives of others. I imagine he found me as dull and disagreeable as I found him, although really, he couldn't possibly judge based on the scanty information I managed to wedge into our conversation. I don't expect to hear from him again.

Caroline and I visited Sainte-Chapelle this morning. It was one of those refreshing mornings that feels warm in the sun and cool in the shade. Intense sunlight provided optimal conditions for admiring the floor-to-ceiling jewel-like windows of Sainte-Chapelle, tucked away in a small courtyard of the medieval royal palace on Île de la Cité. An assortment of ornamental medieval architectural sculptures lay higgledy-piggledy along its perimeter. Modern visitors find it astonishing that Louis IX spent more money on a chest to hold Christ's alleged crown-of-thorns (for which he had also paid a princely sum)—once housed there and now at Notre-Dame—than on the chapel itself. It seems ironic, too, that Marie Antoinette, France's most glamourous queen, spent her final days in 1793 next door imprisoned behind the thick, dank walls of the Conciergerie wearing a plain, scratchy, woolen dress.

I've considered visiting Sainte-Chapelle numerous times in recent decades. I adore it but detest waiting in line. I feel minutes of my life ticking away unless I have remembered to bring a book along or interesting goings-on distract me. This means that many things I would have visited in Paris regularly I haven't seen in years. No wonder I'm delighted by the pandemic's collateral impact. As I approached on the boulevard du Palais, I noticed a crowd control rope hanging between stanchions on the sidewalk in front of the street entrance to the site, but not a soul waited. A guard leaned against the building observing the few passersby. I put on my mask as I walked between the velvet rope and the cool stone façade. The guard checked my reservation and waved me through. In the courtyard, an attendant squirted the obligatory sanitizer onto my palm even though touching anything inside is prohibited.

Signs posted at the entrance and throughout the site advised of the now familiar hygienic regulations in force, and blue arrows taped to the floor transformed the visit into a one-way-only experience. Caroline and I joined a half-dozen admirers in the glittering upper hall of the monumental reliquary constructed to house the smaller one containing Louis IX's cache of Christological treasures. I'm bedazzled every time I visit. Walls melt to form delicate frames around elegantly attenuated windows. Within each appears a stack of biblical scenes configured in an astonishing variety of formats: almonds, circles, diamonds, ovals, quatrefoils, squares, and hybrids for which I have no name. Sometimes, figures appear in the corners of the square fields in which the frames are inscribed, while the spaces outside the frames contain a profusion of geometric patterns.

Blues and reds dominate, conveying the sensation of being inside a shimmering tent of sapphires and rubies. My eyes strained to identify the hundreds of scenes. I wished I had brought opera glasses. This was the first time I stayed as long as I wanted. It felt luxurious. Usually, the human swarm impedes concentration, movement, and pleasure. One can now savor Paris with the easy-going leisure of a VIP or visitor from an earlier era.

As I returned home for an afternoon of writing in le Luco, I took a scenic route past the *bouquinistes* along the Seine. I've always marveled at their very specifically formed boxes. They're custom-fitted to the contours of the wall that protects pedestrians gawking at Notre-Dame from tumbling onto the stone quays below. Marvels of mechanical engineering, they're sufficiently watertight to protect the books, magazines, and prints within. I also wondered about their proprietors: did they inherit them? Do they pay rent? Is there a market for buying and selling them? What do their owners do when they're not sitting on lawn chairs waiting for customers?

In recent years, I've noticed boxes disappearing; one now sees gaps on both sides of the river where they once perched. Like so many countryside towns, this intimate village of book lover-sellers is gradually depopulating, with those who remain, aging and isolated. The little islands of enticing books and prints and the men and women who love them are increasingly ignored by pedestrians. Many have resorted to selling tourist trinkets. I refuse to imagine a Paris without *bouquinistes*, although the only ones saddened by their absence will be those who remember their presence.

Friday 10 July

Yesterday, Mara—visiting for a week from Oslo—and I went to the Musée d'Orsay. We arrived armed with our reservations, happy the museum was less crowded than usual, although it was far from empty. Because it features works of art from my period of expertise —the mid-nineteenth to early twentieth century—I have lots to say, too much, really, about many of the paintings and sculptures there. One of my favorite stories surrounds Gustave Courbet's hideous *Burial at Ornans*. I've never found it attractive (has anyone?), but I'm intrigued by its genesis and early history. It's enormous: ten-feet tall and twenty-two-feet long. The crowd of figures, all portraits of inhabitants of his hometown, Ornans, near the Swiss border, are life-size. Courbet exhibited the gargantuan canvas at the prestigious government-sponsored Salon exhibition of 1851. It would probably have been rejected by a jury for several reasons: the wall space it monopolized, the uneven degree of detail that made it appear hurried and amateurish, the fact that he entered it in the category of history painting with no clear indication of what historical event he depicted. Significantly, it wasn't rejected, thanks to a rule that allowed him to bypass the jury, a benefit accompanying a prize he had won several years earlier.

Burial is in fact a history painting, in a personal as well as a historical-political sense, but the artist withheld relevant information because he thrived on controversy. Few things gave this country boy from a rich farming family more pleasure than outraging the Parisian bourgeoisie. Wiping his mouth with his sleeve at meals, dressing inappropriately, you name it; in a world replete with rules regulating all aspects of comportment, no one could insult the bourgeoisie more successfully than someone acculturated into it—someone who knew and gleefully flouted its rules.

Art criticism in those days split along political lines, and Courbet was clearly a leftie. But *Burial* puzzled even progressive critics. What historical event? Well, several, as it turns out. On a political level, it represented the final compliance of a provincial town with an ordinance passed during the brief restoration of the Bourbon Monarchy two decades earlier. The Restoration government dictated that for hygienic reasons burials should occur in new cemeteries created outside town limits and not beside the church, almost always located at the town center.

France has always had a center-periphery problem, evidenced currently by the suspiciousness with which some provincial inhabitants regard COVID-19 edicts coming from Paris. To demonstrate its orneriness, Ornans continued burying its dead in the old cemetery until 1848, when the Second Republic was declared, and all French *men* were given the right to vote. Encouraged by this measure, Ornans decided to comply with the old ordinance as a sign of support for the new, 'democratic' government.

Here, Courbet documented the inaugural burial, that of his great uncle. His accomplishment in this painting was to combine national, regional, and personal history along with portraiture (Prestige Category Two) of an assembly whose low social status fitted them more appropriately for genre (paintings of everyday life, Category Three). Courbet's cavalier flaunting of bourgeois privilege through ignoring its conventions reminded me, yet again, of Trocadéro Man, who would wait for general boarding of a plane, then, politely if determinedly, stroll past everyone, me in tow, board the plane, flash our tickets, and turn left into the first-class cabin.

Saturday 18 July

Bastille Day commemorates the storming of the Bastille Prison and the inauguration of the decade-long French Revolution. The French refer to it simply as 'July 14th' and celebrate it with a military parade along the Champs-Élysées during the day and a spectacular fireworks display at the Eiffel Tower at night. I tried to figure out a good spot to watch the fireworks. Fearful of contagion, officials closed the most popular viewing spots: the Champ-de-Mars and pont d'Iéna. I decided that the plaza in front of the Panthéon, situated on a hill with a clear view of the Eiffel Tower five kilometers away, would be a good choice.

I couldn't help thinking of how much better a location I enjoyed two years earlier, when not only did I watch the celebration (and hear the concert) from Trocadéro Man's terrace with an unimpeded, head-to-toe view of the Eiffel Tower but in the nights prior, lay in bed nestled beside him on cool, soft, well-worn linen sheets while watching the hourly twinkle. To my astonishment, more activity followed: the trials and rehearsals of the digital visual program projected onto the Tower that synchronize with the fireworks. I wonder how many people realize that in the three or four days prior to July 14th a light show occurs on the surface of the Eiffel Tower after the final hourly twinkling at 1 a.m., one that continues until 3:30-4 a.m., when the first whispers of daylight appear?

On the 13th, thanks to Trocadéro Man's 360-degree view, I discovered at dark small bursts of fireworks erupting at short intervals along the horizon's entire perimeter. Darting back and forth on the terrace, I chanced whiplash as I twisted my head around to see the best bits, usually noticed a tad late from the corners of my eyes. I learned that surrounding towns schedule their fireworks displays for the eve of Bastille Day in order not to detract from the spectacular show at the Eiffel Tower. On the 14th, I hosted a small party, inviting Marie, Gregoire, and a few others, all of whom gasped in astonishment when they saw our breathtaking vantage point. Trocadéro Man opted to view the festivities at a private rooftop party at the museum Cité de l'Architecture et du Patrimoine. Choices like that should have been red flags, I suppose, but I was too crazy in love and enjoying perks to notice. At the time, it seemed as though he was happy to take me everywhere—Barcelona, Meribel, Montreal, Prague, Zanzibar—and introduce me to everyone—siblings, children, cousins, friends, and co-workers. I interpreted these actions as expressions of his confidence in the substance and likely durability of our relationship. In retrospect, it seems I may just have been unaware of the graciousness extended by the French *grand bourgeoisie* to temporary 'other' women. Had I been a mistress? What category of relationship did those in Trocadéro Man's orbit think we had? I still am unable to make a coherent plot summary of that relationship.

This year, Bastille Day occurred on a balmy evening. Mara and I dined at Bistrot l'Estrapade, an old-fashioned restaurant near the Panthéon named after the street where it's located (a stone's throw from Emily-in-Paris's apartment). Such traditional establishments are as essential to Paris as are coffeehouses to Vienna or beerhalls to Munich, and they are an endangered species. Many are 'mom-and-pop' restaurants, whether specializing in hearty homestyle or refined gourmet cooking, and the pandemic has claimed numerous casualties.

The saddest for me is Le Gout Dujour in the Fifteenth Arrondissement, which a friend introduced me to long ago. The restaurant's name was a clever and appropriate play on the surname of the owner/chef—Dujour—and translates as 'the taste of the day', *le gout du jour.* The husband cooked; the wife served. Their limited menu usually had three offerings each—thereby ensuring the greatest quality and creativity—in the categories: appetizer, main course, dessert. These changed daily according to Monsieur Dujour's discoveries at the morning *marché.* A limited wine list paired perfectly with the food. The sedate, relaxed atmosphere with tasteful, simple furnishings and muted colors provided a harmonious atmosphere in which to concentrate on the culinary creations, inspired and unpretentious. There should be special protections for such establishments that maintain and advance local traditions.

Mara and I opted for one of the outdoor tables-for-two lined up against the façade, all bedecked with red-checkered tablecloths; we ordered kir royales while we waited. I enjoyed steamed salmon with fennel and a refreshing glass of Sancerre as we chatted and people watched. The quiet and lack of traffic—human or vehicular—suggested a provincial village more than Paris's most student-dense neighborhoods.

Afterward, on the plaza in front of the Panthéon, we joined a growing throng of mostly masked onlookers unconcerned about social distancing. As it turned out, staying home and watching the event on the old-fashioned CRT TV would have been more satisfying. We couldn't see even a glimpse of the digital show and only the most exuberant explosions thrilled. At least it didn't rain.

We stopped for ice cream enroute home and in the space of one block on the rue Soufflot had three choices. We opted for the Italian gelato shop across the street from the chain Grom, and I was happy to see my favorite, mint chocolate chip, on the menu. We ate as we walked. When we arrived at le Luco, which closes at dusk, I realized that the world, momentarily, felt almost normal. People socialized at cafés or strolled leisurely. As we walked toward the Port Royal, an ambulance siren broke the tranquility, snapping us into awareness that the pandemic continues.

Yesterday evening, Mara and I strolled the Left Bank quays. Along with their twins on the Right Bank, they function as important outdoor social spaces in Paris, offering scenic, traffic-free opportunities for joggers and cyclists. Sometimes, they are the most efficient way to traverse the city. In addition, they provide cool, shady spots for reading or picnicking, sunny spots for sunbathing, and performance spaces for dancers, musicians, and entertainers. This time though, I noticed how quiet the river was; still no tourist boat traffic with powerful spotlights illuminating noteworthy buildings along the riverbanks. The Seine is now so still that you have the extraordinary experience of seeing buildings reflected in it. I worry that it's the absence of many routines characterizing contemporary Parisian life that I have come to love as a new normal. I have difficulty envisioning post-pandemic Paris. I haven't seen an exhaust-belching tour bus or dodged a horde of tourists since my arrival in March and would love for that situation to continue indefinitely.

Part of me—a large part—dreads this fantastic dream coming to an end. I'm willing to wear a mask and social distance forever if that's what it takes to preserve this pristine, tranquil, civil Paris, where the air smells sweet and time moves at a leisurely pace. Paradoxically, my inner experience of time is hurried. Every day seems to rush by with regrettable rapidly. I feel an acute future nostalgia for the moment in which I am currently living.

Monday 20 July

For the past month, I've been rowing once or twice a week. Rowing is by far my favorite physical activity. During summers in Sweden, I developed callouses on my hands that lasted until well after New Year's. I rowed every non-rainy day, usually for two or more hours following a day spent writing before my window, with its view of bucolic pastures inhabited by grazing horses and cows.

In Paris, the best substitute I've found is in the Bois de Boulogne (Bois de Vincennes would be another, more distant, option), the expansive park developed in the 1850s by Baron Haussmann, the man Napoléon III charged with transforming Paris into a bourgeois paradise. With its racetrack, bridlepaths, golf course, tennis courts, and numerous pedestrian paths, it serves as the main outdoor recreational venue for the privileged residents of the Sixteenth Arrondissement.

The rowboats are wooden and narrow, unusual in this fiberglass age, giving one the impression they are the same boats Renoir once rowed. While heavy, they move quickly and are pleasurable to row because the oars are not fixed to the oarlocks, the usual, infantilizing protocol. One of the joys of rowing is a sense of freedom. For some incomprehensible reason, an unknown pessimist deemed rowers incapable of holding on to the oars, risking becoming one-oared, or worse, oarless, a frustrating assumption. Situations often arise that necessitate the shortening of an oar. Fixing them creates an irritating handicap: imagine a steering wheel restricted to a narrow range of motion. As a result, I'm as happy as I can possibly be rowing in an urban environment with bonus views of the Eiffel Tower.

The rowing lake is almost one-mile-long, with two wooded islands at the center that provide the illusion of countryside. Once I pass the obstacle course of boats with young families, romantic couples, or groups of girls spinning in circles with no idea of how boat-rowing works, I'm home free. I find soothing the repetitive sound of oars turning in the oarlocks and of droplets falling onto the water from the oars during the pushing motion. My cortisol level plummets, and I am back in Tolg, or Casco Bay, where my father taught me to row as a child. With the devil-may-care child-rearing attitude of the 1960s, my parents allowed me to row alone for hours without a life jacket and often far from sight, as I explored the Royale River around the shore corner from our cabin, perched on an escarpment overlooking Cousin's Island. The fact that there was a four-hundred-yard tide and not getting back on time meant being stranded on the quicksand-like clam flats for hours never signaled danger for any of us. My parents just assumed a twelve-year-old could manage without oversight.

On the larger island in the Bois de Boulogne lies a charming wooden chalet imported from Switzerland in the nineteenth century that serves as a restaurant. I always imagine the Impressionist era when I pass, probably because of its abundant images of waterside leisure. I envision Manet, Monet, and Caillebotte in their silk top hats and accompanied by Berthe Morisot and Eva Gonzales in their stylish muslin dresses taking the ferry on a sunny summer afternoon in the 1870s for luncheon or a drink on one of its terraces. Beyond, at the far end of the lake, a small waterfall cascades, and near it lies a patch of thorny blackberry bushes.

On my first row, I arrived unprepared for berry picking. Not surprising: who could imagine berry picking in Paris? My hands were nearly shredded by thorny branches as I determinedly loosened ripe berries from their white cores, collecting them in the plastic bag I happened to have along. After that, I came outfitted with leather gloves and a plastic container. Pedestrians on the footpath above looked on curiously as I stood in the boat stretching to reach and then to pull toward me distant prickly branches with my gloved hand while I selected the ripest berries with the other. I am pretty sure that I'm the Bois's only berry picker because the not-as-ripe berries I leave for my subsequent foray are always there when I return.

Children tug at their adults, point toward me, and ask them to explain what I'm doing. Adults sometimes inquire.

"Why are you picking those berries?" they wonder.

"To eat," I respond.

"What kind of berries are they?"

"How do you know they are edible?" is another popular question.

When 'because they are blackberries', doesn't suffice as an answer, I wonder if the questioner requires the confirmation of comestibility conferred by shopping in a USDA-approved grocery store and what they would do if required to forage in the wild. I never dreamt it possible to combine my two favorite summer activities within Paris city limits. This truly is *my* city. The only other time I rowed in France was two years ago, when Trocadéro Man took me to the Grand Canal at Versailles. Yes, it was impressive, but now I wonder why he never mentioned the rowboat rental in the Bois, his neighborhood park.

Tonight—as I often do—I took my dinner over to le Luco and picnicked. The stone benches surrounding the basin make perfect tables. I chose one on the shady western side and people watched as I nibbled my slice of pork-pistachio terrine and carrot salad. I stayed until closing—a time that changes with the seasons—because I adore the park rangers' closing ritual. Around twenty minutes prior to closing, blue-uniformed rangers secure the gates to the secondary garden entrances and station themselves at the principal ones. Simultaneously, a half-dozen rangers gather at the center of the upper terrace where the chestnut tree-edged lawns begin. They chat among themselves until exactly fifteen minutes before closing.

On a signal from their leader, who keeps his eye on the clock atop the former palace, now senate building, the rangers disperse, blowing their whistles and calling "*Fermeture! Fermeture du jardin!*" (Closing! The garden is closing!). Several rangers head toward the south gate on the rue August Comte along the picnicker-filled lawns. Two descend the steps to the lower level and pursue different routes around the basin. Others head into the greater park, threading among the trees on the east and down the various paths on the west that connect the sculpture-containing enclosures. There are memorials to Massenet and Chopin, to Watteau and Delacroix, even a one-third life-size *Statue of Liberty*, on whose book is inscribed 'November 1889', one hundred years after French revolutionaries confiscated all church property for the benefit of 'the people'.

At the signal, park visitors fold their blankets and newspapers, close their books, put away their toys, pack up their picnics, and head toward the exits. My big evening decision is whether to linger in le Luco for this heartwarming, centuries-old ritual, or to walk to the Eiffel Tower for the first twinkle. Were I willing to take public transportation I could accommodate both, but that would nullify the leisurely, atmosphere-absorbing stroll I enjoy.

Friday 31 July

Today, I would have returned to Stockholm from my rendezvous with Mark in Iceland. That episode now seems long ago. I celebrated by going on a date with Go Dutch Man, with whom I had chatted several times before *confinement* and broke off contact once I'd 'met' Mark. He wrote me a touching, regretful, I-will-fantasize-about-you-forever message that inspired me to give him a call.

Go Dutch Man lives in Neuilly, a nice suburb on the west side of Paris. We met at Café Vavin, and he bored me within minutes. He never inquired about me but yacked incessantly about the career in international business from which he had recently retired. We ordered dinner. I kept hoping things would improve and wondered if I were being unreasonably fussy. He asked for the check and promptly informed me of my share of the bill. *That* was the first time a man of my generation has ever just assumed we would split the check. To make matters worse, when we got up to leave, he offered to walk me home. I suppose it was a gentlemanly gesture, but it didn't seem like one after having to cough up my share of dinner. Then, with no prior physical contact or encouraging signals, he grabbed me and kissed me on the lips, a move I rebuffed.

Why, then, did I think it a good idea to accept a second date for tomorrow to see a movie, *Parfum*, preceded by dinner at an inexplicably popular chain restaurant, Entrecôte, that serves frozen *frites* and tasteless, over-tenderized steaks? Apparently, because I don't totally trust my inner voice. It seems to have steered me wrong in the past but perhaps that is because I was not as spiritually evolved. I couldn't differentiate between hormones and my inner voice. But can I now? Has the Mark incident disrupted my fragile equilibrium?

Chapter 7
August: A Château Weekend & Dating Adventures

Sunday 2 August

Caroline has been living a nomadic life in Paris the past few months, staying with various friends. She has been itching to get out of town before she begins her fall lease at the apartment on the rue Mouffetard I told her about and where I have stayed several times. And now, she is on a bike trip through the Loire Valley, where she will ride fifty to seventy kilometers per day. She tried to talk me into joining, but I am happy in Paris for the moment. The last time I biked any distance was in the summer of 2011, when I rode forty kilometers—partly over cobblestone roads capable of dislodging fillings —from Greifswald to Stralsund and then—exhausted but fortified by a beer on the town square—took the train back. I can't envision biking that and more on consecutive days.

I'm delighted, however, that she left me her cumbersome, three-speed, Dutch bike. It must have been the product of an experimental era in Dutch bicycle manufacturing when bikes were made of lead. While I can hoist most bikes onto my shoulder, this one I can barely lift off the ground.

Riding in traffic has made me nervous since 1997, when I was hit by a car in a Munich suburb. It was driven by a woman who waved me across the street at a stop sign and then gunned the motor, purposefully knocking me to the ground. Clearly a psychopath, she jumped out of her car yelling in German, "it's not my fault, it's not my fault!" Well, it was, and two electricians who had been working on a nearby utility pole witnessed the event and rushed to my aid. As I lay dazed in the street with a pancake-sized bruise forming on my shin and blood trickling down my leg, staining the lining of the leather pants I thankfully wore, my tank-like Mercedes 200 drove by with six-year-old Hanna flailing in the passenger seat and screaming to her dad, "Stop! There's Mamma!" Hanna had refused to enter her kindergarten classroom that day, the only time in her life my cheerful and compliant child adamantly refused to go to school. After cajoling by her teacher and father failed, her perplexed dad bundled her back into the car and drove the twenty minutes home. She could not explain her obstinance at the time other than saying, "I knew something wasn't right."

After shopping at the Rennes-Raspail *marché* this morning, I filled my water bottle and embarked on my first Paris bicycle adventure. Heading directly to the boulevard Saint-Michel with its dedicated bike lane seemed the safest bet. My body entered a state of hyper vigilance, aware of every object moving around me. I decided to restrict myself to flat stretches on this first outing since I doubted whether I could shift the sticky gears successfully. I pedaled across the pont Saint-Michel and noticed that the throngs crowding the quays on both sides of the river would make biking difficult, so I headed west on streets. A few blocks north on the Right Bank, the terrain ascends, first gently toward the Grands Boulevards, then steeply, culminating at the hilltops of Montmartre and Belleville. I decided to stay close to the river. I could have threaded my way through the vacant commercial streets of the First and Eighth Arrondissements but chose instead to ride along the river, which offered intermittent shade. I dislike being in the sun, and by the time I reached Trocadéro, my moist shirt and pants adhered uncomfortably; perspiration ran down my back. Now, tourists, mainly French, were admiring the Eiffel Tower and Africans were hawking trinkets, baseball caps, and bottles of water. *It's over*, I thought, *the magic is over.*

This experience differed dramatically from my first, post-*confinement* visit, when I stood there alone, no humans in sight. After crossing pont d'Iena back to the Left Bank, I inserted myself into the bike lane that runs along the Seine, back to the boulevard Saint-Michel and home. That was enough excitement for a first foray.

Last night's date with Go Dutch Man was a predictable disaster. Dinner at Entrecôte was awful, and I had to pay my share. He informed me of how much I owed him for the movie ticket plus handling charge, so I paid him that, too. It's easy to understand why he is single. I was relieved, however, to see fewer than a dozen moviegoers in a cinema with a seating capacity of two hundred. As on all public transportation and in all auditorium venues, alternate seats had signs with red Xs and the message "leave this free." I leaned as far from Go Dutch Man as possible during the film, a strategy that successfully discouraged romantic overtures. Afterward, he asked for my phone number, and I said, "no."

Instead of heading home, I wandered. I crossed the boulevard Montparnasse to the Fifth Arrondissement, past the Panthéon and down the rue de Bièvre, where a small gallery hosts temporary, small mural paintings that usually remain for several months. The current one—a black and white, Picassoesque assortment of distorted faces and figures—bears the message in red: "There are no accidents. There are only surprises, hopes, fortuitous circumstances, and propitious accidents." My twenty-eight-hour acquaintanceship with Go Dutch Man qualified, I figure, as a propitious if unpleasant accident.

On the quay, a brass band played Balkan tunes for a small mostly maskless audience surrounded by the refuse of picnic dinners: wine bottles, cups, bits of baguette, takeout containers. I returned home via Shakespeare & Co. and rue de la Huchette, normally packed like a subway car at rush hour on a late summer evening but now strangely desolate. I continued past the Roman baths and late medieval mansion that now comprise the Cluny Museum, structures once surrounded by fields and cottages and that now seem out of place at the busy commercial intersection of the boulevards Saint-Germain and Saint-Michel.

How many times did I swish by this intersection on the back of Trocadéro Man's *moto* in the spring of 2018? Sigh. I turned south onto Saint-Michel. As I approached le Luco, I heard strains of Dixieland jazz. On the broad sidewalk in front of Le Petit Journal were a dozen occupied tables and a band playing in front of the entrance. The headquarters of the eponymous illustrated daily, whose doors closed permanently in 1944 under the German occupation, is now a jazz club. I lingered at the corner and listened until they stopped playing at 11 p.m. It was heartening to hear professional live music again. I wished that Jean, my favorite dance partner, had been there. No one danced, although the music begged for it, and the toes of listeners tapped rhythmically. A notice in the window advertised live music five nights a week. Now the Eiffel Tower has competition for my evening attention!

Thursday 6 August

I've been video chatting nightly for the past week with Bruno in Dijon, a slight, balding, bespeckled man who seems nice. Dijon is a charming city where I can envision living. Bruno runs his own surveying business and has independent adult children. We don't have a lot to talk about though. He's not terribly intellectual, not that I care about that (or do I?), but culture does provide conversation fodder. He's a musician, a clarinetist, which I like. I've always found the woodsy tones of clarinets soothing. Perhaps a placid, kind, tolerant, drama-free fellow is what I require. Bruno is eager to meet, but I'm not comfortable hosting him in my small apartment, nor am I willing to stay with him because I prefer to avoid the pressure to initiate a physical relationship until I feel ready. Or interested. Right now, it's hard to tell.

I went to Le Petit Journal on Tuesday and Wednesday, sitting alone, sipping my Pernod, and enjoying the music. Big band swing music played by a quintet on Tuesday and Chicago-style blues on Wednesday. Pandemic summer couldn't be better. While my Italian, German, and American friends are languishing, unable to enjoy the pleasures of summertime, I'm sitting at an outdoor café in the cool air of a Paris evening on a boulevard Saint-Michel devoid of traffic, listening to great music and breathing air perfumed by le Luco's greenery. It doesn't get better than this, and I appreciate the privilege of these moments profoundly. Life in Paris feels normal in a way that seems far better than what normal typically entails nowadays. The U.S. seems downright terrifying. COVID-19 rages out of control, shopping has become a frightening ordeal that many evade by online ordering and home delivery, and fear mounts that the nation could continue its descent into fascism should Trump be reelected. I, on the other hand, am reveling in the benefits of the pandemic.

Rosa and Nathalie are on vacation this week, at least that is where I have sent them in my well-progressing novel. To a farm near Fontainebleau. It seems appropriate that I am on a little vacation too, my first overnight outside Paris. Jim's count boyfriend, Pascal, gave him permission to invite me for a long weekend in Brittany that includes a reunion of nobility on Sunday. I'm excited. Although I have friends descended from noble families—des and de las, vons and vans —I've never attended a more-or-less artistos-only event.

Jim picked me up shortly after noon, stooping under the burden of an ungodly magnitude of groceries. If I didn't know we were headed to the grand estate of a nobleman, I would assume he was outfitting a fallout shelter with a year's supply of food in case of alien attack. He explained that food at the château was often raunchy. *Hmmm*, I thought, *what does that mean*? I would soon find out.

The sweltering weather made matters worse. Jim, gentleman that he is, refused my help. We trod to Gare Montparnasse as perspiration blurred his eyesight. With one block remaining, a kind fellow heading to his parents' home on the coast for the weekend helped Jim carry groceries bursting from a caddy so heavy that its wheels were beginning to fall off. One expects such civility in France. It makes it a delightful place to live and evokes memories of how nicely people in the U.S. behaved toward one another when I was a child.

Pascal, a bouncy, gregarious gentlemen in his mid-70s, met us at the station in his ancient, disintegrating, rusty, grey, non-air-conditioned Citroën station wagon. I presented him with a five-hundred-gram box of delectable chocolates crafted by Jean-Charles Rochoux on the rue d'Assas, one of the premier *chocolatiers* of Paris, because I didn't have time to visit Mococha. The countryside enroute was pleasant but unremarkable: fields, woods, buttercup-flecked pastures of lazy brown cows, and the occasional farmstead. We exited the main country road onto a smaller one and then turned into a space between two ivy-covered stone buildings, one of which must once have been inhabited by a *gardien*, a gatekeeper, as is still customary on French estates. Pascal rents his *propriété* as a destination wedding venue and was sacrificing a weekend of income to host extended family and friends for annual potluck dinners on Saturday evening and Sunday afternoon.

Initially, I was disappointed not to have been assigned a room in the seventeenth-century château or the early nineteenth-century *manoir* on the other side of a tall hedge. But Jim assured me I had the best room on the estate. He led me past the *manoir*, through a romantic arbor with a small pond surrounded by benches and flowers, to a long red brick building with a variegated flat tile roof and several doors. My segment resembled an English cottage, with aromatic rose trellises flanking the entrance, and above, a darling dormer containing a window with a bright blue frame that matched the door.

Once inside, I found myself immersed in my childhood dream. 'The library' was a spacious room with floor-to-ceiling bookshelves on all four walls. Pascal calls it the library not because of its original usage—both the château and the *manoir* have libraries—but because it is where his thousands of books, organized thematically by Jim, live. The fireplace is the only non-readable object occupying wall space; my bed stands far enough from the wall to permit access to the shelves. Oriental rugs cover the stone floors, and worn, saddle-leather armchairs with wooly throws on their backs invite leisurely reading. It's a cool space in both senses. On this estate without air-conditioning and in this blistering heat, I'm honored to occupy the chilliest among the numerous available bedrooms. With a small kitchen, sitting area, and bathroom adjacent, I couldn't be more content and can already envision overstaying my welcome.

Before we convened for late afternoon iced tea on the lawn in front of the château and beside its topiary garden, Jim gave me a brief tour. The turreted, peach-colored château with red-brick and limestone decorative details would be as at home in the Netherlands as in central Brittany, where it resides. The sloping slate roof reaches almost the two-story height of the building it shelters. Its symmetrically paired dormers—one large, one small, with differing pediments—flank a fancier, central dormer with a broken voluted pediment separated by a round ocular window surmounted by yet another small pediment, like a chuppah on a wedding cake.

The main floor consists of a hallway with a patterned tile floor and many pairs of mounted antlers, an elegant stairway, and a long, narrow kitchen—a modern addition since kitchens are usually located in the cellar or in a separate building out of public view. Formerly, this was the space where servants retrieved food from dumbwaiters sent up from the cellar kitchen to serve in the adjacent dining room. The dark-wood-paneled dining room has hunter green walls on which are scattered ancestor portraits. A pair of leaded stained-glass windows admit so little light that a lugubrious darkness prevails regardless of the time of day. On the opposite side of the château entrance is a *salon* containing a baby grand piano, bookcases, and a surfeit of upholstered furniture. Both rooms have coffered ceilings with geometrical *marqueterie* designs and central tiled fireplaces. Furnishing throughout are a hodgepodge: harmonious, unpretentious, exotic, comfortable.

Pascal occupies the master suite on the second floor. It has its own chapel, embellished by gold fleur-de-lis on salmon-colored walls. It's choc-a-block with religious statuary in wood and porcelain and framed prints and paintings of saints—some post-beatification others mid-martyrdom—hanging on the walls. The big curiosity, however, is a long narrow sign leaning against a wall, a souvenir of German occupation during World War Two that reads: "*Sicherheitspolizei Kommando. Aussenkommando*" in the *Fraktur* script favored by the

Nazis. The German Security Police commandeered the *manoir* during the war.

Due to penury—a huge problem for the nobility since the beginning of the Industrial Revolution—the château fell into disrepair after World War Two, and the family moved into the *manoir*, where they remained as the château deteriorated. The *manoir* is far more inviting: genteel yet unpretentious. There, one finds down-stuffed sofas in chintz and leather; ancestor, pet, and estate portraits; Chinese furniture and vases; and needlepoint footstools. Carved marble fireplaces adorn the many light-filled rooms, whose walls are painted in cheerful tones of yellow and blue.

The five of us (Pascal, Jim, me, Pascal's best friend—a duke, and Humorless Estate Manager) dined in the *manoir* garden under the shade of an ancient oak. Dinner was not what I had envisioned, even after Jim's warning. Pascal is a skinflint, a quality obvious from the car he drives and the lack of any permanent staff aside from the manager. Thus, I was not surprised by the dinner's modesty. Served with cheap, unmatched tableware and miscellaneous plates and glasses of the sort one finds at Goodwill stores, it consisted of a stew Pascal concocted from an incompatible assortment of leftovers accompanied by a beverage he (proudly) made himself from wildflowers growing on the estate—a meal one might expect at a youth hostel potluck. Eventually, a bottle of wine arrived as an afterthought, contributed by the duke, who owns a vineyard in Burgundy. The cheeses were not delicacies either local or from further afield but factory-produced, pre-packaged ones purchased at Aldi. We sat and chatted after dinner about the pandemic and weather and travels—accomplished and anticipated—until it became too dark to see. Had we been in Sweden, there would have been candles.

Monday 10 August

It was a fascinating weekend. We breakfasted in the château dining room each morning at 9 a.m. and since guests began arriving on Friday, the number seated at the table for twenty varied. I brought oatmeal since Frenchmen are unsure how to accommodate those who don't eat bread, the standard French breakfast food, a smidgen better than Italy, where cookies are standard. Had I not drunk coffee, they would have found me incomprehensibly exotic.

I eventually pieced together Pascal's history. When his parents died, he inherited two estates, one of which he sold to a cousin. Although the sale eased his financial burden, the estate where he now lives, disintegrating for decades, posed a challenge to restore and maintain, with its more than a dozen habitable buildings and a current sleeping capacity of more than one hundred. The estate is in the middle of nowhere, not particularly near any historical sites, and it lacks amenities such as a golf course, swimming pool, water-frontage, or stables. Gradually, he transformed it into an event site, renovating buildings as revenue permitted. The daunting task of furnishing dozens of rooms was accomplished through the generosity of Pascal's downsizing or redecorating aristo friends, who donated unwanted linens, furniture, books, beds, rugs, paintings and sculptures, silver, crystal, and china. With his faultless aesthetic sense, Pascal has created an inviting, shabby-chic atmosphere inside and out. Former stables, a bakery, a saddlery, servants' and guest quarters, have all been outfitted to provide homey accommodations.

As guests arrived throughout Friday and Saturday, with some stragglers arriving on Sunday morning, they searched out their preferred lodgings. No doors or buildings on the estate are locked. It was like being at a fancy adult camp. Pascal usually rents the entire estate from Friday noon to Sunday evening from May through September and can arrange for catering, entertainment, or anything else one might desire. The barn has been converted into a spacious high-ceilinged party space with a large, modern, well-equipped kitchen.

Having toured most of the buildings on Saturday morning—the kind of *Architectural Digest* adventure I adore—Jim and I went for a walk in Pascal's forest after lunch. We traversed the parched orchard where sweet *mirabelles* ripened, snacking as we went. The forest isn't manicured as Swedish ones are; one seldom encounters rotting fallen trees in Swedish forests because there, wood=heat=money and forests are routinely thinned to make growing room for less aggressive (and more valuable) species. We rested in a clearing, and Jim regaled me with stories of his crazy upbringing and eccentric friends. On the way back, we visited buildings we'd missed, including the hunting lodge, unrenovated and inhabited by numerous, taxidermed creatures: squirrels, wild boar, foxes, birds, and a herd of deer heads affixed to the walls.

I returned to 'the library' for a pre-dinner nap and found a shoeless Duchess Charlotte, recently retired from a career as a Chinese-to-French translator, sitting sideways in one of the leather chairs, legs slung over one arm and immersed in Nicolas Mathieu's 2019 Prix Goncourt winner, *And Their Children After Them*. Embarrassed, she admitted not having read it previously and asked if I minded her staying.

"No," I replied, removing my shoes and slipping under the down quilt on the bed.

In other worlds, one would be embarrassed for having invaded another guest's private space, not for having neglected to read a prize-winning novel. But this is France, a nation of avid readers, where keeping abreast of contemporary literature is as important as knowing who won the world series is in the U.S.

One of the most popular French TV shows airs for ninety minutes on Wednesday evenings and is called *La Grande Librairie*—The Big Bookstore. Journalist François Busnel has hosted it for more than a decade. Each week, he interviews up to a half-dozen authors whose recently published books he has thoroughly digested, an awe-inspiring achievement. I watch it, too, since it's an expedient method for keeping culturally *au courant*. At pretty much any social occasion, if stumped for conversation fodder one remarks on the latest episode of *La Grande Librairie* or the books or authors it featured, even foreigners with less than perfect French will be embraced as compatriots.

On Saturday evening, a barbeque was staged in the forest but in a different part from where Jim and I had been earlier, on the other side of the road from which we had arrived on Thursday. The younger generation of nobles assumed responsibility for setting up tables, transporting food, and keeping the fire going. Dinner consisted of the usual picnic fare: grilled hamburgers and sausages, potato salad and chips, beer, wine, water, and soft drinks. I had envisioned an updated version of Watteau's *Embarkation for Cythera*, an early-eighteenth-century painting that depicts aristocrats on a country outing. Elegantly dressed, one imagines them dining on foie gras, roast pigeon, oysters, and champagne. There was little in either the comportment or attire of this gathering that signaled centuries-old privilege. The *grand bourgeois* world of Trocadéro Man conformed more to my expectations of the upper class but I guess now they are, since commerce replaced land as a source of wealth two centuries ago.

The dining table was fully occupied at breakfast on Sunday. Counts and countesses, dukes and duchesses, princes and princesses, marquesses and marchionesses. And the untitled: me, Jim, and Humorless Property Manager. More people arrived during the afternoon, and no one wore masks at any point. I took mine off when Pascal picked us up and did not put it on again until I got out of Charlotte's car a few hours ago. The reunion could certainly have been a spreader event. Pascal intended for guests to wear masks except while dining and drinking, but there we were, almost seventy people of all ages and from many different directions and carrying with us who-knows-what germs. We sat at tables for six at prearranged places. The duke provided one bottle of wine per table.

The guests I chatted with pursued a wide variety of occupations: fire chiefs and real estate agents, lawyers, teachers, and nurses. In that sense they were modest and normal. But each one knew their lineage back for centuries and exactly how they were related to one another. There were many distant cousins. Predictably, conversation differed a bit from the usual. It's not often one overhears people saying things like: "we didn't have enough guest room at the château, so my father bought the neighboring village." Or "you know how expensive château roofs are? It's a good thing they don't need replacing often. I had to sell one of my titles to pay for it a few years ago." Or "the prohibition of fox-hunting is destroying British culture."

The general sentiment prevailed that France has gone to hell in a handbasket since the execution of Louis XVI in 1793. One fellow told me his ancestor was chief advisor to Louis XV (reigned 1715-74) and another, that her family returned from Italy when Napoléon came to power in 1799, only to find their properties ransacked by revolutionaries during the 1790s. Every person there knew exactly what their ancestors did during the French Revolution and afterward. Keeping these memories alive seemed a major preoccupation. These, of course, are the children of survivors, admittedly privileged ones, and their sense of irreparable and unjustified loss reminded me of the attitude expressed by the grandchildren of Holocaust survivors.

After lunch in the barn, a concert was held in the château's *salon*. A pianist and tenor, obsequious acquaintances of Pascal's, performed for the several dozen guests who remained after lunch. The air was humid and suffocating despite all windows being open, an optimistic attempt at inviting the feeble breeze to waft in. Following the concert, coffee and cake were served. Incomprehensible arguments about food and music erupted, after which most guests departed, some in a huff, permitting the estate to return to tranquility.

Jim and I hitched a ride back to Paris with Duchess Charlotte. As we parted ways, I was glad to learn that while Pascal didn't mention it, he did enjoy my chocolate—milk only, as Jim had instructed. He squirreled it away, not sharing it with anyone, including Jim, who reported that the box was half empty by the time we left.

Sunday 16 August

Since returning from Brittany, I've spent most days writing in le Luco. Not on Wednesdays, however, Marché Monge day, when I usually stop for a *noisette* (espresso with a splash of milk) at my old hangout, Café Contrescarpe. Place de la Contrescarpe is one of the oldest, least-spoiled squares in Paris despite its status as a weekend tourist attraction. A Roman arena and remnants of a medieval city wall are nearby, as are many of Paris's most prestigious schools: École Polytechnique, Collège de France, École Normale Supérieure, Sorbonne, Louis le Grand, and Henri IV. The Symbolist poet Arthur Rimbaud lived down the street in a building whose first floor is now a restaurant named in his honor, and Hemingway and his first wife, Hadley, lived for a while around the corner, across the street from the Hotel des Grandes Écoles, where I stayed on my first visit in 1974. Students often go to place de la Contrescarpe for the cheap eats offered at lunchtime at the *boulangeries*, gyro joints, or numerous *crêperies* on the adjacent rue Mouffetard.

I sat outdoors in a back row, less accessible to the occasional beggars. Fewer tables were occupied than in normal times. Romany musicians played for a while on the roundel at the center of the *place*. Last time I was there, they were, too, and I tipped them €5 for an excellent thirty minutes of music. I asked them to play "*Tamburaši samo svirajte*" (Just play, tamburitza musicians), which took them by surprise. Less the specific request I think, than the fact that someone knew their repertoire. Today, they recognized me and opened with it. True professionals. Since my first visit to Paris, most of the businesses around place de la Contrescarpe have changed hands but not this café, which remains one of my favorites.

Hanna bought a ticket to visit in mid-October. Finally! I haven't seen her since Christmas 2019, and that was only for a few brief days with lots of friends around. Our last alone time was on Paros last August: a week or two in Greece has been a tradition of ours for more than a decade.

Although I've continued to video chat most evenings with Bruno in Dijon, I went on a date today with an appreciatively younger and more dynamic man, Clément. A child psychiatrist, he lives a block away from Parc des Buttes-Chaumont, a neighborhood that has become trendy in recent years. It was warm and I wore my favorite Agnes B blouse with three-quarter-length sleeves and gold heart buttons, which I should not save for special occasions but do. My mother was a hedonist who loved beautiful clothes and saw no reason to save them until they went out of style or no longer fit properly (my tendency), but my father was a conservative, sweatshirt-and-chinos man, who saved nice clothes for special occasions. Although I have followed in his wearing-the-same-thing-at-home-every-day footsteps, I should be more mindful of the fact that men's fashion doesn't evolve at the rapid pace of women's.

Clément met my bus, and we walked around Paris's hilliest small park. He was handsome, animated, interesting, and well-dressed; he reminded me a bit of Trocadéro Man, probably due to his *grand bourgeois* upbringing, although I couldn't tell if he, too, smelled like springtime and fresh laundry. Throngs were out, and we strolled the shores of Bassin de la Villette, with its busy restaurants and play-grounds. We had a lovely time, ending with dinner at a gluten-free pizzeria in the Seventeenth Arrondissement to which we took an Uber. As I boarded the bus home, I looked forward to our next rendezvous. Clément is extremely busy now because psychological problems have mushroomed in the wake of pandemic restrictions: living in too-close quarters, home schooling. His father is a well-known writer I admire, and I'm hoping to meet him, too.

Tuesday 18 August

Today, I took my first long distance train trip: to Troyes to meet Bruno. Troyes is a lovely town of half-timber buildings inhabited since Roman times, and the site of a famous centuries-old cham-pagne fair that enriched the town the way significant religious relics did churches. He drove from Dijon, where he lives, and met me at the station. A petite (my size) bespeckled and balding fellow, he dressed in everyday clothes: a zippered poplin jacket, plaid sport shirt, and hunter green chinos—indicative of a working-class back-ground. Bourgeois men or those so acculturated usually wear blazers or dress business casual for first dates. We arrived at lunch time. He met me at the station, and we headed toward the center of town. I had hoped he would make reservations at a nice restaurant, but he hadn't. His first impulse steered him to a small café that served sweets and sandwiches, but my gluten intolerance furnished a plausible excuse for moving on.

We wound up at a popular bistro. When the waiter came, Bruno ordered first: the least expensive salad on the menu. The French generally eat their main meal at lunchtime, and I assumed Bruno would as well. I also assumed that as a gesture of hospitality he wouldn't order the cheapest thing on the menu and would invite me to order first. I ordered the same. When he asked what I would like to drink, I responded, "water," and he didn't inquire what kind (of bottled water) but ordered a carafe of tap water. I have nothing against that and normally drink tap water myself, but were I trying to impress a date, or enjoy something inhabitual, I would have ordered a liter of Badoit or whatever water came in a glass bottle.

Bruno knew the old part of town well enough to guide me down the most charming streets and to show me the loveliest courtyards and churches. The town resembles a full-scale Christmas village, with houses painted in shades of rose, yellow, orange, and green. Exterior beams are often carved. I saw heads of chubby-cheeked angels with low-relief wings, roundel profiles of helmeted knights with pointy beards, and devils with pointy ears, narrow eyes, and downturned mouths. The corner of one building is supported by an upright log upon which a vine bearing ripe grapes is deeply carved, surmounted by a full-lipped head of Bacchus or perhaps the building's original owner. Made wealthy by the champagne trade, Troyes's inhabitants considered their facades important aesthetic expressions and embellished them with an attentiveness usually reserved for interiors.

The cathedral is Baroque and spectacular, with an undulating interior gallery and many sculptures. There's a curious sculpture of a sleeping, curly-haired, bearded man wearing seventeenth-century peasant attire and barefoot but wearing what look like spats. His weary head rests on his left forearm, which in turn rests on a plinth; his right arm hangs limply at his side. Elsewhere, a robed peasant woman in a turban holds up the Veronica cloth with a low relief carving of Christ's head wearing a crown of thorns for visitors to see.

The stained-glass windows are not jewel-like, but painterly, in shades of yellow, white, and mauve in pale, bloody nuances that make one wonder what substance was used to produce them. Some scenes are violent: in one, a lion presses its paw on a fallen man's head as it wraps its jaws around his neck, its furrowed brow and staring eyes communicating intense concentration. Happier moments are also represented: a royal feast depicted in brownish tones, with the baldachin and king's crown in yellow-gold, the color also used for the musical instruments—a lute and a harp—as well as for decorative details on the guests' clothing.

About an hour before my departure, Bruno took my hand, and we walked hand in hand for the rest of the afternoon. He behaved gently, kindly, although by then we were running out of conversation topics. I felt awkward. He's definitely not for me, nor I for him, but he will make a lovely partner for some lucky woman. We embraced and kissed before I boarded the train, but by then I knew that the next conversation would be the one where I tell him our relationship has no future.

Friday 21 August

Today is Hanna's thirtieth birthday. I wish I could celebrate it with her, but neither of us feels comfortable boarding a plane just yet. She and Dani have invited a few friends for a picnic celebration in the park adjacent to their apartment building in Stockholm, where it stays light until well after 9 p.m. We discussed the fun things we'll do in Paris when she comes in October, and I promised to make her the wild blueberry-and-lemon pie with whipped cream that she loves. It became a summer tradition in Sweden during blueberry season.

Yesterday was Trocadéro Man's birthday. Even though he never called after *déconfinement* in May as promised and ignored my birthday in February, since he declared that he would like to remain friends, I sent him an animated card with a horse cantering in a pasture, a motif appropriate to a polo-playing equestrian. He replied immediately "*J'adore*" and sent me a picture of his newborn first grandchild. I congratulated him, and he promised to call when he returned from vacation so we could see an exhibition together. I think we both know that won't happen; it's been three months since *deconfinement*, and he's made no effort at contact. I do wish we could remain friends since I enjoy his wit, charm, and intelligence, even absent all the seductive romantic gestures. I would also love to have continuing access to his idyllic, seldom-used chalet in Quebec. It's the best wilderness oasis I've found since relinquishing the cottage in Tolg.

Clément and I have been playing text-and-photo-tag. He proposed visiting Parc Saint-Cloud—an André le Nôtre-designed park that abuts the southwest corner of Paris—this Sunday but has not initiated plans. I'm beginning to think, sadly, that he's not ready for a new relationship. He calls and asks how I'm doing as if truly interested as opposed to desperately grasping for conversation topics as is the case with Bruno. Clément has called from trains, cars, bicycles, and from a swimming pool in Caen. He's adorable.

I probably—no, definitely and compulsively—spend too much time on this dating project, but I am also finding it a fascinating sociological experience. As I survey my twenty choices of the day and men who take the initiative to contact me, I look first at pictures, rejecting anyone who: is overweight, takes bathroom mirror selfies, shows cars/motorcycles/tattoos/large fish, includes ugly settings like parking lots or cafeterias. I also pass on those who sport weird, attention-getting hairstyles that advertise I'm a wild hippie (long, stringy hair), or I love 1950s rock 'n roll and vintage cars (long sideburns and slicked-back hair), or I'm super hip (a modified mohawk), or who just appear to be dullards. My judgment might sometimes be wrong.

Next, I look at where they live. If it's Paris or somewhere sunny and beautiful, sure, I'll meet you. In a depressing suburb or a part of France that suffers months of cloudy weather, then no. I wilt under those conditions, and my environment is, I have realized, the main determinant of my happiness. Because most men write the same things: music they like (jazz, classical, blues, rock), humor they like (Desproges), what they are (respectful, kind, patient, loyal, curious), the thing they can't be separated from (usually stuff: glasses, cell phone—only rarely qualities like honesty and integrity), more singular specific qualities attract my attention. One productive aspect of this project is learning more about French geography. For any fellow who looks promising, I google his location, often having to reduce it several times in order to see where it lies in relation to familiar places. I don't want to live in the north: it's too cloudy, rainy, and flat. If I like what I see, I turn to pictures of the town and region. Charm and nearby water are important. I've started a list of locations I can imagine living by myself.

Friday 28 August

Yesterday, I called the Bois de Boulogne boat rental to tell them I was coming. I've had to call upon arrival several times, and it has taken up to a half hour for an attendant to appear. I totally understand—school is in session, people are back at work, and sometimes I'm the only customer. Still, I don't like to while away my time waiting. When I arrived, the station was unmanned. Since they leave oars in the boats and the boats are hooked to their neighbors by chains, it's possible to liberate one boat and hook its neighbors back together.

A personal trainer working with a female client nearby told me I was not allowed to do this, but since he had no authority over the boat concession, off I went. Once on the lake, I became preoccupied with possible consequences to my rogue action. I figured responses might range from sending the police to arrest me to asking me how long I had been out upon my return. And if no one was there, I'd just put the boat back where I found it and pay for my hour on the next visit. I'm an honest person. I took my usual tour around the islands, visiting the heron and ducks, picking berries. On my way back, I noticed a couple in a boat (I'm the only one I've ever seen rowing solo) and knew the attendant must be there. I could stop thinking about what I would tell the police. The attendant recognized me and asked how long I had been out. I told him and paid. No lecturing, no yelling, no fine, no jail.

Today is the first day of an outdoor mask mandate instituted by the French government because COVID-19 numbers are rising. It's unpleasant wearing masks in warm weather. Will people walk more slowly to avoid overheating?

I met Reem for coffee at Rotonde this afternoon. It was wonderful to see this young woman whose intelligence, energy, and character portend a brilliant future; we're Facebook friends, so we keep in occasional, virtual contact. She's Canadian and now studies at Sciences Po. When teaching turned to distance in the springtime, she, like many students living in tiny apartments, decided to return home and is now back for a visit, trying to decide whether to return to France.

We first met in July 2016, when she was one of twenty high school students from across the globe participating in a month-long educational summer program in Greifswald, Germany that I designed and ran. My idea was to offer a program different from any other: an authentic college-prep program that involved taking a course with an actual American college professor, immersion in local culture, and singular experiences I arranged through contacts. It was a program that gathered students from more than a dozen countries and from diverse socio-economic backgrounds. It was the only scholarship-offering summer-in-Europe program that was an equal opportunity enterprise catering to teens unable to afford the $6-8,000 fee that such programs typically charge.

The program was small, compelling 'haves' and 'have-nots' to interact, and they lived in suites of two double rooms with balconies, which fostered friendship. Unlike most educational situations, no activities were inaccessible to the financially underprivileged; that was a consideration when I selected Greifswald as the site. There was plenty to do, just nothing expensive. It was also the only program offering an authentic college level course (International Studies) with an American college professor, membership in a local teen social group, internships with local businesses and institutions, German language instruction, bicycles for all, and an enriching array of activities made possible by my extensive friends and colleagues networks: private meetings with journalists and politicians, behind-the-scenes museum tours, visits to beekeepers and physics labs, attendance at professional sustainability conferences.

I ran it on fumes for two years, together with a partner, and abandoned it in 2017, when we were unable to attract outside funding or sufficient participants. The program was so palpably beneficial that we planned to expand it to Spain and France, with relevant language instruction and activities tailored to the locales. Our students have gone on to study at Harvard, Yale, Pomona, Georgetown, Oxford University in the UK, and prestigious universities elsewhere in the world. Several students, inspired by our fabulous International Relations professor, are pursuing diplomacy professionally, while others are becoming successful in other realms - entrepreneurship, law, marketing, medicine, photography, sustainability, tourism.

We had envisioned an alumni association too, and that has worked a bit via Facebook, but we had also planned reunions every five years at the original sites in order to reinforce the close friendships that formed and to promote networking. Reem regretted that we had no reunion in June 2020. The pandemic was a good excuse, but frankly, I'm demoralized by my inability to raise money and recruit students and have moved on. As a teacher, I'm nonetheless gratified to have made a positive difference in the lives of these young people and am delighted when they keep in touch.

In cheerier news, it's been a lovely week of dates with Jean-Claude. We first met for drinks at Café Vavin on Saturday, and that went well enough that he invited me for dinner at the nearby seafood restaurant Bistro du Dôme on the rue Delambre. On Sunday, we met for a pre-cinema walk in nearby Montmartre Cemetery. I showed him my favorite grave monument, that of Monsieur and Madame Pignon, portrayed life-size in bronze on an elegantly carved double bed in the dress of their era, circa 1900. Monsieur, a lamp entrepreneur, rests on one elbow, a book in his other hand with a finger inserted to mark his place. He looks up at visitors as if they have interrupted his reading aloud to Madame, who lies beside him, eyes open. I thought about how I might self-memorialize, but no obvious possibilities presented themselves.

I also showed Jean-Claude one of the most famous landmarks of modern sculpture: Constantin Brancusi's *The Kiss*, which marks the grave of a young, female, Russian medical student who committed suicide in the wake of an unhappy love affair. Or rather we saw where it is—due to a strange controversy the sculpture is now encased in a plywood box and guarded by security cameras. We inadvertently happened upon the forlorn mausoleum of Trocadéro Man's family, which I hadn't realized was there, another *madeleine de Proust*. Afterward, we saw a beautiful and inspiring Saudi film, *The Perfect Candidate*, about a young female medical doctor who runs for political office.

On Monday, we attended the Christo-Jeanne Claude exhibition at the Centre Pompidou, where I enjoyed rewatching the wonderful documentary about *Pont Neuf Wrapped* made by the Maysles Brothers, which I first saw at a private showing in New York before its release. Also on display was the equipment used in installing the wrap. It was the first time I've noticed museum curators intent on showing visitors the sophisticated technical aspects involved in what appears to project witnesses as an uncomplicated aesthetic gesture.

Tonight, Jean-Claude took me to dinner at Le Petit Journal, where we enjoyed a mediocre dinner and terrific jazz. I wish I felt more of an emotional charge in his presence. If I wrote a partner description, he would tick all the boxes: he meditates, exercises, is interested in and knowledgeable about history and culture, loves travel, and has bourgeois politesse. I'm not sure how to explain my reaction. Is it because I have attained a kind of semi-detached ability to live in the moment? He's just not 'the one'? I'm still unconsciously attached to Trocadéro Man? Another reason? I no longer feel attached to Trocadéro Man; my time with him seems to have settled comfortably into the past. When I encounter reminders of him, they evoke memories, not feelings.

Chapter 8
September: Back to Normal?

Tuesday 1 September

This is the longest I've gone without boarding an airplane in decades—six entire months. I don't even have reservations to go anywhere. I'm forgetting airport codes. In normal times, I'm on planes at least once a month. I don't miss airports, however—they're just the pound of flesh exacted for the privilege of travel. I'd love to see friends, but on the other hand there's something wonderful about not being pressured to go anywhere because one can't or shouldn't. My only friends whose travel has been little impacted by the pandemic are younger ones with visas or second passports. When I feel comfortable travelling again, I'll have to remember to use the vouchers I've been issued for cancelled flights.

Today, I went somewhere new: Château de Vincennes. An Englishman I befriended two years ago often walked in the Bois de Vincennes, so I figured it must be worth a visit. Baron Haussmann designed the park for the enjoyment of the working classes inhabiting the adjacent Twelfth Arrondissement, situated at the opposite side of the Right Bank from the Bois de Boulogne. I took the *métro*, changing at the never-pleasant Châtelet-Les Halles stop, whose underground maze rivals Times Square in its length, hectic crowdedness, and aroma. As I ascended into the sunshine, the formidable fifteenth-century stone fortress rose before me. It's the tallest fortress in Europe and must have offered fabulous panoramic views back in the day when it helped to see the enemy approaching. Like Versailles, the Château originated as a hunting lodge and only subsequently and briefly became a royal residence. In a fit of jealousy, Louis XIV had his finance minister, Nicolas Fouquet, imprisoned here, incensed that an underling would build himself a residence—Vaux-le-Vicomte—more splendid than the king's. Other illustrious prisoners included the Enlightenment philosopher Denis Diderot, editor of the first encyclopedia, and the infamous Marquis de Sade.

Over the centuries, the broad protective moat has transformed into a carpet of verdant lawn, now home to a family of rabbits. Inside the spacious château precinct, circumscribed by formidable masonry walls, the freestanding delicate Gothic chapel beckoned. Likely designed by the same architect as Sainte-Chapelle, it has similar proportions, with mini-spires atop each pencil-like buttress that function like spacers between tall, pointed windows. Vincennes has squattier proportions and rounder window arches than Sainte-Chapelle, so it was likely constructed earlier. Its windows are also plainer, functioning mainly as light-admitting surfaces rather than dazzling Christian-themed jewels. I was disappointed to find it closed, but that's a good motivation to return.

The feminine silhouette of the chapel contrasts dramatically with the towering, virtually windowless, and intimidatingly masculine château, which dominates its surroundings like a sentry. Protruding rounded stairwells anchor each corner, utilizing the same design as the Bastille prison, stormed by a revolutionary mob on July 14, 1789 and subsequently razed. There's little evidence of the château's former domestic use other than a small library, several elaborately carved fireplaces, and Gothic vaults with ribs embellished by figural and vegetal ornamentation. One room contains frescoes in earth tones that depict fifteenth-century peasants engaged in seasonal activities, including apple picking and wheat harvesting. In another, an imposing triple-domed church resembles Saint Mark's in Venice.

The prison doors—thick planks of oak joined by crisscross patterns of riveted iron braces with double-crossbar locks—seem impregnable. Their tiny windows with sliding panels operable from the outside would permit only limited transactions: food, supplies, letters. Steps with edges worn into rounded shallows by thousands of feet over the centuries convey a palpable sense of time passing. I imagined men in Renaissance or Baroque silk tights and tunics and during the Enlightenment, powdered wigs and waistcoats. Chisel marks on the risers preserve the memory of the stone masons' labor. I imagined them at work and wondered how they looked, worked, and what their lives were like.

Afterward, I wandered in the adjacent Bois, where I encountered a small lake with row boats, an alternative if I tire of the Bois de Boulogne. Then, I stumbled on a nudist precinct. One could not mistake it for anything else: sun worshippers lay scattered in a meadow exposing their largest organ to the invigorating rays of the midday sun. On my way out of the park, I noticed a sign: "You're entering an area where the practice of naturism is authorized."

The experience reminded me of an earlier event. In the mid-1990s, I researched the surprising frequency of nudity in German painting over the centuries. This led to an investigation of contemporary naturism. Someone told me that the archive of the FKK (*Freikörperkultur*, literally 'free body culture') movement was in Kassel, so there I went. I inquired at the art museum and was directed to a naturist park nearby. Within two minutes after getting off the bus, I felt awkward dressed in a skirt and flats for a day in the archive as I inquired of nude passersby about the archive location. All were polite and thoughtful, but none had heard of such a repository. Finally, a man suggested going to FKK headquarters in town. Back I got on the bus.

A ten-foot-tall stockade fence protected the in-town sanctuary. I rang the bell and an athletic middle-aged man carrying a twelve-foot-long two-by-four opened the gate. I wondered about splinters.

"Good day. May I help you?"

"Hello. I'm a scholar who's searching for the FKK archive. At the art museum they told me it was in the park, but it wasn't, and someone in the park suggested trying here."

"Ah, I don't know anything about it, but someone is in the office." He pointed to a nearby building with a sign reading 'office'. "You can ask her."

I thanked him and took stock of my surroundings. It looked like a holiday trailer park. A few dozen trailers parked under large leafy trees looked like they'd been there a long time. They surrounded a swimming pool, tennis courts, and a playground. In the office, I saw the back of a woman seated at a desk typing on a computer. I knocked at the wooden screen door. She turned, noticed me, and got up. The woman, middle-aged with a blond, jaw-length bob, wore only glasses and a wedding ring on her right hand. Feeling overdressed, I introduced myself and posed my question. She looked puzzled and informed me that she didn't know of *any* FKK archive anywhere in Germany. Not all research trips are successful.

Friday 4 September

Children have returned to school, and teens now flood my neighborhood at lunchtime and in the late afternoon. I predict a second pandemic wave judging from their carefree behavior. While schools might dutifully enforce mask wearing, distancing, and hand washing, students behave differently on their own. They remove masks while eating, of course, but they do it in small tightly packed groups on steps, in doorways, in squares, and in le Luco, offering each other bites of pizza, spring rolls, and crepes. They share food and drink freely, chatter gregariously, and remain unmasked after dining. They have also discovered cigarette smoking as a legitimate excuse for mask avoidance; teen smoking has escalated steeply since springtime. I know that closing schools complicates life for parents and may not be optimal from a pedagogical viewpoint, but unless these kids begin observing regulations, the near future looks bleak for France pandemic-wise.

Have lipstick sales plummeted, I wonder? Lips are rarely visible with the indoor-outdoor mask mandate, except, of course, while drinking and dining. I've stopped wearing lipstick unless I have plans to dine with someone. Smiling at people also presents a challenge. A recent article in *Le Monde* offered tips on how to smile with your eyes. And masks have joined the fashion front. While most people remain content with standard blue and white medical masks, others have seized the opportunity to make fashion statements. French government officials wear dignified black or navy masks that harmonize with their business suits, while fashion forward women like Nancy Pelosi and Queen Elizabeth II have pioneered outfit-matching masks. Others prefer making alternative statements, with masks proclaiming their admiration for the paintings of van Gogh or Monet, their nostalgia for cartoon characters, or their sense of humor, donning masks depicting various configurations of expressive lips. For me, the real downside to outdoor mask-wearing is that it inhibits my ability to smell. The streets of Paris now offer a delightful bonanza of scents: hops wafting from bars, croissants and baguettes from *boulangeries*, flowers from *fleuristes*, old books and leather from *libraries*, wood oven pizza, crepes, gyro meat, and, more generally, flowers and other growing things in parks and planters. This is especially true in the absence of the usual traffic density.

Today, I was invited to Jean-Claude's for dinner. He had been planning a delicious gluten-free feast for the past week. It was a heartfelt testament to his thoughtfulness as a potential partner, a gesture I deeply appreciated. I can't remember the last time a romantically interested man offered to make me dinner. While he was enthusiastically determining a menu, finding recipes, and shopping, I was becoming increasingly anxious, knowing that staying overnight was a strong possibility, one that for him would ideally entail sex. I've struggled with the reasons for my hesitancy to sleep with him; I guess I just don't find him that physically attractive, although at our ages seeing age-appropriate people who make you tingle with anticipation happens less often. A lot less. I know he would have respected my choice not to sleep with him even if he found it disappointing, but I'm not in the mood to confront the subject at all. Although that's exactly what I did when I called him yesterday to cancel before he bought the scallops. I feel certain that

I'd never want to sleep with him. Do I need to figure out why? Is it just one of those things? Either you find someone attractive, or you don't? Jean-Claude expressed understanding about the whole awkward thing. I said I'd really like to keep seeing him if that was OK, but I'm also pretty sure this is his signal to move on, and that impulse is probably correct.

Sunday 6 September

Jim invited me along to visit his artist friend Aristide today. Aristide lives in Menilmontant, a neighborhood of contrasts, with hideous high rises inhabited mainly by immigrants looming over crooked lanes occupied by artistic alternativo types. Aristide is the latter and resides on a tranquil, block-long cobblestone street in a ground-floor apartment that was once a shop. It has large, curtained display windows and a now purely decorative front door. Upon arrival, we entered a long dark hallway that opened onto an enclosed garden packed with a chaotic array of plants, flowers, sculptures, and patio furniture. Inside is a spacious studio with a barebones cooking corner, a serviceable toilet, and dining, living, studio, and sleeping areas.

Around 1900, the Swedish artist Carl Larsson wrote an international bestseller, *A Home*, that advised readers to consider their homes authentic extensions of their personality. He illustrated it with twenty-six watercolors of his own home, which inspired Ingvar Kamprad's IKEA aesthetic. Aristide's home does just that. It's eclectic and eccentric, distinguished by an appealing, antique-shop *horror vacuii*. My eyes flitted along the walls where his and others' paintings grace the walls asymmetrically along with beautiful but empty frames. Dining chairs and tableware are mismatched and surfaces pleasantly congested with an intriguing array of seashells, *objets*, microscopes, and mysterious scientific instruments. Books lay everywhere, arranged on shelves and stacked on floors and tables.

Aristide works in a wide range of media, letting his impulses guide him. Lately, he's focusing on creating his own books, or rather re-creating or collaborating with them. A photographer by trade, after completing a privileged 'military' service in Washington where his job was buying champagne and wine for the French embassy, he affixes his own photographs of people and places and sometimes drawings into preexisting books. Each book is a surprise: you're never sure what awaits when you open the cover. With some, I turned many pages before coming to one of Aristide's interventions that occur at irregular intervals.

Many of these books are large, old, and beautiful, with tooled leather bindings and images on their covers. Once inside, I was captivated by elegant scripts. Many are in Arabic or Farci that, because of their incomprehensibility, were for me as for most viewers merely decorative. Aristide doesn't make these for people who understand the texts but for those who appreciate the aesthetic experience of engaging with a book this way—in a purposeless, joyful voyage of discovery. Aristide is a true creative bohemian, and I felt happy and carefree in his company.

Aristide served us a delicious vegetable soup he made, accompanied by a salad and a large, crusty, round peasant loaf, which I of course couldn't eat, although it smelled wonderfully. Aristide spends months at time in Cairo, and he and Jim chatted about their mutual friend who lives there. Afterward, we strolled around the neighborhood, heading west toward Belleville. We passed the birthplace of Maurice Chevalier and Concert du XXe Siècle, a defunct cabaret on the boulevard Menilmontant where he first performed.

We walked through the mountainous Parc Belville, whose overgrown vegetation reminded me of the Central Park Rambles except that it offers panoramic views of the city. Paris appears to collapse in such vistas: the square towers of Notre-Dame appeared just to the left of Tour Montparnasse and the colorful blue-red tangle of tubes on the Centre Pompidou to its right. Further to the right, the shimmering golden dome of Invalides poked up from a field of grey roofs and beyond that, the Eiffel Tower, whose pinnacle seemed to touch the clouds. From here, the relative smallness of Paris becomes apparent. The rolling hills to the south formed a bluish frame encircling the urban panorama.

A painted bedsheet hanging at the community center

announced in blue and green lettering "House of Air. Belville Park. A House for Everyone and Everything." Along a narrow path leading out of the park lies what can only be described as a neighborhood inhabited by cats. They're not homeless exactly, it's just that their homes are too small to shelter humans. Someone or some group—I'm guessing older women with nothing better to do (I saw several reading or knitting on nearby benches)—have created individual domiciles for feral cats. More than a dozen small cartons and crates lie among the bushes, each covered in black plastic to keep the interiors dry. Shag carpeting or terrycloth towels line the studio-homes, and they have cushy floors made from throw pillows or fabric-covered foam. Each has a brick foundation and steps made from rocks or pieces of wood. Inside, a full food bowl awaits and by the steps outside, a water bowl. These cats live a life of freedom and comfort of which domestic cats can only dream. Paris is a city committed to taking good care of its homeless, human and feline.

Many parts of Belleville—like Menilmontant—catapult you back in time to a slower-paced, village-like Paris. As Aristide, Jim, and I meandered, I felt as though I'd landed in a vintage film: two-story buildings with shutters flanking their windows, fading stenciled signs, small shops whose proprietors leaned against the doorways chatting with passersby, elderly bereted men sitting in small squares reading newspapers.

For me, the big surprise was the streets Edgar Poë and George Lardennois. They lie atop one of Paris's taller hills and are lined with variously sized private homes built long ago, when this neighborhood was an independent village. At their westernmost end is Butte Bergeyre, from which one could hang glide across the valley to Sacré-Cœur. It's a serene corner of Paris that feels like a high elevation West Village, a West Village with a vineyard.

Friday 11 September

A few months ago, an intriguing man got in touch: a world-renowned scientist once considered for a Nobel Prize. Someone who does not *need* a partner but would enjoy the life enhancements it can provide. Torn between pursuing a career in research or as a concert pianist, he's done both. Just the kind of high achiever I find appealing. He's busy, I'm busy, and he lives in a far corner of France but said he would get in touch when he comes to visit his daughter in Paris. Despite many weeks of silence, he did as promised. We met on Monday. I had a hankering for Greek food, so I suggested Grand Café d'Athènes on the rue Faubourg Saint-Denis, which prepares Greek cuisine as well as I.

Daniel was handsome, youthful, and clean-shaven, with a thick head of white hair and intense blue eyes. I've been astonished by how old people in their mid-60s can look since few of my friends do. It felt, finally, as though I had met someone from my world and at my vibrational level. He doesn't require someone to hang out with because he's bored in retirement, seemingly the case for many men I have dated. Instead, he's busy preparing for a piano competition. He seems just the right combination of independent and companionable, and we have sufficient overlapping interests. He, too, speaks several languages and has friends everywhere, something that I'm beginning to realize sets such individuals apart in a significant way. When one has and spends time with friends at their homes in various geographical locations, one becomes quickly immersed in their cultures and learns their very different ways of being in the world. When we parted, Daniel promised to call and play me the pieces he was working on. The first time we spoke I had asked him to play for me, and he happily complied, playing Chopin's challenging "Fantasie-Impromptu" on his Bösendorfer. We also share a preference for Romantic piano music. Although I have no expectations, Daniel seems promising.

On Tuesday, Duchess Charlotte, who had driven Jim and me back from the aristo reunion in Brittany, invited me for lunch at her lovely, compact apartment located in a medieval building in the Fifth Arrondissement, half a block from the Seine. Martha Stewart would have felt immediately at home. We ran into each other two weeks ago on the rue Mouffetard as I headed to Marché Monge. She invited two other guests: an anthropology professor at the Sorbonne and the sculptor Marina Donati, who keeps a studio across the cobblestone lane and is the daughter of Surrealist painter Enrico Donati.

Lunch was traditional and unpretentious: a soup course followed by a main course of fish, potatoes, and green beans, and finishing with salad and cheese, dessert (crème brulée), and coffee. Bourgeois Frenchmen are particular about dining etiquette, so I'm glad I know not to cut large lettuce leaves (they should be folded using knife and fork into a bite-sized packet) and the order in which cheeses should be eaten. Some practices one can discern by watching, but for others, one must discreetly ask non-judgmental friends (such as proper use of knife rests—between courses only—otherwise *on* the plate). It's been a long time since I've socialized in that way—a meal indoors at the home of friends—the first time since the outbreak of the pandemic. We wore masks getting there but removed them upon arrival. I'm not sure why unmasking indoors feels unthreatening to me here when friends in the U.S. refrain from even seeing their own adult children indoors.

Afterward, we visited Marina's studio, a well-organized space with drafting tables and shelves filled with plaster and clay maquettes, bronze sculptures, and art books. The studio opens onto a small, walled rose garden. An interior spiral staircase leads both up and down, although we weren't invited to see where to. Marina regaled us with tales of her childhood growing up in New York and of Uncle Marcel—Marcel Duchamp, the pioneering modernist genius and her father's best friend—who delighted her with magic tricks. She told us how her mother dreaded visits from Surrealist artist Max Ernst, a mean drunk, hostile and insulting when inebriated. As an art historian, it was thrilling to hear first-hand accounts of those pillars of twentieth-century art.

As a parting gift, Marina gave me several catalogues, including one documenting an exhibition of her work decades ago held at a gallery owned by a relative of Trocadéro Man. In Paris, he and his history seem inescapable. In the evening, I chatted with a new fellow, Olivier from Grenoble. He's a musician and artist. I like both his music—he plays bass in a blues band—and his art. The few men I've encountered who claim to be artists have produced work I find so amateurish and kitschy that I didn't want to meet them knowing they would ask for my opinion, and I would feel uncomfortable both lying and being honest.

Thursday 17 September

Today is Grandma Irene's birthday. My mother's French mother was born 119 years ago in Buffalo, a city founded by the French, who called it *'Beau Fleuve'*—beautiful river—because of its location on the Niagara River near the eponymous falls. It seems strange that my grandmother was born more than a century before the moment in which I now find myself. I should have questioned her more about her childhood before she died three decades ago. I do remember her describing ice deliveries by horse-drawn cart in the era before refrigeration. She and her mother, Barbara, were extraordinarily entrepreneurial for their time: both women founded moving-and-storage companies. Barbara made a fortune during Prohibition smuggling alcohol from Canada, and Irene started her business in her home, transforming it into a multi-million-dollar enterprise now owned, ironically, by the grandchild she and my grandfather liked least. "She's such a selfish little dickens," Grandma Irene would say.

Grandma Irene rarely called me by my name but rather by Angel, which is not wholly accurate. On my birthday cards, she always wrote the exact time of my birth: 11:30 a.m. She was obese when I was growing up. After a heart attack at age sixty, she lost weight and became a runway model locally in Buffalo. Ever since I can remember, she had snow-white, frizzy long hair that she wore in a tidy bun or French twist. She was also culinarily adventurous, although she never left the U.S. except for Canada, which was closer than the adjacent county. I remember finding tins of fried grasshoppers and chocolate-covered ants on her pantry shelves. She and my grandfather wintered in Fort Lauderdale and occasionally visited the Okefenokee Swamp. That was about as exotic as her life got.

Grandma Irene loved visiting me in New York. She came with my mother and found everything about the city thrilling: the noise, the crowds, the filth. Her sense of wonder made me see my life there in a vibrant new way. We spent lots of time together when I was growing up and afterward, whenever I came to town. She taught me to cook (my mother was only good at baking), embroider, and knit. I still have a few crewel projects she never finished and that I have always meant to but have not. Their nostalgic grip won't permit me to discard them, either. Hanna's middle name is Irene, and I like to think that her serenity, beauty, and adventurousness are my grandmother's legacy.

Yesterday, Hanna gave a concert at Larry's Corner, a music shop and concert venue in Stockholm run by an American ex-pat hippie who moved there for love in the 1970s. In accordance with unenforced distancing regulations, attendance was limited to twelve, and Larry required his audience to wear masks. I watched via Facebook. Hanna played alone, without her band, The Sedations, and treated her audience to new tunes accompanied only by her on guitar. She ended the performance with her sing-along "If You're Alive You're Not Alone," an appropriate tune for this moment of relative social isolation. It's been a joy to watch her mature as a musician. When Hanna was three, she wrote her first song, "The Kitties are Lasting Too Much," with lyrics as nonsensical as the title suggests. Over time, her lyrics have become smarter and her music more sophisticated, but they remain authentic reflections of her essence: full of playfulness, insight, and surprises.

On Monday, I chatted with my best male college pal, Dave, who has continued to live in Buffalo, where we both grew up. He mentioned having been a boy scout, something I had difficulty envisioning of my blues-loving, bar hopping buddy. In that context, he mentioned a fellow scout, Ben, and I almost fell off my chair. They didn't live close at all back then, and I couldn't imagine how they could have belonged to the same troop since I thought all scout troops were school-specific. I asked if there had been a Jewish boy scout troop, and yes, there had. Ben was in my elementary school class from second to sixth grade. We attended different junior and senior high schools and lost contact. Nonetheless, Ben played a huge role in my life unbeknownst to him, and I always thought he would find it amusing. I decide to write to him and share the tale.

Ben was responsible for my deciding that Roman Catholicism was a stupid religion. I fell in love with him the minute he set foot in my class: his freckles, red hair, intelligence, and kind, friendly manner captivated me. We lived on opposite sides of the baseball fields beside the elementary school we attended, and I could see his brown corner house from my bedroom window. As a Catholic, I got released early on Mondays to attend Religious Instruction at the local parochial school. Toward the end of the school year in second grade, I asked my nun-teacher what would happen if I married Ben, a Jew. Without pause she replied, "you'd go to hell." And that was that. At seven-years old I wanted no part of a religion so harsh that it condemned you to eternal damnation for loving someone. I don't know if the nun was anti-Semitic, but I knew instinctively that her assertion was wrong.

I first shared the Ben story with Aunt Margaret—Sister Mary Leona, my mother's paternal aunt and a nun in the order Sisters of Mercy—when I was fifteen or sixteen. She was mortified and told me that Nun-Teacher was wrong and that I should have reported the incident so my misunderstanding could have been corrected. But I never questioned the knowledge and authority of Nun-Teacher. My mother blamed this malicious and mal-informed nun for my atheism.

Emerging out of the blue and probably long forgotten, I sent the anecdote to Ben in a Facebook message. He replied almost immediately, finding it as amusing as had everyone else. In scanning his FB page, I realized that were I to run into him, I would recognize him immediately. Most people change drastically in appearance between seven and sixty-something, but not Ben. If outer appearance reflects inner truth, Ben has retained his childhood integrity. And just as one might have predicted, he has had a happy and wildly successful life with wonderful children and a beautiful wife. I hope someday that our paths cross.

Tuesday 22 September

Last Thursday, my travel buddy/colleague/former student Thor arrived for a long weekend because it was the *Journées de Patriomoine* (Days of Patrimony), an annual event when throughout France historical sites normally closed to the public are open. Popular ones, like the Luxembourg Palace, have very long lines (or require reservations). I feel fortunate to be in Paris this particular year when one doesn't have to compete with foreign tourists. Still, some sites were crowded even if rainy weather may have stifled attendance.

For Saturday, I mapped out a route in the Sixth and Seventh Arrondissements that began with a house museum and ended with a concert. We walked through le Luco, past the line of lucky folks waiting to see the inside of the Luxembourg Palace with its murals by Delacroix. I could probably arrange a private viewing since most culturally important sites make accommodations for scholars purporting to study works of art or architecture otherwise off limits, and perhaps someday I will. We were alone at our first stop: the Auguste Comte Museum on the rue Monsieur-le-Prince. I love exploring the residences of people who lived long ago. Recently, when walking home from rowing in the Bois de Boulogne, I stopped by the Balzac Museum, a wonderful house-museum located in the author's former residence. Located in the Sixteenth Arrondissement and surrounded by a garden in a location that must have been the countryside in the mid-nineteenth century when the writer lived there, it's now a forlorn spot surrounded by tall, white apartment buildings at the edge of a motorway entrance.

A visit to Comte's modest and charming suite of rooms with their period furniture didn't take long. Despite the rain, the rooms were luminous, infinitely more pleasant than the somber rooms inhabited by Delacroix during the same era. When we descended to the street and approached the boulevard Saint-Germain, the streets vibed a kind of adult Halloween: masked people wandering in groups from landmark to landmark searching for intellectual sweets. Lines formed at the many temporarily accessible public buildings. We headed to the Institut de France, home of the illustrious Académie Française, guardian of French linguistic purity. Established in the seventeenth century by Cardinal Richelieu, abolished during the French Revolution, and restored by Napoléon, its forty members are known as 'The Immortals' and possess tremendous prestige in this book-loving land. It has always been under the direct 'protection' of the head of state: Louis XIV, Napoléon, now Macron. It has included famous philosophers, politicians, scientists, writers, and even, currently, art historians: Paul Rosenberg, former director of the Louvre and Jean Clair, former director of the Paris Picasso Museum. Its setting is impressive: situated on the Seine, the wood and iron pont des Arts leads straight to its main entrance. With a classical Roman temple façade—a triangular pediment supported by Corinthian columns—and especially its dome, it's an easily identifiable cousin of the Invalides and Panthéon domes on the Paris skyline. The interiors are as sumptuous and stately as one imagines, and I learned that its elegant library is open to the public.

In the afternoon, we ventured to the Seventh Arrondissement. The interiors of the former palaces we toured had been so transformed into serviceable government offices that whatever original period charm had existed has vanished. It was chilly, and I wore gloves. Some of the attendants whose job it was to ensure that visitors sanitize their hands even in venues where there was nothing imaginable one would want to touch were confused by my refusal. Some insisted, so I removed my gloves, sanitized, and put them back on, while others understood the absurdity of such a gesture and let me enter with my germ-ridden, gloved hands. Attendants eagerly distributed brochures and gave informative talks that we skipped, both of us more interested in the past than the present. We visited the Museum of the Legion of Honor in tribute to my Uncle Jim, made a *chevalier* (knight) shortly before his death a few years ago. The award acknowledged his service during World War Two as a ball-turret gunner, the most hazardous job on a B-17 bomber, one with a mortality rate of sixty percent. Uncle Jim had been lucky. His small stature would also have suited him for a career as a jockey. This small museum is ostentatiously, palatially elegant, with gilded molding and candelabras, mirrors, crystal chandeliers, and ceiling paintings. I picked up a brochure to send to my cousins.

Just as it started to rain, Thor and I ended our day at the basilica of Sainte-Clothilde, which I sometimes pass on my Eiffel Tower pilgrimages. It has a spacious square and small park in front, where children roller skate and scoot. Built in the mid-nineteenth century when the neighborhood was growing, Paris's Chief Architect, Franz Christian Gau, designed it in a Gothic Revival style to harmonize with the other grand churches of Paris. Its stately demeanor suits the surrounding bourgeois residential buildings. As everywhere, a sign notifying concertgoers that masks were required stood at the entrance beside a table with two bottles of sanitizer. Sheets of paper that read 'leave this space free' were posted at regular intervals in the pews, but companions could sit side-by-side, and we did. It was a contemplative, hour-long concert on an organ famous for its outstanding sonority; the composer César Franck was the church's first organist and remained in the position for thirty years, until his death in 1890.

The program explored the temporal expanse of organ composition from J.S. Bach to Jean Guillou with pieces, including one by Franck, selected for their suitability to this particular organ. I learned from an organist friend that organs differ tremendously, with some perfect vehicles for one period of music but not for others. I also learned that since one doesn't perform on one's own instrument, organists need to spend a day or two rehearsing, so they can become familiar with an instrument's mechanics and expressive possibilities. Because organs are significantly more complicated than pianos or tympana—two other instruments that one rarely transports to gigs—organists are individuals with temperaments that embrace the novelty of discovery. My organist friend compared it to the thrill of a new romantic encounter.

The pandemic has altered my sense of time. Weekends and weekdays seem indistinguishable. For me, this is a somewhat normal situation except when I'm teaching and have a schedule dictating my activities. My nightly walk to the first twinkling of the Eiffel Tower does provide a distinct sense of time passing. It never starts before 8 p.m., the time when it begins for much of the year, progressing to 11 p.m. at the summer solstice. Now, it's back to 9 p.m., and on my way this evening, streetlights were illuminated for the first time. This—rather than the equinox or falling leaves or gutters filled with chestnuts—seems to me the true marker of the arrival of autumn in Paris.

Wednesday 30 September

Thor departed yesterday, following a spectacular dinner the previous evening at the reliably delicious and traditional Josephine Chez Dumonet on the rue du Cherche-Midi, which specializes in Thor's favorite French dish, *andouillette*—pork tripe sausage. It's my least favorite dish (as a child, Hanna referred to it as 'poop sausage' based on its smell and taste), so I ordered the *coq au vin* to which Josephine added its own gourmet twist.

I have returned to my usual rhythm of meditation followed by jumping rope, breakfast, writing in le Luco, lunch, more writing, dinner, and chats with friends from the forests of Sonoma to the cobblestone streets of Budapest. Normally, I turn up for visits in these locations at irregular intervals; chats now substitute for visits. During this old fashioned-feeling pandemic time, analog communication feels appropriate. My ability to make free landline calls to anywhere ignited my virtual social life, and now I usually talk to several friends or to family most evenings before or after my two-hour Eiffel Tower promenade. Today, I lunched with Caroline at the Grand Mosque after shopping at Marché Monge, where I saw both purple- and orange-colored cauliflower.

In France, the fruits and vegetables available in open-air markets chart the passing of the seasons. Even though I find myself in a metropolis, I feel earthbound, connected to nature in a way I never do in New York or Stockholm, where (except for chanterelles and strawberries in Sweden) one finds similar offerings year-round. *Terroir*—literally 'place' but redolent with associations of soil, nostalgia, and authenticity—is respected in France with quasi-religious reverence. Discussion about the specific geographical locations from which one's food comes and the subtle differences in taste it causes is common among the French; even supermarkets often identify the origins of their domestic produce. Attention to the subtilties of terroir, to the sensual pleasure of food, elevates what for many is mere survival to one of the supreme joys of life.

Yesterday, I lunched with a colleague, a former runway model living a luxurious life with homes here and there since becoming the trophy wife of a Frenchman old enough to be her father. Afterward, she introduced me to the Nordic Library, located in an extension of Labrouste's architectural masterpiece, Bibliothèque Saint-Genviève, across from the Panthéon. I've passed it many times when it was closed, and a Rhodesian Ridgeback slept curled up in its bed just behind the glass entry door. While I would love to support the library by using its resources, it lacks the archival materials I require to complete my *Denmark* book, and the reading room is too depressing for me to concentrate on writing.

Monday was a cultural highlight. Jim and I went to soprano Sabine Devielhe's recital at the elegant Theâtre des Champs-Elysées. I experienced an extraordinary feeling of normalcy and my first live classical musical experience since Fall 2019, when I attended a performance at the State Opera in Berlin. Settling into the comfortable, red-upholstered barrel chair for an evening of music felt exhilarating. Delvielhe sang a program of works by Debussy, Fauré, Poulenc, and Ravel in an angelic voice that dampened my anxiety about being in an enclosed space with nearly every seat occupied. We walked there from place de la Concorde, which at dusk possessed a quasi-musical beauty with its lampposts, lions, obelisk, Pradier's allegorical sculpture of Lille, and the Eiffel Tower silhouetted in tones of dark grey and black against a pale golden sky. This Paris—Paris without too many people or vehicles, Paris of quiet beauty—lasts only for the eternity of the moment I am in, and I know there won't be many more such moments once the world returns to 'normal'. I want this image, this feeling, to permeate my being so that its trace remains even after its reality has vanished.

Chapter 9
October: Shrinking Boundaries & New Possibilities

Saturday 2 October

I'm suffering from dating fatigue. It initially seemed a practical way to improve my French, gain insight into French culture, and possibly find a romantic partner, but lately, it has become tedious. Regardless of how fussy I try to be in choosing the men I meet, there is a certain uniformity. Many seem lonely and intellectually unstimulating or pretentious. I'm reflecting more on why I should look for a partner in the first place.

Partly, because I'm used to it. I've lived in partner relationships continuously since the age of seventeen. I like having someone around, someone whose habits, recreational enjoyment, culinary preferences, and lifestyle sync with mine. Swedish Ex ticked most of the compatibility boxes. Demonstrably enthusiastic, energetic, affectionate at first, he taught me to ski. For years, we enjoyed the same food, music, people, and places. Had he not been a gaslighting philanderer, everything might have been fine. I loved our lifestyle of winters skiing and writing in Lapland, summers rowing, berry picking, and writing in Tolg, periodic autumns and springs teaching, and otherwise traveling, mostly to visit my friends. Perhaps I should arrange my own agreeable lifestyle, like Sharon Stone, by replacing a man with a dog, although part of me does want to find a human companion. I sleep better when I can touch someone with whom I have an intimate relationship. I'm beginning to think that Internet hunting is not the best strategy. Since it's much too late for me to walk hand in hand for decades along the path of life with someone growing closer all the while, I require a more glove-like fit at the outset.

Tuesday 6 October

While searching for something interesting and free to read on my iPad, I came across Daniel Defoe's *A Journal of the Plague Year*, first published in 1722. It's an imaginary memoir of the bubonic plague that ravaged London in 1665, when the author was five-years old. I first read it as a teenager. The plague's early stages resembled, eerily, those of the current pandemic: a few safely distant cases making the headlines, soon receding in the wake of more exciting political and climate disaster news. Then, regularly occurring cases, unignorable and closer at hand. Weeks of statistics rising and falling accompanied by sighs of relief and fearful whispers. A mass exodus of the affluent to their country houses with servants and possessions in tow, signaling a worsening crisis. Those left behind, wary of one another, cloister at home, leaving their safety zones only as necessity demands. Inspired, a few days ago I shelved *Rosa and Nathalie*, now two-thirds written, to begin an authentic journal of the pandemic year in Paris—the one you are now reading. Good thing I followed Hanna's advice to journal and keep track of my daily doings, something I have never done in the past despite the best of intentions.

This evening, Jim and I went to the exquisite Athénée Théâtre, to whose name that of one of its most illustrious mid-twentieth-century directors, Louis Jouvet, has been added. Built in the 1890s, Athénée Théâtre Louis Jouvet shortly thereafter premiered Oscar Wilde's *Salomé*. Until Jouvet took over in 1934 and transformed it into an avant-garde mecca, the Athénée functioned primarily as a vaudeville venue tucked away in a stately courtyard near Opéra Garnier. We saw *Crœsus*, a German Baroque opera by Reinhard Keiser. The stage is taller than it is wide, with small, steep balconies and ornate, Grande Epoque décor. The busy walls are embellished by carved and gilded cartouches, flourishes, garlands, masks, musical instruments, and putti. Mask wearing in theaters seems sufficient to ward off undesirable germs, so it was a wonderfully normal-feeling evening.

Today's news featured concerns about Trump's health. Apparently, he has contracted COVID-19 and is hospitalized. French journalists assume his health is more fragile than White House spokespeople let on. In fact, journalists regard any news coming from the White House with suspicion because they harbor—regardless of their position on the conservative-liberal spectrum—an inherent mistrust of information emanating from it.

Friday 9 October

This evening, I had a date with Richard, a short spry British expat with a wry sense of humor. We met at Espace Krajcberg, which occupies the former studio of Jewish-Polish ex-pat artist Frans Krajcberg. Krajcberg's father was a shoe salesman and his mother, a political activist. She did several stints in Polish prisons and was hanged by the Nazis in 1939. Frans escaped into the forest, joined resistance groups, and eventually the Russian army. After the war, he returned to reclaim his family's apartment but found it occupied by virulent anti-Semites. Rather than fighting for his property, he left Poland forever and decided to become an artist.

Krajcberg emigrated first to Germany then to Paris, where he stayed for several months as a guest of interwar Cubist painter Fernand Léger. Krajcberg found post-war Europe depressing, with its mountains of rubble and trash and doily-like bombed out buildings, so he departed for Brazil at the suggestion of fellow Jewish emigré Marc Chagall. Upon arrival in São Paulo in 1948, Krajcberg immersed himself in the local art scene, attending exhibition openings and searching in vain for supportive collectors. Frustrated by his failure, he then withdrew to the tranquility of the Amazonian jungle. There, Krajcberg found his passion: championing the cause of indigenous Amazonians to preserve their culture and their rapidly vanishing rainforest home.

He returned to São Paulo when his home and all his artwork were destroyed by arson in 1955. In 1957, Krajcberg and the Abstract Expressionist painter Jackson Pollock won top cash prizes at the São Paulo Biennial, a stroke of luck that enabled Krajcberg to return to Paris, where he achieved sudden success and joined an avant-garde circle that included Jean-Paul Sartre and Alberto Giacometti. In 1960, Krajcberg moved into the space we visited in the heart of artists' Montparnasse, a few blocks away from Giacometti's studio. He continued to visit Brazil and Amazonia. Channeling the activist spirit of his mother, he fought for its preservation. Krajcberg died in Rio de Janeiro in 2017 and is celebrated as a father of the Anthropocene. Krajcberg's former glass-walled studio is now a gallery dedicated to his work and that of others engaged in the struggle for environmental sustainability. I'm touched by his love and concern for nature and impressed by his facility with languages. He was a kind and empathetic man. I'm also surprised that I didn't know about this exhibition space, a five-minute walk from my apartment.

The exhibition showcased photographs by Krajcberg's Brazilian friend Sebastião Salgado, a former Magnum photojournalist and conservationist who works exclusively in black and white. A film he made with Wim Wenders, *Salt of the Earth*, was nominated for an Academy Award in 2015. Salgado's photographs are exquisite. Their rich tones convey profound emotion. Sweeping aerial views of mysterious billowing tree canopies and bright dense clouds contrast with heartbreaking scenes of strip mining and deforestation. In one image, determined natives hold up their hands beseechingly, pushing metaphorically against unstoppable corporate power in a fruitless effort to protect their homeland. On a beach crowded with seals, one turns back toward us, its mouth open in a cry—a warning or a plea? By capturing the fragility and magnificence of the earth and its creatures, Salgado intends to inspire action.

Afterward, Richard and I enjoyed a relaxing evening of ex-pat chit chat over *galettes* (main course crêpes made with buckwheat flour) and a *pichet* of hard cider at Plougastel, my favorite crêperie among the multitude of competitors on the rue Montparnasse. I had wondered what motivated such a crêperie-dense block—more than a dozen establishments line it—until a friend explained that Breton peasants moving to Paris after World War Two arrived at Gare Montparnasse, which opened in 1940, the year the German occupation of Paris began. *Of course*, I thought, since crêpes originated in Brittany. The Bretons settled nearby, often naming their restaurants after the villages they had forsaken. Plougastel, for instance. Despite what in many ways was a perfect summer evening, neither of us felt that thrill of attraction we both craved.

Thursday 15 October

I've just returned from a three-day-long date with Olivier in Grenoble; I'd been chatting with him for several weeks. He's a retired academic and a semi-professional blues musician and artist, whose meticulously crafted works displays humor and intelligence. I agreed to visit partly because I was curious about Grenoble, a fascination that began with the 1968 Winter Olympics held there. I remember sitting riveted to our recently acquired color TV watching skiing superstar Jean-Claude Killy win gold medal after gold medal and thinking that Grenoble looked like a winter paradise. I was seized by the same uninformed fascination that enchanted Frankie the Fixer when he opted for 'Lilyhammer' as his Witness Protection Program venue based on watching the 1994 Winter Olympics. Lillehammer, Norway, however, is exactly as lovely as it appears whereas Grenoble is not.

I have always harbored a soft spot for bass players and artists and was thrilled to escape Paris for a few days after more than seven months of sleeping in the same bed, a record for me. The first-class train car was comfortable and sparsely populated; the lovely hilly landscape enroute was mesmerizing. I didn't tell Hanna what I was doing; she would have counseled against it. A crazy idea in pandemic times and perhaps even dangerous, she would warn. Maybe he's a psychopath. But Olivier didn't feel threatening. He was a responsive communicator, and we shared the banalities of our existence in missives exchanged almost daily.

Strangely, Olivier didn't meet me on the platform. Instead, he waited in the station/shopping mall. He looked exactly as his photos: friendly blue eyes, shaggy white hair, a thin, athletic physique. A seventy-year-old in a younger body. We drove directly to his house in his ratty van. While in the car, it would have been nice to have a tour of the town and its environs. We were in the Alps, and there must be charming things to see even in cloudy weather.

Olivier's house is in Fortuny, an adjacent suburb and a twenty-minute walk from the city center. To enter the house, one traverses a short drive/carport and garage, narrow and dark with a jungle of plants. From there, through the art studio, whose walls are lined with workbenches and tidy boxes of supplies. I kept my two cashmere sweaters on. The fireplace is immaculate and unused, and there are no rugs to buffer feet from the icy-cold, white tile floors. Olivier did provide a loaner pair of his daughter's sheepskin slippers, but those—even with two pairs of socks—didn't thaw my frozen feet.

The house has a sound-proof music studio, kitchen, dining room, and *salon* downstairs, and three bedrooms upstairs. Beyond the *salon* is a glassed-in veranda with a jumble of plants and a few bamboo chairs. Outside, an unused swimming pool extends the entire width of the yard and has an arched cover that blocks a view of the garden. It is an eyesore that—along with the high walls around the small property—contributes to a sense of claustrophobia. The decor evokes frat house taste: cheap, soulless furnishings possibly selected from overstock in the sale hall at IKEA. They make youth hostel interiors look worthy of a spread in *Architectural Digest*. I slept both nights in the guest bedroom with a partial view of the mountains from my window. Although I slept well in the cool air, the rest of the time I shivered in a turtleneck, two sweaters, and a lightweight down jacket.

Olivier dressed in tattered old clothes. You'd think, given his objective of attracting a mate, he'd dress better. Surely, leftovers from his administrative and academic life hang in a closet some-

where. Outfits he wears for gigs would likely have been an improvement. His profile pictures showed him in shirts with collars. Not one
shows a threadbare, stretched out, faded knit shirt with frayed collar
and cuffs. Olivier was a good cook though and mindful of health.
He prepared all meals from scratch: steamed veggies, brown rice,
salads of various sorts, fish. He used fingers rather than a knife to
push food onto his fork and spit food a bit while eating. With meals,
we drank water as delicious as the pure cold water of Lapland. Still,
it's unusual for Frenchmen to not at least offer wine to guests. He
liked talking about himself and required no encouragement to tell
me his life story. He never asked about mine, and when I began to
tell him he seem disinterested, walking away or looking elsewhere
and interrupting with personal anecdotes, rarely asking me to carry
on after the interruption. He never suggested either dancing or
playing music together, and when I did, he didn't respond. Mermaid
behavior (not talking) worked well.

Olivier missed many opportunities to initiate physical contact.
After lunch on Day 1, we walked along a depressing river in a
scruffy field strewn with refuse and surrounded by industrial buildings. He could have taken my hand but didn't. That evening, we
watched "Throw Down Your Heart" with Bela Fleck at my suggestion. It's a heart-warming documentary about the origins of the
banjo in Africa. He could've sat beside me as I pressed myself
against the wall heater trying to keep my teeth from chattering but
didn't. The next day, we took the tram downtown. He walked
several paces ahead of me, like a Saudi prince, and never held doors
open.

The art museum has a good collection of nineteenth- and twentieth-century art that I was happy to see for the first time. Olivier
wandered ahead like a stray cat, never engaging in conversation.
Maybe he's shy or has Asperger's, I thought. Standing together before a
painting, discussing and admiring, would have offered the possibility
of a physical and intellectual, if not spiritual, connection. I know a
lot about art—a student once described me as the Einstein of art, a
funny, flattering, entirely exaggerated assessment. I eventually found
him in the lobby, as if he had driven me to a colonoscopy and was

waiting patiently for me to come to. Apparently, there is no good café in Grenoble since we hopped back on the tram and returned to his house. At one point, he mentioned how important tactility was to him, and I said it was to me too, hand on the table, unflinching when he touched it. He withdrew his within seconds, and that was our last physical contact until he dropped me off at the train station. We didn't even hug but just 'made the kiss'—the kiss-kiss on each cheek—with masks on.

On my way back to Paris, I thought about the Frenchmen I've dated. They've been either aggressive or physically distant. Only Trocadéro Man felt normal. Actually, he felt a whole lot nicer and qualitatively different than normal. Am I wasting my time trying to meet a partner? Should I just go about my activities and let fate decide? I don't feel desperate, am happy alone, and am becoming bored by this sociological experiment, even if I am happy to notice my French improving. Perhaps I should just concentrate on my inner compass and have an amazingly wonderful life on my own with my friends and future dog.

Monday 19 October

A 9 p.m. curfew went into effect on Saturday, a measure irritating to restaurant and café owners, who fear, like everyone else, *réconfinement*. For me, the main inconvenience is hurrying home from the 8 p.m. Eiffel Tower twinkle.

On Monday, I returned for my second pneumonia vaccine to the doctor recommended by Jim. I had no idea there was such a thing until recently. Since COVID-19 attacks the lungs, it seemed a prudent measure. On my first visit, I was surprised by the informality; it looked and felt like the 1960s. Most French doctors operate independently or belong to very small practices and survive without staff, office or medical. Dr. P's office occupies the ground floor of an ugly, dirty, white corner-building on a seedy street in the Eleventh Arrondissement. It consists of a shabby waiting room and three dorm-room-sized offices with windows overlooking a narrow corridor, whose windows face a dreary street. Grey metal chairs upholstered in orange plastic, many of them leaking yellow cotton-candy stuffing, line the waiting room. No TV or magazines. Each of the three doctors sharing the space has their own small room furnished with a desk, visitor's chair, refrigerator, and examination table.

When I first visited and requested a pneumonia vaccine, Dr. P wrote out a prescription that I filled at a pharmacy and then put immediately in the refrigerator because both doses must be kept chilled. I opened the box and couldn't figure out which dose came first—they were different sizes—so I brought both to my appointment. Dr. P kept the second dose until my next visit. At the end of my initial visit, Dr. P asked for my *Carte Vitale*, the national health insurance card. With it, all medical treatment and medicine is more-or-less free. I told him I didn't have one, and he apologized and seemed genuinely embarrassed, informing me what I already knew from previous adventures in French medicine: I had to pay full fare for the visit. He accepted only cash or debit cards. I pulled a €50 note from my wallet—I didn't have the exact amount—and he reached for his own wallet to give me change, €25. He then hand-wrote a receipt and noted, also by hand in his paper calendar, the date and time of my next appointment.

The French, indeed all Europeans, are perplexed by the American medical system. They consider healthcare a civil right like education and a for-profit insurance system undemocratic. Americans misunderstand European healthcare systems, which differ from country to country. In Sweden, for instance, healthcare is free after the first $200 of co-pays, and only those with private insurance choose their own doctors. Otherwise, you begin at the local clinic. If specialized care is required it refers you. In France and Germany, you choose your own primary care doctor and pay monthly fees related to income (for most people around $150 per month), never receiving additional bills for care, whether immunization or open-heart surgery. In Germany, when you begin working you choose either the national system or a private one, which is often cheaper at the outset but whose premiums rises steeply with age. And switching is difficult. Thus, if you opt for private insurance (which gives you access to luxurious rehab, private hospital rooms, and sometimes expedited care) and then lose your job in middle age and are unable to pay the higher monthly premiums, you shift to the public option. My physicians in Germany and France, whom I chose, provide personalized service far superior to that I have received to date in Purgatory.

Sometimes, European doctors don't charge at all. Like the time one of my summer program students ran out of Ibuterol inhalers for her asthma. She feared not being able to get one and how much it would cost if she could. I took her to my doctor the next day. There was no problem getting an appointment since German doctors usually have walk-in hours. The receptionist filled out one short form with her, and within fifteen minutes we saw the doctor. The doctor didn't recognize the medication and sent us to the pharmacy downstairs, instructing us to return with the name of the proper medication so she could write out a prescription for a close equivalent. We did, she did, and there was no charge for the office visit.

At the pharmacy, the inhaler cost €15, which astonished the student, who normally paid $45 per inhaler, with insurance. When she returned to the hotel, the student excitedly shared her story with the others. The tale impressed only the Americans, who exclaimed: "WOW!" "Oh my god!" "You're kidding!" while the Europeans, South African, and New Zealander looked on with puzzled expressions, unable to understand the reason for jubilation.

"If you had a German insurance card it would have been a lot less," one German student dryly commented.

Also incredible from an American perspective was the fact that the doctor trusted the inhaler belonged to the student and that she needed this medicine. When I broke my foot in Paris in 2018, I had no idea what to do after seeing the X-ray which showed a jagged bone terrifyingly displaced, its ends perhaps half an inch apart, and the French emergency room doctor blithely assuring me that it would heal. I naturally wanted it to heal in its original configuration and not like some poorly repaired puppet. My French was insufficient at that point for an argument or to request a second opinion. I called my American doctor of twenty-five years, the man responsible for all my health-related advising for most of my adult life. I wanted to send pictures of the X-ray (which they give you immediately in France) to ask his advice. I didn't expect him to accept responsibility for the decision I would make, I just urgently needed professional guidance. I knew there was a very small window during which the bones could be properly aligned.

I never spoke to the doctor, protected as he was behind a barricade of unempathetic office staff. The nurse told me that the doctor could not comment unless I came in person, an untenable position defended by the office manager. I asked if I came to the office whether the doctor would need to see an X-ray.

She responded, "How else is he going to make a decision about the best treatment?"

To which I responded, "I can send pictures of my foot immediately. I just want a recommendation of what to do."

But she held firm. No office visit, no advice. My desperate pleas and references to the Hippocratic Oath fell on deaf ears. Thus, I did nothing, and the bones grew together crookedly. When I came for my annual physical a few weeks later, I was informed by the receptionist that I was no longer a patient. I asked whose decision that was.

"The office manager's," she answered.

"But what about the doctor?" I asked.

"He doesn't make those decisions," was the curt response.

After twenty-five years. That would never happen in Europe. Or, I imagine, anywhere else on the planet. The 'socialized' medicine many Americans fear, would be the kind of competent, compassionate care their parents and grandparents remember, complete with home visits when necessary, all for virtually free.

Wednesday 21 October

It's strange walking to the 8 p.m. Eiffel Tower twinkle in the streetlight-lit night. Instead of studying architectural details, I now focus on shop windows and apartments. I adore gazing into apartments; I'm curious about how others live. Some leave the wood of their half-timbered ceilings unpainted, while others coat them in ceiling white to create visual coherence. These apartments have relatively low ceilings and generally date to the sixteenth or seventeenth century. Those with high ceilings and floriated plaster borders around them date to the eighteenth or nineteenth. Some have crystal chandeliers, built-in bookcases, and overdoor panels painted with bucolic scenes that evoke palatial elegance; others suspend paper-balloon ceiling fixtures and are outfitted from IKEA, evidencing a modern, economical aesthetic.

Usually, amber lights define the contours of the Eiffel Tower beginning at dusk and change to white twinkling ones for five minutes on the hour, like so many blinking stars affixed to the steel beams. Tonight, it switched to unlit. No twinkling. Eiffel's Tower of Three Hundred Meters became a strange, black silhouette against the darkening blue-grey sky. I looked around to see if there was a blackout but no, apartments and streetlights remained illuminated. I suddenly realized it was likely a moving, if witnessed by few, commemoration of martyred history teacher Samuel Paty, beheaded by Islamic terrorists on October 16th. Earlier in the day, a parade was held in his honor, ending with a memorial service at the Sorbonne, where Macron gave a poignant tribute.

Paty was assassinated because he held a discussion about freedom of expression in his junior high school class. The subject centered on the terrorist attack of *Charlie Hebdo* offices, an event that inaugurated a bloody year of Islamic terrorism in France. On January 7, 2015, the Kaouchi brothers, members of *al-Quaeda*, entered the office of the provocative satirical weekly just before lunchtime. They executed eleven journalists in retaliation for the newspaper's publication of caricatures of the Prophet Mohammed. Since its founding in 1969 in the wake of the student riots of 1968, *Charlie Hebdo* has published many caricatures of religious and political figures past and present.

I stood alone in the darkness for the full five minutes paying homage to the dedicated and compassionate teacher. I gazed at the respectfully darkened silhouette of Paris's most iconic symbol, reflecting on the unconsidered risks taken daily by teachers dedicated to fostering open-minded examination of societal values and individual rights in democratic societies. The sudden re-illumination of the Eiffel Tower snapped me out of my reverie. As in meditation, I lost track of time during those five minutes, which seemed much longer as my mind wandered the labyrinth of unanticipated dangers involved in educating youth. Certainly Paty, the father of two small children, could never have imagined even in his most dystopic dreams how his last day would end. I hurried to make it home before the 9 p.m. curfew, too absorbed in my thoughts to window gawk.

Thursday 22 October

It was a chilly rainy day, and I went on another meet-for-drinks date. This time with Gabriel, a semi-retired management consultant and a passionate, accordion-playing freemason. He's also a Wagner-loving opera buff who suggested meeting at the café beside Opera Bastille, a location convenient for us both. The 91 Bus from Vavin goes directly there. I was ten minutes late due to sheeting rain and rush-hour traffic. He sat at a corner table, waiting to order until I arrived. Gabriel has slightly greying black hair, is trim, kindly-looking, and wore a collared shirt and navy wool sweater. He was also my height—in other words, short. The French are generally shorter than their European neighbors, a subject that Gabriel raised.

"You know why?" he asked.

"No idea."

"Well, Napoléon drafted all tall robust Frenchmen into his army and most of them died during his disastrous Russian campaign. Frenchmen have been short ever since."

I wasn't sure I bought this argument, but I understand so little about genetics that his explanation seemed plausible. I did know that after walking all the way from France to Moscow the French army was forced to turn back in December 1812, when the terrified inhabitants of Moscow burned their city—constructed principally of wood—to the ground, leaving no shelter and no riches for Napoleonic troops to plunder. Disappointed, Napoléon and his army returned to France. The mortality rate was sufficiently high among French conscripts that by the time Napoléon's army arrived in Leipzig in October 1813 for the Battle of Nations—a bloody battle that left more than one hundred thousand dead in three days of fighting—it consisted mainly of unwilling conscripts from the Germanic and Slavic territories he had conquered.

I ordered an *apero spritz* and Gabriel did the same. French men on dates often do this, they order whatever their dates do. I thought this was a Swedish phenomenon. There, whoever orders first, whether drinks or food, is usually the one who determines what the rest of the herd will have. "Me, too," they often respond when queried by wait staff. Germans tend to order what they actually want, the way Americans do. I haven't noticed this propensity for ordering the same thing in other French social contexts; it simply seems to be an effort at establishing common ground when dating. In any event, we had a pleasant time and I felt neither repelled nor attracted. The time passed quickly, and we left in a hurry to honor the 9 p.m. curfew, he to the suburban train taking him to Fontenay-sous-Bois, a northeast suburb adjacent to Paris and the Bois de Vincennes, and I, to the 91 back to rue de la Grande-Chaumière.

Sunday 25 October

Another rainy day. I unfurled my umbrella and crossed the boulevard Montparnassse to La Coupole at 10 a.m. to meet Caroline and a group of Anglo-American expats for coffee. The ringleader was a gregarious fellow from Brooklyn. It's been a long time since I interacted with a group of American strangers, and I was struck by how differently Americans socialize. The French are much more interested in your thoughts and experiences than on personal accomplishments or where you live. Caroline, an extrovert, is starved for human contact and seeks it out and I, an apparent introvert, do not. I have plenty of friends in Paris and see them often enough. In addition, I have no burning desire to meet fellow Anglos when I'm abroad. National origin or native language are insufficient reasons for friendship. Do you love cooking, dancing, dogs, playing music, traveling, reading, and nature? That's what I would like to talk about no matter where you're from!

I didn't linger and spent the rest of the day indoors writing until it came time to meet Gabriel for a free organ concert at the church of Saint-Jacques du Haut-Pas, on the other side of le Luco. Rain pelted as I walked down the rue Auguste Comte, and I was glad I wore my Gore-Tex-lined Frye boots. Gabriel awaited in the narthex. The church interior was cold, dark, and humid, prompting thoughts of how unpleasant it must have been to attend church during the winter in the pre-umbrella, -waterproof clothing, and -central heating era.

The concert was sparsely attended, understandable since it was one of those days when the appeal of sitting snuggled on the sofa with a good book while chocolate chip cookies bake in the oven might easily trump the most delightful of concerts. Several dozen music lovers sat in chairs facing the altar, a frustrating situation because the organ and organist were behind us. I wished we were in the Marienkirche in Greifswald, which devised an ingenious solution to the directional problem: the back of the pews tip to allow the audience to face in either direction depending on whether the main attraction is occurring on the altar or in the organ loft. Back in Purgatory, I'd have to walk for weeks to attend an organ concert in a centuries-old church. In Paris, I can do that every Sunday if not more often. Gabriel and I held hands and spoke little between pieces. He has strong hands with thick fingers. The hands of a peasant. If you guessed he was from farm stock, you'd be right.

Afterward, we went for hot chocolate at nearby Café Saint-Jacques and stepped back into the 1930s. Frames containing auto-graphed photo portraits of illustrious customers packed as tightly as puzzle pieces lined the moss-green walls, and brass chandeliers resembling giant spiders with twelve upturned legs and glowing balls of light for feet provided dim lighting that Swedes refer to as *mysbelysning*, cozy lighting. In other words, sufficient for reading the expression on your companion's face but not a newspaper. The black-painted Danish modern furniture had moss green, leather-upholstered armchairs with salmon-velveteen backs, a décor that imposed such serenity that arguments would be unthinkable. The silky, barely sweetened chocolate garnished with fresh, unsweetened whipped cream, *Chantilly* (purportedly named after the château where it was invented), amplified a sense of harmony, tranquility, and warmth, a welcome sensation on a raw, wet, dark Sunday afternoon.

We talked about possible excursions from Paris. I mentioned wanting to visit Vaux-le-Vicomte ever since hearing the tragic tale of Louis XIV's finance minister, Nicolas Fouquet, who had hired the stellar triumvirate of architect Louis le Vau, painter Charles le Brun, and landscape architect André le Nôtre to design his estate southeast of Paris. At the housewarming celebration in 1661, the young Louis XIV became so jealous that he ordered d'Artagnan, one of the Three Musketeers, to arrest Fouquet, who spent the next twenty years in prison, where he died. Louis XIV then commanded the three to design Versailles, whose extravagant cost initiated the pecuniary problems of the French state that eventually led to revolution more than a century later. We decided to visit tomorrow.

Monday 28 October

Vaux-le-Vicomte was just as lovely as I'd imagined. Gabriel picked me up in his Citroën at 11 a.m., and we stopped for lunch in nearby Plessis-le-Roi at what appeared to be the only restaurant in town, a modest locale bustling with workers, a spot where everyone knows one another. Sated, we headed to Vaux-le-Vicomte. From the parking lot, we walked down an alley of plane trees and entered a forecourt with a portal guarded by over-life-size nutcrackers. The absolute symmetry of the château and gardens conveys aesthetic refinement, order, and control—of nature, the built environment, and the finances of the French state under Fouquet's stewardship. The moat surrounding the château and parterre is decorative because by the time Vaux-le-Vicomte was constructed Île de France was secure from foreign invasion.

The main façade, with its central, cupola-topped dome surmounting a triangular pediment, references the grandeur of classical Rome; rectangular wings sprout from its sides like a pair of compact appendages. Sober Doric columns constructed of stacked stone lifesavers support the cornice of the central section, where dentilation alternates with figured metopes of animals portraying either cats with extremely fluffy tails, or imaginative squirrel-feline hybrids. The dark-grey slate Mansart roof caps the pale limestone structure like an anvil, reinforcing the impression of control. Landings positioned at thoughtful intervals on the front staircase allow guests to be impressed but not breathless upon arrival. Grandeur without intimidation.

Inside, it is all Baroque brilliance. Glittering gilded-and-sculpted frames on walls and ceilings surround mythological paintings that require neck-craning to view. Some figures seem descendants of Michelangelo's Sistine Chapel sibyls. Enormous tapestries line some rooms, their original purpose to keep the interior warm in wintertime, an experience poor Fouquet never got to enjoy. The elaborately patterned parquet floors have designs in many different woods and patterns. Crystal chandeliers, now electric, originally required a team of full-time candle-men to keep their lights burning, a feature that also warmed the capacious yet reasonably proportioned rooms. The dining room was set for a party, with more than a dozen tables bedecked with silk cloths, a forest of crystal glassware, stacks of plates and bowls, and wings of silverware at each place. Some children and parents rented costumes at the entrance to experience the château in appropriate period attire.

We explored Le Nôtre's gardens, magnificent even in flowerless late October. The best view is undoubtedly via drone, but elevated spots at the far end of the gardens provide satisfying observation points. We wandered until dark instead of moving closer to the château for the *son-et-lumière* show as we should have. We watched it alone from a parterre at the end of the garden. Twinkling lights in frequently changing colors illuminated the château's main contours, and a projection of Vaux-le-Vicomte's history accompanied by narration projected onto the garden façade. Gabriel and I held hands for much of the afternoon and leaned on the balustrade side-by-side to watch the show. I kept thinking: *if he is ever planning to kiss me now would be a good time.*

Finally, he did. Not particularly affectionately or tenderly, more a kind of functional kissing. And, once his tongue penetrated my mouth, he didn't seem eager to remove it. It rested there like a piece of warm liver, reminding me of a horse secure in its stall for the night. To cut that short, I suggested going closer to the château, so we could see the performance we had stayed to watch. We hurried in complete darkness, me hoping that I wouldn't stumble over an unseen obstacle. We got close just as it ended. Because Gabriel seemed unconcerned about arriving home past curfew, we sat on a bench by the château and made out for a bit. Pretty much the same as at the balustrade except longer. He was earnest and urgent, seemingly delighted by this new closeness. We didn't talk much on the way home. While I like tranquility, it seemed strange to have nothing to say at this inaugural stage of a potential relationship. He did say a funny thing on the way back to Paris. What we did, even in French, is called 'French kissing', and he, having never kissed an American before, had wondered what 'American kissing' was like. Now he knows.

Wednesday 28 October

Today, Gabriel invited me to lunch at Bouillon Chartier on the rue du Faubourg Montmartre. When Faubourg is added to a street name—as it is to the rue Montmartre north of the boulevard Haussmann, one of the Grands Boulevards demarcating the former location of a protective and long-since dismantled city wall and the transition from the Second Arrondissement to the Ninth—it indicates the part of the street that once lay outside Paris city limits. Chartier initially lay along the edge of the megalomaniacal urban renewal project of Napoléon III and Baron Haussmann and a stone's throw from two of Paris's major department stores: Au Printemps, founded in 1865, and Galeries Lafayette, founded in 1893, around the same time as Chartier. I often walk visitors through it just to experience the cavernous space packed with long tables, where one will likely be seated beside strangers. There's a second—more florid—Art Nouveau branch of Chartier near me on the boulevard Montparnasse. Both offer the same menus of home-cooking favorites. The food reminds me of the soggy, bland, if hearty, offerings at Amish restaurants in Pennsylvania.

Chartier was one of a handful of cheap restaurants established for workers when Haussmann's urban renewal project destroyed most worker housing in central Paris and replaced it with the pale, stately, architecturally embellished buildings with decorative black-iron window grates that today epitomize Paris. Workers who had lived previously near their workplaces found themselves exiled to ghettos outside city limits; they had to walk or take horse-drawn busses from their drafty tar-paper shacks to jobs in the city center, a trip that could take an hour or more in the days when the work week consisted of six ten-hour-long days.

Gabriel's choice surprised me, but I think he chose Chartier because he loves history and isn't fussy about food. I'm more epicurean. All I thought was, *tough, dry meat and overcooked vegetables*, and I wasn't disappointed. Chartier has not changed since I last ate there in the early 1980s. Waiters charm tourists as they write orders on the white butcher paper protecting the red-checkered tablecloths and rapidly tally the bill when it's time to pay. While the adding skills of Chartier waiters might impress American tourists in an era when their countrymen require mechanical assistance to perform that task, even those good at mental math are awed by the abilities of wait staff at Munich beer halls. There, nothing is written. When it's time to pay, the waiter asks what you ate and drank and—knowing menu prices by heart—performs correct mental math. German beer halls are one of Europe's many public venues based on the honor system.

Gabriel forgot his wallet, so I paid. Thankfully, we hadn't dined at Arpège, which I am dying to try but will not pay for myself during the Year of No Income. From there, we went to the Museum of Freemasonry on the rue Cadet. I became interested in freemasonry because I discovered that many pivotal figures in my Denmark project were freemasons, and I'm intent on discovering what aspects of freemasonry may have inspired the land and social reforms they initiated. This was my chance to visit with a freemason who might be able to answer my questions.

I got in free with my 'magic museum card' but had to pay Gabriel's entrance. The museum is dark with spot-lit cases displaying decorated ceramicware and embroidered aprons of varying ranks. Freemasonry is a rigidly hierarchical organization of lodges or, as I like to think of them, covens, with scout-troop-sized memberships. Many objects on display date from the eighteenth century, when Freemasonry formally organized in London. Symbols abound: smiling suns emanating vibrating rays; creepy, single, open blue eyes (the 'all-seeing eye' in Freemason lore); pentagrams; ladders and stairs; scales; carpenter's squares; and compasses. There's even a porcelain *Statue of Liberty*, or *Liberty Enlightening the World*, as it's formally known. The foundational values of Freemasonry are moral self-improvement and contributing to the improvement of society along egalitarian lines, principles for which Frédéric Auguste Bartholdi's *Liberty* was a fitting symbol, especially considering the number of Freemasons among America's Founding Fathers.

Gabriel invited me to spend a few days in Fontenay-sous-Bois, and I agreed to come on November 4th. He has devised a legitimate-sounding excuse to get around the *confinement* distance restriction: translation work for his business. He seems a kind and stable fellow with whom I perhaps could develop a happy relationship. Or should there be chemistry at the outset? We enjoy similar activities: tennis, chess, and playing the piano. Even if a fling reassures me that I have moved past Trocadéro Man it would be time well spent. I feel as though I might not totally escape his hold if I don't sleep with someone else. I told Hanna about my blasé feeling toward Gabriel, and she replied, "Good Mamma, you're not controlled by oxytocin. Now you can find out if he's a man who makes you happy." Hanna, the Self-Help Songwriter, is always right.

Tonight, President Macron appeared on TV. He doesn't do this often. In fact, his televised appearances are rare. In recent months when there's been a missive from on high, Prime Minister Jean

Castex announces it. This was an especially important proclama-
tion, however. COVID-19 numbers have risen steeply for weeks,
overwhelming intensive care units throughout the country. I think I
predicted this in September. There are two new virus strains—a
British and a South African one—that are more contagious, require
longer hospitalization, and have higher mortality rates. For these
reasons, France will return to *confinement* beginning October 30.
Everything will close except essential services: food and wine shops,
pharmacies and newsstands. And this time, thankfully, parks will
remain open. The government has realized that contamination
occurs almost exclusively indoors and that Parisians, many of whom
live in tiny apartments—sometimes converted closets—need fresh
air, space, and exercise.

After Macron's broadcast, I spoke to Hanna, who will cancel her
visit scheduled for next week; there's little to do in Paris now except
stay cooped up in my small apartment at a dark and rainy time of
year. We're heartbroken. It's the longest we've gone without seeing
each other. The last time was Christmas 2019. We are grateful for
the Internet, however. We chat while she bikes, and she introduces
me to the ducks she feeds near her Stockholm apartment. It's a less
frustrating situation than when I was in Europe for months at a time
during my twenties, and the only means of contact with my parents
was letters and the occasional extremely expensive phone call made
from a post office. Still, Hanna and I plan to spend Christmas
together, hopefully in Potsdam with our German family, although
conditions shift with sufficient regularity that we are hoping more
than planning.

Chapter 10
November: Cocooning in Réconfinement

Tuesday 3 November

Réconfinement went into effect yesterday, spurring another mass exodus from Paris over the weekend. A procession of young people dragging suitcases headed up the rues d'Assas and de Rennes and the boulevards Raspail and Montparnasse toward Gare Montparnasse; similar scenes have likely unfolded around every other train station in Paris. Double-parked cars again clogged the streets of the Sixth and Seventh Arrondissements as residents loaded children, dogs, suitcases, and toys for another prolonged stay in the countryside, or perhaps just to foist the kids on *Grandmère* and *Grandpère* for a few weeks of much-needed relief. Shuttered windows in the upscale neighborhoods of Paris indicate their inhabitants have fled. News sources estimate that five hundred thousand inhabitants, twenty-five percent of the total population, have left.

My *voisinage* is again depopulated; even the trash bins are empty. Communal trash and recycling bins are usually located in building courtyards, often in small sheds that previously functioned as outhouses. As late as the 1980s, some Paris apartments still lacked indoor plumbing. Repurposed outhouses are one of those banal elements of the urban landscape whose original function one rarely considers, like the small fountains of running water also found in most courtyards, evidence of the government's centuries-old conviction regardless of regime—monarchical, Napoleonic, republican—that free potable water is a civil right, as do the disappointed inhabitants of Flint, Michigan.

Today is Election Day in the U.S. and several of its aspects puzzle Europeans. For instance, why isn't it held on a Sunday as in France and Germany, making it easier for citizens to vote? Why, if it must be on a Tuesday, isn't a national holiday declared? Why can't voting occur via a secure internet site (as in Sweden) and why are there insufficient polling sites to obviate inhumanely long lines that discourage, if not preclude, voting by the old and infirm? In some countries, it's illegal for citizens *not* to vote. Several American friends express cautious optimism about the likelihood of a Biden victory that they hope will realign the U.S. along a course of civility, egalitarianism, and sustainability. The U.S. COVID-19 numbers are also rising, nearing 100,000 new cases per day. A hospital ship has docked in the Hudson River, and hospital parking lots are filled with refrigerated morgue trucks.

Monday 9 November

Pragmatic French citizens have devised workarounds that allow them more than the government-sanctioned degree of freedom during this second *confinement*, which has no endpoint in sight. An ethical and mostly honest person, I obeyed all rules of the first *confinement*. However, once mask wearing was mandated indoors and out, I strictly abided by the indoor rule but only wore one outdoors when traversing congested areas or passing others. In other words, I used common sense, which seems uncommon to those who still haven't fathomed the hygienic recommendations repeated incessantly on newscasts and on advertising surfaces throughout Paris. Incredibly, in this society that lacks a large cadre of militant anti-maskers, one still sees individuals who find that employing their mask as a chin support or mouth-only covering suffices.

Most people have realized that exceeding the one-kilometer limit requires only a simple change of address on one's *attestation*. I suppose you're in trouble if the police also ask for identification that reveals your actual place of residence, but I have yet to see police control pedestrians. If you want to stay out later than permitted, all you need is a 70+ person at the place you are headed to text you a 'I've fallen and can't get up' plea. My friend Gail has suggested coming for dinner soon, and we plan to give that strategy a whirl.

In the meantime, Gabriel and I used it to enable my visit to him. Last Wednesday morning, I walked down a deserted rue de Rennes in the blinding morning sunshine to the boulevard Saint-Germain and stationed myself in front of Café Deux Magots, our agreed rendezvous point. Gabriel selected this spot because it lay on his usual route from home to business address; you couldn't really call it an office because he rarely goes there. We both filled out *attestations* alleging that I was performing translation work that required an in-person meeting. This first violation of the one-kilometer rule made me apprehensive; I felt my heart beating faster. I arrived first and he, several minutes later. We tossed my backpack into the trunk and proceeded east on the boulevard Saint-Germain, crossing pont National and continuing northeast around the Bois de Vincennes to the covered food market in Fontenay.

After parking, we made new *attestations*, now conveniently down-loadable with the standard information—name, birthdate, home address—pre-filled in. All we needed to do was indicate the purpose of our mission and the time and date. Gabriel, apparently, had never before filled one out. Glancing over his shoulder, I noticed that his birth year, 1950, differed from that noted on the dating site, 1955. Is this a red flag? When questioned, he explained his concern that younger women such as I would not be interested in a man his age. I responded that women whose primary criteria was age should not interest him anyway. And it works in the other direction, too. I often find men my age unadventurous and unenergetic but would never lie to attract a younger one. Gabriel shrugged his shoulders asserting that women he had met on the site had also lied about their age. Two wrongs don't make a right, as my father used to say. It violates 'be impeccable with your word', the first of Don Miguel

Ruiz's Four Agreements. While Gabriel considered this insignificant, for me it represented an ethical standard to which I could not subscribe.

"Shall I take you home?" he inquired? "Is this a deal breaker for you?" I softened as he looked at me hopefully with his brown Bassett-Hound eyes.

Maybe I should have said 'yes', but I considered the situation from his viewpoint: a minor offence intended to optimize possibilities. How can you tell when an action is a warning and when it's a triviality? I would like to have clear signals. Perhaps my microexpression interpreting skills need honing. Feeling optimistic, I overlooked this deception; it seemed innocent enough although past experiences had been triggered, and my early warning system switched on. We bought salmon and vegetables for lunch and bananas and yogurt for my breakfast. Like most Frenchmen, Gabriel's morning meal consists of bread and a bowl of warm milk diluted with coffee. He seemed stymied by my gluten intolerance and non-carnivorous tendency.

After shopping, we parked in front of Gabriel's stately, nineteenth-century building set back from the street. Located half a block from both the Bois de Vincennes and the suburban train, it's in a very convenient location for nature lovers who travel frequently into Paris but prefer living in the suburbs—a situation I can't envision. I grew up in the suburbs, and once I turned thirteen, they represented for me the worst of two worlds: city and countryside. Leafy without really being nature and inhabited without the culture and commerce of cities. A world, for me, of vastly constrained possibilities. As a teenager, I often rode my bike into downtown Buffalo to explore book and record stores, shop at the army-navy store, and visit museums and Forest Lawn. It was a poor excuse for the urban activities I envisioned enjoying in New York, where I knew I would one day live. Having read *The New Yorker* since birth (like everyone else, I began with ads and cartoons), I was well-oriented. When—long before the backpack era—I mail-ordered my first Danish Book Bag from Chocolate Soup, a boutique on Madison Avenue that advertised regularly in *The New Yorker*, I consulted a map, so I knew its location. In my imagination, I lived on the Upper East Side, which was where, serendipitously, my college boyfriend grew up. With my bookbag slung over my shoulder I was the envy of my school mates, who cradled textbooks in their arms as they walked to and from school, trying to keep them from sliding off into snowbanks, rain puddles, or crosswalks.

Gabriel carried the groceries but didn't offer to carry my backpack. A tall black iron fence with bars spaced like those of a jail cell protects the building. He pressed the gate's five-digit code and pushed it open. We entered a verdant garden that must be glorious in spring and summer and passed residents' mailboxes to a code-enabled glass door. I saw a staircase but no elevator.

"What floor do you live on?" I inquired.

"The last one," he replied.

And he did not mean the (non-existent) penthouse but the sixth floor. I may have rolled my eyes. I recalled my broken foot of 2018 and wondered what Gabriel would do if that or worse happened to him. He went first up the broad creaky staircase. There are two apartments on each floor. He was huffing and puffing by the time he reached the third landing. My shoulder muscles tightened in such a way that I knew an application of Voltaren would later be necessary to relax them and prevent a headache.

At the half-landing between floors five and six is a toilet. I prayed it was not the one I would use. At the top are three doors: to a studio apartment owned by another tenant, to a hallway where each of the other ten apartments had their *chambres de bonne* (maid's rooms, now mostly storage), and to Gabriel's apartment. As I entered his apartment, I stepped onto a Bokhara rug covering a hole in the floor. His foyer has five doors: one leading to the bathroom (thankfully), a second to an office, a third to the living room, the fourth to a tiny music room/library, and the last to the kitchen. His bedroom is off the kitchen and contains a very crowded wardrobe and a double bed with only enough space for a night table on one side. The window was open, the room freezing.

"Look," he proclaimed proudly, "I have a view of the Eiffel Tower!"

And sure enough, peeking up from the horizon between two leafless trees in the neighboring yard was a thumbnail-sized Eiffel Tower. I couldn't help comparing the view unfavorably to the vista from Trocadéro Man's penthouse. Still, it was wonderful to see my beloved from home.

"Wow, that's splendid!" (a word I use a lot in French), I exclaimed.

I steamed the salmon and put it atop the salad I customarily eat for lunch. Although Gabriel munched politely, he clearly was not a fan of meal-sized salads. Afterward, we played chess. Again, Trocadéro Man surfaced in my consciousness. Gabriel won, although not easily, and I am a terrible and inexperienced chess player. It took ninety minutes for him to win, and he didn't have a lot of pieces left when he did. In contrast, Trocadéro Man was such a skilled player that after three or four moves I felt paralyzed and hopeless, at which point he'd offer to switch positions. I always happily assented. But after another few moves, he again had the clear advantage.

"Do you want to switch again?" he'd politely ask. It never felt patronizing.

"Yes," I'd admit again. We'd turn the board 180 degrees. Several moves later, I was again in desperate straits.

"Again?" he would ask quietly.

"No," I'd reply like an antelope taken down by a lion and accepting its fate as the rest of the salivating pride closes in. I usually asked why he moved where he did and what eventualities the move positioned him well for. I learned a lot but found my ineptitude frustrating. There was simply no way I would ever beat Trocadéro Man at chess unless he were on his deathbed in a non-responsive state.

Dinner that and every subsequent evening with Gabriel consisted of a boxed soup. He never bought them in advance, so each day entailed a trip to Naturalia, a new experience for a man indifferent to organic eating. One day, we biked along the Marne River. We rode more than the permitted ten kilometers, but because he has never been controlled I didn't worry. The river snaked through suburbs of comfortable bourgeois homes built circa 1900.

We rode back via Joinville, the now seldom-used Hollywood of France, where soundstages still stand.

I slept by the wall and had to balance my water bottle on the bedframe's upper corner. I drink regularly at night, and the dryness in his apartment trapped me in a frustrating cycle of drinking, coughing, and getting up to pee. This entailed slithering out of the bed at the foot end, traversing barefoot the kitchen with its freezing tile floor, entering the foyer, then the bathroom, by which time I was wide awake. I didn't sleep well, and his apartment felt cold. As did Trocadéro Man's, for that matter. Although I grew up in Buffalo, where we wore thick socks and sweaters all winter long, in my adult life I have kept the indoor temperature warm, around seventy degrees. Swedes, even in Lapland and despite daytime temperatures of minus twenty or less Fahrenheit, keep their homes warm enough that they run around in t-shirts.

Gabriel let me crank up the temperature a bit in the rooms I occupied. At night, he prefers warm air and I, the healthier opposite; I can sleep outdoors in winter if the comforter is warm enough. We spent the rest of our time playing music, reading, or working. I thought of Rapunzel in her tower prison. For me, it's too much trouble to schlep up and down five flights of stairs every time I want to go outdoors. If only he had a terrace or balcony. I imagined what fun it would be if he had a slide from his apartment into the back garden or at least a large basket one could step into and lower oneself down in, as the monks used to do at the monasteries in Meteora, Greece. Nonetheless, I stayed five nights. We took several walks in the Bois de Vincennes, and he showed me the lake with rowboats, the riding stable, and the site of an Asian exhibition that occurred in the 1930s.

Wednesday 11 November

Yesterday was a warm, grey, autumn day, and I met Caroline in le Luco for lunch. *She* likes my salads. We had a huge choice of where to sit despite park workers having collected most of the green metal chairs for their wintering. For our dinner rendezvouses during the summer, we were lucky if we found two chairs together near the basin. Today, the atmosphere was a bit melancholy: couples lunching, individuals reading, chatting on the phone, or napping. No more children pushing their little wooden sailboats around the basin, and the toy boat rental kiosk was closed. Flowers in the planters along the balustrade have changed from invigorating bright pink petunias to pots of calming orange and yellow mums. We discussed where to go and what to do, short and long term. Caroline is feeling a bit out of sorts after ending a relationship in the U.S. and trying to figure out whether to stay in France, in Paris, or to find somewhere she would have more freedom and that was in closer proximity to 'real' nature. It's a difficult time to make decisions with the pandemic making life unpredictable.

I talked to Hanna this morning, and we discussed Christmas possibilities, deciding that if we can't spend it with our German family perhaps she should spend it with Dani's family in Italy. There's nowhere we would rather be than at Walt's in Cleveland, where we and her dad normally celebrate with a chosen 'Christmas family' of two dozen mostly musicians and their families. It's a joyous occasion filled with music and dance—Croatian, Greek, Hungarian, jazz, Norwegian, Polish, Serbian, Ukrainian—until dawn, with a steady stream of guests coming and going all night long: drinking, dancing, eating cookies, playing music, catching up.

Today is Veterans' Day in the U.S. and Armistice Day in France. Also the day Jim and I had tickets to see Anna Netrebko's recital at the Philharmonie. I never received notification of its cancellation, so that is something to investigate tomorrow. We were pleased that we could change our tickets from the 8:30 p.m. to the 2:30 p.m. performance the day after the curfew was announced; we never imagined *réconfinement*. The only healthy attitude now is a Zen-like 'whatever-happens-was-meant-to-be' approach.

The commemoration in Paris began with the traditional ceremony at the eternal flame that marks the Tomb of the Unknown Soldier, located beneath the Arc de Triomphe. At 6 p.m., a solemn ceremony for French politician and Holocaust survivor Simone Veil began; she died last year and today was interred at the Panthéon.

These events formed ceremonial bookends to a day and in a city whose effervescence is dampened by *'le deuxième confinement'*. A long blue carpet led to the entrance of the Panthéon, and the plaza before it was transformed into a forest of blue lights. Portico columns were illuminated red, white, and blue. On the façade, images relating to World War One—which ended on this day in 1918—were projected.

Macron delivered an homage to Veil's patriotism after which a choir sang the first verse of *The Marseillaise*. Veil is the fifth woman to be buried in the Panthéon. I would have walked the ten minutes to see the procession along avenue Sufflot had not news reporters announced that—aware of circumventing measures—police have increased control of *attestations*, and I'm not sure if my going there would be considered 'taking air', one of the new legal reasons for leaving home. The Panthéon is slightly less than one kilometer from me as the crow flies, but not by foot, so it may have been OK, but it was also cold, dark, and wet. In addition, one could watch it on TV, including the ceremony inside, an event limited to the invited. I decided to watch the festivities from the comfort of home.

I spoke with Gabriel twice today. We seem to be developing a comfortable routine of contacting each other. New relationships are weird when you're in your sixties. He cherishes memories of his year of military service in Nicaragua as a young man and seems excited about the prospect of accompanying me to Costa Rica in January if it's possible to travel there. I'm yearning to escape a sunless sky and bone-chilling cold. In preparation, Gabriel's taking his camera to the repair shop tomorrow and will buy a guidebook because he gets bored staying in the same location for long. Me? I could stay alone at that little paradise of Playa Lagartillo for months. I long to spend early mornings cradled in the warm sand watching pelicans frolic and waves lap the shore, afternoons in a hammock reading, and ending the day with a visit to the howler monkeys, followed by sunset on the beach. But I am delighted that he is on board; it would be nice to share the experience (and, at this point, the expense).

I finally finished evaluating a half-dozen articles on Serbian Symbolist art and poetry and returned them to the publisher. I had

to restrain my obsessive urge to fix them all and hope the comments
I made will help the authors improve their final drafts. Twenty-five
hours of *pro bono* work seems sufficient. Despite my semi-impover-
ished circumstances, I feel reluctant to ask for money because Serbia
is a poor country and my curator friend, through whom the request
came, was generous with his time during my September 2019 visit
to Novi Sad. It was one stop on a wonderful folk-music-filled
odyssey visiting friends in Hungary and Serbia with musician-friend
Walt.

Thursday 26 November. Thanksgiving Day

Thanksgiving always evokes memories. I remember the suffocat-
ingly warm, turkey-fat-infused air at my grandparents' house, men
in the family room watching college football, and my mother and
grandmother in the kitchen preparing dinner while my mother's
willowy vodka-soaked sister-in-law leaned in the doorway chatting. I
usually stayed outdoors, walking along the creek in the backyard
talking to the mallards until it was time for dinner. Grandmother
Irene named some of them, and I eventually could identify several
by their appearances and behavior. Mallard ducks have
personalities.

After dinner, Granddaddy retrieved the giant jar of pocket
change he had accumulated during the previous year. We four
cousins sat on the living room floor dividing it as the women cleaned
up after dinner and the men returned to football. I, the eldest, took
charge. Granddaddy poured the coins—which made a tinkling
sound like waves receding on a stony beach—into a mountain the
middle of our little circle. We then sorted: silver dollars, half dollars,
quarters, dimes, nickels, pennies. We distributed our fortune starting
with silver dollars and working our way down to pennies. One for
you, one for you, one for you, one for me. It took more than an
hour, and I'm sure our parents were happy to see us absorbed in a
collective task. Many coins were so shiny that I suspect Granddaddy
supplemented the gift with rolls of coins purchased at the bank. He

may have pre-counted the cache as well because it always came out evenly.

Grandmother was expert at all textile handicrafts and contributed the pouches for carrying our loot. I still have several of them. Each year, she created a new design in four different color schemes. One year, they were round and crocheted in cotton string with a contrasting lining and zipper closure. That one was handy for stashing joints, and I kept it in the secret pocket sewed into the lining of Grandmother's hand-me-down black curly-lamb jacket that I wore in high school. Another year, they were made from doubled rectangular layers of felt, each in contrasting colors. These had an envelope-flap closure cut with pinking shears and fastened with a loop and button. Our monograms were embroidered in the lower right corner in gold thread. Each year, our grandparents announced at the beginning of the process that the money was intended to provide us with funds to purchase Christmas gifts for family members; I think I was the only one who did.

In the snowy winter darkness, my mother drove me to the Williamsville Water Mill on one of the evenings it was open late. Located in a nearby town, it had been owned by the same family since the early-nineteenth century. It ground wheat and corn and produced cider in the fall. It also had the gift shop where I purchased my Christmas gifts, mostly small objects in pewter or porcelain. In advance, I added up the total of my Thanksgiving revenue (usually between $12 and $15), and upon arrival, I deposited my heavy, jangling pouch at the cash register. I kept a running mental total as I chose suitable gifts. The proprietors were kindly and undoubtedly amused; they assembled my gifts at the register as I shopped.

Once the items had been rung up, I poured my coins into a mound on the countertop, and a patient mill family member counted out the money. This was apparently as memorable an event for them as for me. I visited the mill only sporadically after I left home at seventeen, but when I was in my thirties, I stopped by to purchase their superlative corn meal. The gregarious balding man at the counter, whom I did not recognize, asked me if I were the little girl who used to do her Christmas shopping there, carrying her money in a homemade coin pouch. I was so touched by his remembering that tears welled up immediately and streamed down my surprised face. The family has since sold the mill and its property. Now, I think it's a café.

Since my mother's death in 2008, I began spending Thanksgiving with my aunt, uncle, and cousins in Vermont in the years I was in the U.S. and before Aunt Cleo died. I loved joining this family—my family—and participating in its Thanksgiving Day rituals: the Macy's parade, dinner at 1 p.m., *Jeopardy* followed by *Miracle on 34th Street*, and the next day making the round of downtown stores, which give twenty percent discounts to shoppers wearing flannel shirts. This year, Thanksgiving was just another day, although I did send out e-cards to those I thought might appreciate them. Hanna is now in the U.S. spending the holiday with her dad, who undoubtedly made his mother's cornbread stuffing.

Today, Paris was sunny, with a bracing chill in the air. After lunch, I bundled up and headed over to le Luco, where I wrote for the afternoon. It was hard finding a chair with most of them now stacked in a corral near the *pétanque* courts. But two young women on the west terrace using four chairs departed just as I arrived. When my fingers turned blue, I returned home.

I called assorted ex-pat friends around Europe and spoke to Gabriel in Champagne, where he was rewiring his childhood home. When I called, he was entertaining—I assume his farmer brother and others—and said he would call me at 11 p.m., which he did. His guests interrupted constantly, and he conducted a simultaneous conversation with them, which I found rude and annoying. They had apparently drunk too much champagne. Or just enough. I kept the conversation short, taken aback by comportment I considered discourteous. We had discussed his coming to stay with me when he returns on Saturday, but because he delayed his trip there due to a spike in COVID-19 cases, I mandated a week-long quarantine and a negative test before we get together. Getting sick is too high a price for premature togetherness.

Sunday 29 November

Today is the first Sunday of Advent. Yesterday, the government extended the restrictions for venturing outdoors for recreational purposes from one to three hours and from one to twenty kilometers. Parisians celebrated. More than one hundred thousand largely unmasked people, including many 'yellow vests', demonstrated on the Right Bank at place de la Republique and place de la Bastille. They followed their usual protocol of materialist terrorism: cars set afire, cash machines vandalized, shop windows smashed, merchandise stolen. Demonstrators were reacting to two events: police violence caught on video and a pending law forbidding civilians from filming police. The galvanizing event was the release of recent footage that recorded four police beating a man of African descent outside a recording studio. The four offending police were arrested immediately, their behavior denounced by President Macron as "embarrassing." At no point did police officials attempt to justify the violent response.

Stores reopened yesterday. I went to Picard, the frozen food chain, on the rue Edward Quinet near the Gare Montparnasse, and saw lots of people out shopping. I should assemble a Christmas package for Hanna because we won't be together. Spiking COVID-19 cases has led to travel to restrictions, with the result that Germany is now impossible; she has decided to stay in the U.S. until January. Mail in Europe is now almost as slow as in the U.S.: Hanna sent me a package with items I might want in Costa Rica that took three weeks instead of the usual five days to travel between Stockholm and Paris. That's still significantly better than the U.S., however: I mailed two checks to the U.S. in June that still haven't arrived and sent replacements in October that haven't arrived yet, either.

Caroline called to report that Palo Alto friends own a spacious home in the Old Town of Antibes and will rent it to her for a fraction of the usual monthly cost. She wondered if I were interested in sharing. ABSOLUTELY!! Costa Rica, my first choice, seems ill-advised if even possible at this point. Gabriel and I consulted

COVID-19 statistics there, and they spike whenever tourists are let in. Healthcare there is supposedly good, but I have no desire to find out firsthand. Gabriel likes the idea of Antibes as well and offered to drive me down and leave his car because he is unable to stay for the entire six weeks. Perfect! Although I've never visited Antibes, I found nearby Nice delightful on earlier visits. There, the charming, green-shuttered pink buildings of the Old Town lie a short walk from both the beach and the bus that takes you west to Marseilles, east to Italy, and north to picturesque mountain villages. I can already smell the lavender.

Hanna called. She tested positive for COVID-19. She traveled from Stockholm to Purgatory on November 20th with extreme caution; she has barely left her apartment since April, when she returned from Vietnam. She wore goggles, an N-95 mask, and a visor. She neither ate nor went to the bathroom. She took three flights: one within Europe, one transatlantic, one to Purgatory. She took a test on the 23rd and received a negative result on Thanksgiving, the 26th, and thus felt safe celebrating with her dad on Friday. Just to be sure, she took a second test on the 25th that today was reported as positive. Now, her dad will get tested on Tuesday and the friend she hung out with yesterday is isolating. I have faith in her robust health and optimistic attitude but also realize that this virus has had a devastating impact even on those who seem invincible.

Caroline and I took advantage of our greater freedom today. I walked over to her apartment on the rue Mouffetard, and from there we strolled past the Mosque, down to the quay, and east to Bercy. We crossed pont Bercy to the Right Bank and wandered through Parc de Bercy, very urban, with small precincts landscaped in creative ways. We explored Bercy Village, an assemblage of former wine storage warehouses, now an outdoor shopping mall. We talked about dating, complexity theory (her specialty), upcoming plans/wishes, and I revealed part of my list of things that make me cry when I think about them. She asked about the plot of Paul Gallico's magnificent story *The Snow Goose*, which as I related it demonstrated the truth of my assertion.

We stopped at a *patisserie* that offered gluten-free treats: a coconut macaroon called a stone (*un pierre*) even though it was moist and chewy. We were not permitted to 'dine in' because of current regulations, so we took our coffees and sweets to a bench across the street. Thus fortified, we continued to the Bois de Vincennes, which, since it was Sunday, was packed with dog- and children-walkers, *pétanque* players, and people feeding ducks. We wandered the Bois's circuitous paths, slippery with damp leaves, until dark and took the *métro* home. It was my first time underground in more than a month, and I was relieved to see people correctly masked (noses covered) and distanced, even if many of the 'don't sit here' stickers posted on alternate seats in April have disappeared.

On my way home from the *métro*, I first heard, then spied, a party raging on the boulevard Raspail. Three tall windows indicating a spacious *salon* were open. Smokers crowded by them, leaning against the elegant, waist-height, Haussmannian window guards. Further in, heads bobbed up and down to ear-splitting house music, signs of absent parents. This is the kind of situation that becomes a 'spreader' event. I wondered where the police were. Do Parisians not call them in such cases as they would in Germany, Sweden, or the U.S.? The government can make regulations and schools can enforce them, but wild parties such as this pose the real danger. The fact that there's a curfew—widely respected but rarely enforced—offers no obstacle to scofflaws. I've seen similar events unfolding in the spacious apartments of the privileged youth of the Seventh Arrondissement during my treks to the Eiffel Tower.

Lately, I've spent a lot of time thinking about what conditions I require for happiness and have concluded that most are within my control. The one that's not, at least in the same way (and is perhaps dispensible), is a partner. I don't think about that much anymore, though because I'm happy and not lonely. Although would I be were Gabriel not in the picture? I like to think yes, that I've achieved psycho-emotional equilibrium. I'm not even sure if I want to reexperience a grand romantic passion. They end in either death or grief, and the latter is harder to recover from—like everything else—the older you get. Perhaps for the spiritually enlightened, they end in gratitude and acceptance. Now that's a goal worth striving for!

Clearly, my environment plays a crucial role in determining my happiness. I must be somewhere beautiful, and water must be nearby—a lake or river for rowing or waves lapping the shore. I'm as fascinated by the movement of water as I am by clouds, perhaps because of time spent during my childhood along shores of Lake Erie, the Niagara River, and the coast of Maine. The weather must be mostly sunny. It can be cold, like Lapland or Buffalo, or warm, although ideally not hot and humid. I require seasonal changes in vegetation but not necessarily dramatic temperature variations.

I don't want to live amid poisonous plants, insects, or animals that would interfere with my enjoyment of nature, and that includes cicadas. Forests must be nearby, preferably reachable by foot or bike, and there must be excellent local organic food available. The views from my windows must be lovely and my apartment or house light-filled with high ceilings. An airport should be within ninety minutes and a train station even closer. If I live in an apartment, I require an elevator if above the second floor. And I would like to hear church bells ring the hours. Perhaps I should be retirement-location- rather than partner-hunting.

And of course, it must be affordable. I'm looking forward to having an income when I teach in the spring semester, so I can return to buying items such as glucosamine-chondroitin, which for months has felt like an unwarranted luxury. The privileged Always Affluent have little idea of how to survive in a financially limited world. When I, as sole breadwinner of my three-person family, complained to a colleague (married to an ad agency partner) at my first job about the challenge of working eighty-hour weeks while keeping the house clean, the lawn mown, and the laundry done, she commented:

"Just give up one dinner out a week, and you'll have enough for a cleaning lady."

When I told her we never dined out, she stared in disbelief.

She responded dismissively: "Well then I don't know."

Another time, I was the weekend guest of the president of a German manufacturing company with hundreds of factories in dozens of countries. He razed a castle on a hilltop because it was too small and built in its place a luxurious rambling refuge as his principle, but by no means exclusive, residence. After rubbing the cap of his Havana in the small pool of vintage champagne remaining in his glass after dessert one evening, he asked what my salary was.

"How can you survive on that?" he wondered, believing, errantly, that my lifestyle corresponded reasonably closely to his. "That's less than I pay my secretary!"

I haven't met many happy super rich people. I mean genuinely, deeply contented. Like poor people, they're often prisoners of their demographic. There are many places they will not go—public transportation, economy class, distant free lots to avoid parking fees— and things they will not do—mow their lawn, bring food on excursions, borrow rather than buy books, shop in discount stores, attend events with live folk music. And they have pressing worries and suspicions: people befriending them who plan to take advantage of their wealth and connections; managing their portfolios, properties, and staffs; curating the success and happiness of their children; attending or foregoing events where their presence is expected. Sadly, many don't enjoy the freedom their economic privilege bestows even though they could.

Chapter 11
December: An Unusual Holiday Season

Wednesday 2 December

Time seems to move increasingly quickly. What happened to November? On Monday, I went to Laetitia's in the Seventh Arrondissement for lunch. She made a delicious gluten-free eggplant parmigiana. Because I am currently homeless from mid-December until I arrive in Antibes in early January, I planned to inquire about staying for a few weeks in one of the three bedrooms in her rambling apartment with a balcony and a lovely view of Les Invalides but changed my mind. Her apartment was arctic! I donned my lightweight down puffer jacket over my two cashmere sweaters and wrapped a cashmere pashmina around my neck but still yearned for gloves and earmuffs. When I excused myself to go to the bathroom, contact of my bare skin with the icy cold toilet seat startled me. The thought of removing clothing to take a shower was abhorrent. There is no way I could survive a month in such a cold apartment. I envisioned sitting fully dressed in bed working in a ski hat and fingerless gloves. Still, we had a lovely time discussing books, movies, travel, and the turbulent state of the U.S. On the way home, I'd hoped to find Christmas presents for Hanna and Dani but felt uninspired. I suspect it's because I feel overwhelmingly frugal.

Yesterday was supposed to be sunny but wasn't—the grey monotony of Paris winter absent its usual indoor distractions is becoming oppressive. I met Gabriel at the *Fontaine des Innocents* at 2 p.m. I chose a route through le Luco, exiting on the east side of the Senate and taking a few minutes to read on posted information panels about the renovation of the Medici Fountain, under wraps since I arrived in March. Sculptures will be replaced by copies and cracks in the basin repaired. It should reopen in Spring 2021.

I took small streets through the Sixth Arrondissement, crossed the boulevard Saint-Germain, headed down the rue des Saints-Pères to the Seine, and walked over to Shakespeare & Co. to order *The Snow Goose* for Gabriel as a Christmas present. Ahead of me, an American woman was placing a large order, pestering the salesman with questions, hesitating and changing her mind as she proceeded. Because I didn't feel like waiting, I crossed the pont Saint-Michel and arrived at *Fontaine des Innocents* a few minutes early.

I read that this was the oldest fountain in Paris and originally situated against a cemetery-adjacent convent wall. In 1787, when all Paris's cemeteries moved outside city limits for hygienic reasons, the fountain, scheduled for demolition, was spared thanks to the protest of the pioneering historic preservationist Quatremère de Quincy. Designed by architect Pierre Lescot and sculptor Jean Gujon around 1550, it had one unsculpted side that required decoration in its new freestanding location. Augustin Pajou was hired for the job. I decided to figure out which façade he carved. A three-hundred-year difference *should* be detectable, *non?*

I circumambulated a few times. All sides appeared weathered. I made one round looking just at faces, another at body proportions, another at drapery. Then, it became clear. The figures on the south side look different. Their perfect profile faces appear consistent with the mid-eighteenth-century's admiration for classical sculpture. These female figures exhibit the impassive facial expressions of Greek goddesses. And their drapery is not as refined as that on the other three sides. Their proportions are also more normative: the six original figures have disproportionately long legs, fluttering drapery, and expressive faces. They evoke the Mannerist School of

Fontainebleau, which dominated French art in the sixteenth century during the reign of François I (who brought Leonardo da Vinci to France where he died in 1519). I felt gratified to pass my self-imposed challenge.

It was our first meeting since Gabriel's quarantine after leaving Champagne. He arrived carrying a clear plastic bag that he presented, explaining that he didn't want me to feel cold. I plunged my hand in to find a thick, soft, aquamarine cashmere turtleneck. How wonderfully thoughtful! He must like me! I threw my arms around him and gave him a hug. No kisses until he tests negative. I asked him which side of the fountain had been carved in the eighteenth century and he was pretty sure he knew because someone had told him. But I asked him what qualities indicate that? We walked around the fountain a few times and discussed drapery, bodies, and faces. He noticed all the same things I did. Because he loves learning he found it fun.

From there, we walked up the rue Saint-Denis and into the church of Saint-Gilles, which, after Sainte-Chapelle, has the most beautiful stained-glass in Paris. I love the window with Jacob wresting the Angel. The pink-winged angel towers over Jacob and stands calmly in a contrapposto position wearing a gold robe and purple cloak: quite fashionable for the sixteenth century. Jacob, endowed with portrait-specific features, wears an elegant red velvet robe and lunges tentatively with outstretched arms toward the angel while shooting observers a furtive glance. He stands precariously at the edge of a sea, threatened on land by a snarling dog and in the sea by a large fish with the toothy muzzle of a crocodile. Was it a portrait of a young worker? Someone's son commemorated but not remembered? Delacroix surely must have known it when he painted the same subject across the Seine in his chapel at Saint-Sulpice, although he represented Jacob and the Angel at a different moment: engaged in physical combat.

While there, I remembered the beautiful decorations on the rue Montorgueil, so we walked up that mainly pedestrian street toward the Grands Boulevards, where the best-known covered passages are located. It was sad to see the second story glazed-tile sign advertising

Au beau cygne (At the beautiful swan's) missing a third of its tiles. It was even sadder to find the eighteenth-century sign *Au Planteur*—the centerpiece of one of Paris's most magnificent and sadly dilapidated wood facades, now of a greengrocer—defaced by two spats of black paint. They drip down the center, separating a colonist from a black-skinned African clad only in red-and-white striped shorts and three golden bracelets. The colonist, in contrast, is impeccably dressed in a white-linen vested suit à la Tom Wolfe and a wide-brimmed hat; he holds a long-necked clay pipe in his right hand. Although the African appears to offer a plate with what looks like—but could not possible be—a slice of New York cheesecake to the colonist, it's impossible to tell beneath the veil of black streaks. The façade is rotting, but the street number, 12, nailed in place centuries ago, survives. It's the only wood street number I've seen in Paris.

I never tire of wandering Paris's more than a dozen covered passages. There, one sees artisans busy at work, vendors selling stamps and autographs, shops overflowing with books whose covers are art works in themselves, proprietors absorbed in their reading as they wait for customers. I wonder how these, and other small enterprises, survive. How many antique postcards or small wooden toys must one sell to pay rent and employees? Near me, on the rue Vavin, there's a tiny candy store of a type I remember from childhood but haven't seen for decades. It sells what we called penny candy, although everything undoubtedly costs more nowadays. Do shop proprietors own their buildings, gaining rent income from others, so it doesn't matter how much they sell? If they've been there a long time do rents stay low? Do government incentives support certain kinds of traditional businesses? I remember a Munich friend explaining that the few remaining farms within city limits receive special tax dispensation intended to keep traditional culture alive. The same is true of coffee houses in Vienna.

With cafés and restaurants closed and tourists absent, the passages were desolate, even the normally bustling Passage des Panoramas. This provided a wonderful opportunity to stroll at one's leisure, to be a *flâneur* or *flâneuse* appreciating the beautifully tiled floors, original interiors, elegant lighting fixtures, and mysterious staircases. We stumbled upon Passage du Caire (Cairo), with the longest and narrowest corridors of all Paris's *passages couverts*. I found it once and despite intentions to return had not and couldn't even remember where exactly it was.

Passage du Caire caters to the garment trades and resembles a *souk*—a haunted empty *souk*—with confusing passages extending in all directions and windows filled with weird and fascinating items, particularly mannequins and mannequin parts. I especially like the surrealistic forests of hands resting on amputated forearms and wigless heads with expressionless faces. They remind me of the poignant photographs of Eugène Atget. One emerges disoriented from this maze situated in the Second Arrondissement. There are no clear landmarks, just a charming little square, impossible to find unless you're one of the initiated; it's like trying to find Platform 9¾ at King's Cross Station.

Paris's oldest covered passage—or we could just use the modern name, shopping mall—Passage du Caire commemorates Napoléon's victorious Battle of Cairo in 1798, the year the passage was constructed, during his successful Egyptian military campaign. Passage de Caire replaced one of many religious institutions—a convent—decommissioned during the fanatically secular French Revolution. Originally, Passage de Caire functioned as a center of printing and publishing.

A raw chill infused the air, and it was getting dark. Gabriel and I headed back toward Châtelet-Les Halles, where he could catch the train back to Fontenay. We stopped at a restaurant across from the darkened Centre Pompidou. Its interior was off limits and its beverage offerings restricted to hot wine, which warmed our gullets as we chatted with the frustrated owner about pandemic inconveniences.

Tuesday 8 December

Today would have been my mother's 96th birthday. I will always find it odd that her overly Roman Catholic parents named her for the holy day of her birth, the 'Immaculate Conception'. Thus,

Regina Immaculata. I sent Hanna the letter I write annually on my parents' birthdays that contain memories of their lives and their relationships with me. Each year, I consider reviewing past missives (chucked into the ginormous 'Hanna correspondence' file in my Inbox), but I never do. My housewife mother, who predicted the rise of China as a superpower, would have found the pandemic as enthralling as she found Buffalo blizzards, with their attendant lockdowns. She would've been glued to the news, fascinated by every fresh detail that revealed how various nations and localities grappled with it. And, all the while, baking and enjoying cozy time indoors.

I should never check email before breakfast, but like a crazed addict I seem unable to help myself. Bad news awaited. The unempathetic university administrator who initiated my unwanted fall 'medical leave' informed me that my university was unwilling to extend my medical leave and could only offer me a Leave Without (any) Pay for the spring. Because the U.S. seems even less safe now than it did last summer—in the stranglehold, as it appears from here, of a rampaging pandemic and on the verge of civil war—I refused to return. Well, another eight months of income-free living. But also freedom.

While reason would counsel taking time to consider my situation before responding, I didn't hesitate to say 'no'. I knew it was the right decision. Nonetheless, my heart fluttered as I contemplated a bank account doomed to a steady descent, deprived of its usual ebbs and flows. Now, I'm happier than ever that the renter of my Purgatory home, who has now taken refuge elsewhere, continues to pay five hundred dollars per month despite her absence and will continue to do so until the semester ends in April. The fact that activities on which I normally spend money—music, restaurants, theater, travel—are unavailable facilitate a frugal lifestyle. My German family continues trying to entice me to relocate there, but I feel inexplicably safer in France. In addition, I enjoy my relative solitude, and travel restrictions change unpredictably.

I sometimes wonder about feelings of connection to place. Although I enjoy exploring a wide variety, strong sensations of connection occur infrequently. I never felt them in the Buffalo suburb where I grew up but did on the Maine coast where my family vacationed. I felt them among the forests and fields of upstate New York, where I attended college and spent two summers with Jessica, my Nantucket Retriever, playing tennis, picking wild berries, rototilling myself a little garden, and swimming in the town reservoir. There, one Fourth of July, I was arrested, naked, for trespassing. Many parts of Sweden, where I have no cultural or ancestral connection, feel like home, probably because of their geographical and climatic resemblance to central New York State and Maine.

Greece and France, where I do have ancestral roots, have vibes I experience as familiar even when they aren't. That makes me wonder about genetic impressions. My maternal grandmother's family emigrated from a farm near Colmar in 1832, and my Greek paternal grandfather escaped Ottoman authorities in Anatolia at age fifteen along with several other boys from his village and emigrated to the U.S. shortly before World War One. I first visited Greece in my forties but return most summers for a week or more, often with Hanna. Although I didn't grow up immersed in Greek culture—I first tasted feta in my twenties—it's my favorite cuisine and the location of my favorite beaches. If I knew the language, I might consider moving there.

I hear fewer sirens now, an accurate reflection of the pandemic state-of-affairs in Paris. After spiking a week or two ago, hospitalizations and deaths are now decreasing. Journalists and experts have speculated about the revelations Castex will make on Thursday at 6 p.m., when he announces the upcoming changes to restrictions scheduled to begin on December 15th. They agree, perhaps tipped off by government informants, that there'll be another curfew in hopes of limiting holiday gatherings and their super spreader potential. If the government seeks a swift end to the pandemic, it should send everyone ages thirteen to thirty to a remote island—it possesses several—because they're the main culprits. One can only hope that a curfew will curtail late-night parties whose attendees celebrate like it's the End of Days. Junior high students, *collègiens*, are largely out of control, judging by those attending schools in my neighborhood.

Gabriel spent the weekend at my apartment. On Saturday

evening, we walked to the Panthéon to see the Christmas trees, a V of blue lights, beautiful in the darkness, silhouetted against and illuminating the monumental white marble façade. We continued to place de la Contrescarpe, where light-bedecked trees dripped gold cascades. While I love nighttime city walks in general, there's no city whose hushed empty streets I adore wandering more than Paris's. Silence-induced reverie works the double magic of conjuring vivid images of the past and creating the palpable sensation that one is an integral part of this singular urban organism.

Yesterday, I gave my first Zoom lecture. Alexander, the administrator of Greifswald University's History Department, invited me when he heard about my pecuniary circumstances. I discussed the mobility of art in and around the Baltic Sea from 1750 to 1920 and knew many of the attendees. After lunch, I met Gabriel at Opéra Bastille, and we walked the three-mile-long *Coulée Vert*, a walkway like New York's High Line, punctuated by landscaping and art. His favorite sight was the building on avenue Daumesnil with twenty, supersized white sculptures inspired by one of Michelangelo's *Slaves* that are installed at uniform intervals around the upper story of two facades of a corner brick building.

Wednesday 9 December

Today would have been my parents' seventieth wedding anniversary. They didn't understand each other and should never have married. The summer after graduating from Yale, Daddy managed to charm mother at a classmate's party in Port Colborne, Ontario, a desperate effort to avoid an engagement to Cleo, the woman his Greek father had selected for him, the daughter of his best friend. Instead, Cleo married his younger brother, Jim, and they enjoyed a long and happy marriage. My loving parents, however, modeled a dysfunctional relationship that undoubtedly affected my own.

I noticed the French flag flying at half-mast on the Panthéon as I walked to Marché Monge today. I'm guessing it honors Valéry Giscard d'Estaing, French president during the Gerald Ford and Jimmy Carter administrations, who died on December 2nd. As I approached his stand, Cheeseman greeted me with a warm smile and no mask. I trusted that he was as germfree as his cheeses.

"Bonjour, Madame. How are things going with you?" he inquired.

"Bonjour, Monsieur. Things are going well. It's nice to see all the Christmas decorations."

"Ah, yes, they're lovely. Have you seen the windows at Galeries Lafayette?"

"Not yet but I plan to."

"They are *magnifique*. As usual?"

I responded, *"oui, s'il vous plaît,"* so he cut me a slice of the well-aged, cow's-milk Gouda and another of Brie with truffles.

"Anything else?"

"No thank you. Not today."

He started to reach for a chunk of fresh bread from the huge round loaf behind him. Then, he remembered my gluten intolerance and grabbed a fist-sized round of fresh, wrinkly cheese that looked like it had spent too long soaking in the bathtub.

"Thank you for the present," I said, handing him a €50 note.

"The pleasure is always mine, Madame," he replied handing me change.

I left, thinking halfway home that I should have asked how *he* was doing. Next time.

Caroline showed up wearing a new cloth mask with a floral pattern. I'm fine with medical masks. I still have most of those sent by my Wuhan colleagues, so there's no need to splurge on anything fancier. I paid her the rest of my share of the upcoming rent for the house in Antibes, feeling a twinge that registered the sinking of my bank account. *Will I ever be able to retire?* I wondered. *At least I have a bank account that can survive a gradual months-long plummet*, I thought gratefully.

I can't wait to get to a luminous environment where the sun warms even when the air is chilly. The unrelenting greyness of Paris winter, more noticeable now that enterprises are shuttered, oppresses. I feel lethargic and imprisoned, restless and frustrated. I never suffered light deprivation while living in Lapland despite the sun never fully clearing the horizon for weeks in mid-winter. Because cloud cover is impossible when very cold, Southern Lapland is bathed in light for at least a few hours daily, seven minutes more each day after the winter solstice. Luminosity is augmented by a snow-blanketed landscape that conceals the border between land and water, creating a world of radiant whiteness. At night, the absence of light pollution reveals a star-studded sky. Lack of traffic creates a soundless environment, one so silent you can hear your heart beating. Then, Lapland's other personality emerges. In the spring, when rivers thaw and birds and insects return, nature again becomes noisy. Seasonal changes in the far north are dramatic: silent, cold, dark, and still in winter and raucous, warm, light, and kinetic in summer. Continental cities covered by clouds much of the winter offer only apocalyptic dreariness.

After lunch, I walked to Shakespeare & Co via le Luco, nearly deserted streets, and an equally desolate place Saint-Michel. I continued down the rue de la Huchette, a street that hasn't been this empty during the day since the Nazi occupation of Paris. I wondered when I would dance again at Caveau de la Huchette. Its period décor and swing music transport me back to the 1950s: I can imagine Gene Kelly and Leslie Caron having a tête-a-tête over kir royales at one of the tiny café tables during a band break in the dimly lit ground-floor bar that was undoubtedly dimmed further in those days by clouds of cigarette smoke. Narrow staircases at each end of the room-long bar lead down to the 'cave', with its small stage and dance floor encircled by benches. Young and old dance, and every now and then one sees a couple as athletic and skilled as Gene and Leslie slipping, flipping, and bopping to the envy and delight of onlookers.

At Shakespeare & Co., *The Snow Goose* awaited. I decided to give Gabriel my favorite book for Christmas. I'm not sure why it's my favorite because my life couldn't be more different—at least outwardly—from the solitary fisherman whose story it tells. There's something about solitude in nature and by the sea with which I connect. I admire the fidelity of the goose who always returns to her rescuer, their inter-species relationship exemplifying an ideal and impossible love, without boundaries or conditions. Is this possible with humans as well as animals? How wonderful and terrible to experience such a thing. Wonderful because of the joy generated by two souls merging and terrible because in the normal course of events one will remain to grieve. I'm touched by the heart-rending devotion of the fisherman waiting without knowing the fate of his winged beloved. *My Octopus Teacher* prompted the same response when I watched it recently. I wept inconsolably.

Despite—or perhaps because of—its fame, Shakespeare's is inviting. Like Caveau, it seems a relic of an earlier, more leisurely, era. Randomly positioned comfy chairs for reading occupy cramped book-lined passages, a kind of bibliophile's rabbit hutch. Titles beckon from the shelves. I wish I made time to hang there. I always just rush in and out to retrieve books I've ordered. Now would be a perfect time since there are few customers and outdoors is frigid. Often, and especially in summer, Shakespeare's is packed with tourists ticking off a Rick Steves's 'must' on their Paris 'to do' list.

I returned home at rush hour. Few pedestrians circulated on the boulevard Saint-Michel and shops were not as busy as their proprietors undoubtedly wished. Shopkeepers lingered hopefully in doorways looking this way and that, probably wondering how they will survive this bleak Christmas season. Along the boulevard, a wave of 'for rent' and 'for sale' signs sprang up in the wake of spring *confinement*, and now more have joined. I just hope chain stores don't invade and that the pandemic does not turn out to be the disaster that ruins the Paris I love.

Thursday 10 December

Today, I got my haircut on the rue de Rennes; one never knows how long businesses will remain open, and now it has been five months since my last visit. Afterward, I strolled through the Seventh Arrondissement enjoying holiday displays. Beside the newsstand on the corner of Montparnasse and Rennes, Puzzle Man, bundled up and wearing fingerless gloves, worked a jigsaw puzzle on his folding card table.

Paris displays little holiday spirit. Half-heartedly decorated windows contain hints of red and gold or token plastic Christmas trees. Lingerie shops feature red-and-gold lacy bras and panties, jewelry stores feature emeralds and rubies or jade and carnelian in their windows. More ambitious establishments have installed mini winter wonderlands of fake snow and mannequins dressed in Norwegian-style sweaters. An artistic employee at my corner *boulangerie* has adorned its windows with paintings of reindeer prancing over *Bûche de Noël* (yule-log-cake) hills. The trees in front of Deux Magots are dressed in white lights and, continuing east for half a block, a dozen rustic timber stands sell regional specialties: cheese, sausage, ceramics, and hot wine, whose cinnamon aroma infuses the air.

In normal times, crowds would avidly be engaged in afterwork shopping at this strategically located Christmas market, but now merchants stand between their small popups chatting and probably ruing their decision to pay stand rental fees in this disastrous year. Some small streets around the city, like the rue Cler, a food-shopping street in the Seventh Arrondissement, have strung lighted holiday banners across the street. Occasional whiffs of pine trees at markets and street corners selling Christmas trees advertise the season.

This evening, Castex appeared on TV to explain the rules in effect beginning December 15th. Good news: *Confinement Deux* ends. We no longer need an *attestation* to explain our activities when leaving home. Although the 8 p.m. to 6 a.m. curfew remains in effect, this will be suspended on Christmas Eve, the big, family, gift-exchanging day in Europe. In addition, the twenty-kilometer restriction expires, enabling free travel throughout France. Borders with Belgium and Germany remain closed, however. Restaurants, cafés, museums, cinemas, theaters, and gyms won't reopen for another month at least, although ski resorts are accessible but with lifts non-operational until January 7th, perhaps longer. I can't imagine many opting for ski trips that entail schlepping skis up Alpine peaks as in the pre-lift era. Only *collèges*, *écoles premières* (elementary schools), and *crèches* (daycare) will remain open, due to their lower incidence of contagion. *Lycées* (high schools) and universities continue distance-only education until at least January 20th.

Monday 14 December

Yesterday was Lucia, a beloved holiday in Sweden that triggered regret about the impossibility of reliving happy times past. I thought about 1985, when I was conducting dissertation research in Göteborg and arrived at the art museum early that day at the director's request. On the bus in the early morning darkness, I had noticed more than the usual number of teenage girls with long blond hair. All carried shopping bags. I didn't realize until I arrived at the museum that they were Lucias-for-Hire headed to office parties all over town. The museum staff surprised me with the honor of playing 'Lucia'. They dressed me in a floor-length, white cotton gown with a Peter Pan collar—the kind Marie Antoinette wore to her execution in the drawing made by Jacques-Louis David—and affixed a wreath of battery-powered candles to my head with bobby-pins. I led the traditional procession of star-boys and -girls wearing pointy dunce caps decorated with silver and gold stars and carrying star wands. The entire staff was treated to a breakfast of coffee, saffron 'Lucia cat' sweet rolls with raisin eyes, and ginger thins.

Most people's Christmases will be different this year, but I feel especially disadvantaged despite having much to be grateful for. I'll miss my tree, topped by the serene tree-toting angel Hanna and I chose together on one of our trips to Oberammergau. I'll miss the ornaments, each of which guards a special memory: angels, snowmen, and reindeer that my father cut from plywood and the family painted at the kitchen table, my mother's favorite Gingham Dog and Calico Cat with their red rickrack hanging loops, hand-painted wax and pewter ornaments bought in Bavaria when my parents visited during our year there in the mid-1990s, a yarn couple wearing Värend folk costume given to us by Edith in Kyllekulla the day she took us to the open air museum in Korö, and leather *opanci* dangling from handwoven ribbons bought when visiting Northern Macedonia with my daughter's father before we joined our band,

Zlatne Uste, to play at the Guča festival. The tree comes to life when I light its small candles, a practice that amazes visitors, impressed that my house has not yet burned down.

Lately, my thoughts have drifted to the rituals of Advents past: *glögg* and cookie making, present wrapping, driving to Cleveland in a monochromatic, snow-blanketed landscape, Croatian and Ukrainian food, music, dancing, and friends. This may be the first time in my life that I haven't had a live tree either at my house or where I visit. Because I'll soon move to Menilmontant in the Twentieth Arrondissement for a few weeks while Colette is away visiting her mother, there's no point in getting one. Besides, I have no ornaments, not that they're essential; the aroma of pine or spruce is more important. I have kept my eyes open for ornament souvenirs to commemorate this very strange year but have not seen any that tempt. This year is a dramatic contrast with last, when I cut my first live Christmas tree in a forest near Potsdam together with my sister-in-law, Marita.

I spent a quiet weekend at Gabriel's playing chess and piano, reading, writing, and walking in the Bois de Vincennes. His book-lined apartment is pleasant, and I adore having a teensy Eiffel Tower blinking at me in the distance. Still, I feel like a prisoner in this six-floor walkup. It's *far* to outdoors. But Gabriel is kind, well-meaning, and I like his company.

Today, the electoral college votes, presumably placing Biden one step closer to becoming president. Whatever the outcome, I hope that fear abates and civility and freedom return. Americans who fear socialism because of its ill-informed association with the Stalinist Soviet Union would, undoubtedly, happily embrace the lack of worry it offers. European friends cannot comprehend why some Americans believe the election was stolen and why an electoral college is appropriate in a democracy. They wonder why American media outlets incite fear of the infinitely more humane European system. When I tell my American students that minimum wage in Western Europe is around $15 per hour; that everyone gets five or more weeks of vacation; free university; practically free healthcare and prescriptions, with citizens able to choose their own doctors; a year of parental leave after the birth of a child; and parents receive a monthly check of $150-200 for each child until they turn eighteen, their jaws drop in disbelief. And the drinking age for wine and beer is sixteen. If American youth knew just that detail, there'd be mass emigration.

On Saturday afternoon, I stopped by Collette's, where I will housesit from December 16th to January 4th. Afterward, I'll relocate to Gabriel's for a few days before we drive to Antibes. My landlady agreed to let me apply the month of rent I just sent her for four weeks in December-January to mid-February-mid-March instead. She's allowed me to keep the key. It's hard to imagine that she'll find a spring renter when France's (and Europe's) borders are still closed to Americans. This evening, Gail invited me to kitty sit during June in her apartment at place Blanche, with stunning views of Sacré-Cœur. Now, I just have mid-March to June to figure out and suddenly envy individuals with personal assistants who attend to arranging such details.

A good first for the U.S.: COVID-19 vaccinations are starting but still no news regarding vaccinations in France. I wonder if I will even be able to get one here given my inability to get a flu shot. Priority was given to those registered in the French healthcare system, and by the time the registered had received it, stocks were depleted.

Friday 18 December

How did my time at rue de la Grande-Chaumière pass so quickly? Yesterday, I joined the throngs hunting for Christmas gifts. I stopped at J.B. Guanti, an Italian glove store on the rue de Rennes where I had seen gloves resembling a pair I purchased at the design museum in Copenhagen years ago. Colette had admired them, and I wanted to buy a pair for her in appreciation of her letting me borrow her apartment. I hope my size guess is correct.

The boulevard Montparnasse bustled, and Puzzle Man sat at his card table beside the newsstand working a puzzle. He reminds me of Egg Seller Man on the Market Square in Greifswald: elderly, reassuringly always present, with a face full of character that Walker Evans would have admired. Le Select, closed like all other restaurants, roused its holiday spirit despite the impediments: tables are set as if the doors are about to open for fashionable holiday diners; wrapped presents await beneath a prominently displayed Christmas tree, and a cheery '*Bonne Noël*' painted on the window greets passersby. I stopped by the *papeterie* beside La Coupole for wrapping paper. Because Hanna won't return to Stockholm until late January, there's no urgency to send her package until just before I leave for Antibes.

Thursday 24 December

Had you asked me a year ago where I'd wake up on Christmas Eve 2020, I would have stated confidently 'in Cleveland. At Walt's'. Instead, I rose at 6 a.m. after a sleepless night in my former apartment on Grande-Chaumière. Jim prepared a festive pre-Christmas dinner for two yesterday, buying an extra slice of *Bûche de Noël* just so I could enjoy the mouthwatering strawberry buttercream icing. Before returning from Jim's house, located in a southern suburb, to Colette's apartment in Menilmontant on Paris's north side, I had to swing by my old apartment to pick up Caroline's Christmas present, *Maria Chapdelaine* by Louis Hémon, a poignant romance set in the Quebec wilderness. Caroline is now house-sitting near me in Menilmontant and invited me for Christmas Eve dinner. By the time I walked to Grande-Chaumière from the Port Royal RER station, picked up the book, and hurried to the 96 Bus stop at Rennes-Littre, it was 7:30 p.m. The next bus wouldn't come for another eighteen minutes, getting me to Menilmontant after curfew. Had I not feared the €135 fine, I would have chanced it. But I didn't, so breathless and soaked in perspiration, I returned.

It was an awful night. The apartment was unheated, and I had neither the charger to my nearly depleted phone nor my iPad. I finished reading *A Moveable Feast* at 2 a.m. and couldn't find anything else I was in the mood to read. I lay awake, doing breathwork, visualizations, yoga nidra, meditation, all vain attempts to fall asleep. In the morning, I had planned to go to the Montparnasse post office, where there's never a line, to get a box to send presents to Hanna. Afterward, I intended to walk to Bon Marché, which opens at 10 a.m., to see its interior holiday decorations. But when curfew ended at 6 a.m., I was wide awake and frozen stiff. I decided to take the bus directly back to Colette's to try to sleep. I was a ravenous wreck.

At that hour, the boulevard Montparnasse was dark but surprisingly lively. Parents walked children to school. Others headed to work. Well-lit *boulangeries* beckoned, their window displays brimming with brioches, croissants, and *pains au chocolat*. I thought of Jacque Dutroc's *chanson* "It is 5 a.m. and Paris is Waking:"

> The coffee is in the cups
> The cafés clean their mirrors
> On the boulevard Montparnasse
> The station is no more than a carcass.

At the 96 Bus stop, five people waited. Not the fashionable Euro-French, who mostly inhabit the neighborhood, but two of Asian and three of African descent. And me. The workers and the sleepless. I was happy the bus wasn't crowded and took a seat in the back with my phone ready to snap pictures, my habit when traveling above ground. By the time the bus reached the pont Saint-Michel, dawn had broken, the sky a streaked canvas of dark turquoise against a pale blue ground. Store windows glowed like full-scale, over-illuminated Dutch still lives.

Friday 25 December

Christmas. My first in Paris and my second alone. Like many others this year, I celebrated Christmas via Zoom. The group of around twenty with whom Hanna and I always spend Christmas, are an ecumenical group of Catholics, Protestants, Ukrainian Orthodox, and Jews, mainly professional musicians. I enjoyed it more than anticipated. Musical children performed, adults toasted and caught up, Ukrainians sang. Later, I Zoomed over coffee and cognac with

Nina in Chicago who, as a Russian, celebrates Christmas according to the Julian calendar. For her, it was just another Friday.

Sunday 27 December

Today is German brother Robert's birthday. I realized I hadn't spoken to either him or Inge and Jürgen since late November. I figured they were busy celebrating the holidays. My email birthday greetings received an immediate response. I thought, *ah, they're as eager to catch up with me as I with them*. I didn't expect to learn that Jürgen was dead. A tall, wiry man in his mid-80s with thick, wavy, white hair, he died of COVID-19 alone in a Zittau hospital on December 23rd. He infected frail, diabetic Inge, who experienced mild symptoms and recovered.

I thought back to what I was doing that day. I always want to notice when a monumental event occurs in my life—a sort of disturbance in The Force—the way Hanna intuited that something was wrong that day she refused to go to kindergarten. Was it a coincidence that the day he died was the only night in memory I couldn't sleep? Or was my restlessness more the result of not having my usual doses of valerian tea and melatonin, on whose calming effects I depend?

This devastating news struck me with the intensity of a lightning bolt. Overwhelmed by regret, I tried to remember why I had not spent the summer in beautiful Hainewalde with the adopted parents I love. This cruel reminder that nothing lasts forever and that I would never again enjoy an edifying historical discussion or a father-daughter chat with Jürgen left me bewildered, shocked, and grieving. I opened my phone and looked at pictures from my last visit in October 2019. The last photo I ever took of Jürgen was during our walk to the nearby church and cemetery with its magnificent Baroque chapel, whose exterior is embellished with expressive allegorical female figures. We stood before the family plot, where his parents lay. Jürgen was an expert gardener, and the plot has beautiful plantings that flower in most seasons and rose vines that creep up the wall behind it. He told me—not for the first time–that he was happy he would someday rest there in view of the chapel and church. I left him briefly to photograph the chapel for the umpteenth time but turned around when I was a few feet away and snapped him, stooped over and contemplating. I could never have imagined that would be my last photo of him.

Robert scheduled a Skype chat for the 31st. I just hope I don't disintegrate into a sobbing mess when we talk. It's hard to conceal one's emotions on video, although I suppose in this case there's no reason to.

Wednesday 30 December

Today, the sun shone with the robustness of summer, and I decided to walk from Colette's apartment near Notre-Dame-de-la-Croix to place Monge for the last *marché* of the year. I wound my way down-hill, past Aristide's street—I think he winters in Cairo—and through the gritty and fascinating Twentieth and Eleventh Arrondissements. I continued through the trendy Marais, whose fashionable boutiques on the rue Vieille-du-Temple display tasteful Christmas windows, and over the pont Louis-Philippe. I descended the seventeenth-century steps leading to the quays of Île St. Louis to rest for a few minutes on a cold stone bench along the quay.

Arriving on the Left Bank, I walked up the rue de Bièvre, zig-zagged through narrow lanes to the rue Cardinal Lemoine, crossed the boulevard Saint-Germain, and paused at the apartment where Hemingway and Hadley lived, the one with the dance hall in the cellar. I crossed a vacant place de la Contrescarpe, whose epony-mous café appeared forlorn: windows shuttered, with terrace chairs and tables moved indoors. On the rue Mouffetard, the several open fast-food vendors—independent crêperies, and taco and gyro shops—were either closed or their owners were kibbitzing for lack of customers.

At La Fontaine aux Vins, I bought my usual Côtes de Blaye for dinner this evening with Gail. The female proprietor greeted me effusively, like the regular I sort of was, although they would have a hard time surviving if they had to rely on my patronage. We wished each other a happy New Year's Eve and said '*abientôt*', which presumes that we will see each other again soon.

I was disappointed that Cheeseman had taken the day off, although *Maman* was there along with two young female helpers, one with barely the upper body strength to slice through the ultra-aged Gouda. I stopped by Grumpy Greens Man across the way and the organic fruit and vegetable stand next door to pick up salad supplies. I then retraced my steps to place de la Contrescarpe and followed the rue Descartes downhill, past the house where Verlaine died on the same date, January 8th, but not the same year, as my father. I passed the original École Polytechnique, Trocadéro Man's alma mater, established during the Enlightenment to create a cadre of math and engineering experts to serve the state. École Polytechnique is located on place Jacqueline De Romilly as was Bistrot Descartes, where we dined on our third date before going to Piano Vache to hear Rodolphe Raffalli one Monday evening in March 2018. He had called me on the way, requesting that I order for him 'because I knew what he liked'. And I did. Fish. No wine. Already at that early stage, we had a familiar, confident rapport that I never before experienced after such a short acquaintance. It was seductive.

Bistrot Descartes, a typically tiny Parisian restaurant with tables along both walls that served impeccable French cuisine for decades, was closed last time I passed. Now, its name effaced and contents emptied, its successor, yet another Thai restaurant, is refashioning the space. The open door exposed the process of transformation. The yellowing photographs of the neighborhood as it once was left pale rectangle imprints on the walls, the last sad vestiges of another vanishing era. I mourn its closure because it highlights a regrettable trend. The once ubiquitous mom-and-pop French restaurants, common as *boulangeries*, are becoming relics of the past. Will Paris become yet another Western city where fast food and Asian restaurants replace neighborhood establishments serving local specialties prepared according to time-honored traditions?

I returned to the Right Bank via the pont Louis-Philippe and pursued the rue Vielle-du-Temple north through the Marais, where hip inhabitants walk their miniature purebreds and wee boutiques create fanciful window displays. I crossed the breathtakingly wide avenue Richard-Lenoir, named after an eighteenth-century textile entrepreneur, and headed uphill on the rue Oberkampf, home of bars and clubs, and recently, inordinate amounts of graffiti. Not the beautiful or interesting kind, just the wanton, destructive kind: swirling black scrawls of cryptic words and random letters. A lone humorous one read "Macronavirus."

I remembered walking on Oberkampf back to the Left Bank from world music concerts at Studio de l'Ermitage in Spring 2018. At that time, I had to navigate an obstacle course of partiers spilling onto the streets while bands played in the front windows of bars, a lively scene, especially on weekends. Now, bars have receded in visibility, hibernating during the pandemic winter if they survive at all. Instead, food shops have risen in visibility, along with hairdressers, restaurants offering takeout-only, and cheap dry goods stores catering to customers with roots in the Middle East and North Africa.

In the early evening, I walked down rue Menilmontant and bought a rotisserie chicken with potatoes cooked in drippings, ubiquitous in Paris and almost always delicious. I had promised to provide dinner for Gail, a generous hostess. I took the *métro*. The train was standing room only, and I breathed as shallowly as possible although everyone appeared properly masked. I arrived at place Blanche, where Gail lives, two minutes early and took the opportunity to briefly peruse Paris's most famous red-light district, which surrounds the appropriately named Moulin Rouge (Red Windmill) cabaret; illuminated signs identified sex and food boutiques open for business.

After I pressed the exterior and interior door codes and rode the elevator to the sixth floor, Gail— dressed fashionably as always in black and white—welcomed me. A large plate of oysters and a bottle of Chablis already occupied the table, so that was what we ate and drank. The chicken and potatoes could wait. She told me about her new love and glowed with happiness. I'm looking forward to kitty sitting in June. Her airy, oriental-carpeted, four-bedroom, two-bath apartment with high, decoratively plastered ceilings and a large terrace is a luxury in this expensive city. She enjoys magnificent views of Sacré-Cœur outside and books by the thousands inside.

I returned to Menilmontant by taxi long after curfew. As we sat in her living room watching *Death to 2020*, she sent me a text requesting me to come immediately because she had hurt her back and couldn't move. As it turned out, I didn't need the excuse since I returned to Colette's without incident. What was extraordinary on the taxi ride home, however, was the absolute emptiness of the streets. The taxi followed the major avenues separating the Ninth, Tenth, and Eleventh Arrondissements from the Eighteenth, Nineteenth, and Twentieth, a heavily trafficked thoroughfare in normal times. We sped past cabarets, bars, twenty-four-hour sex shops, and bodegas near to the always-busy train stations Gare du Nord and Gare de l'Est and rocketed down the boulevard Belville to the rue Menilmontant. There was hardly a soul in sight at 11 p.m., not even dog walkers. I saw exactly two humans: one filling his car at a gas station, the other, a cyclist wearing an Uber Eats backpack. The taxi fare was €13.60, but in these hard times it seemed appropriate to give the driver a €20 and not request change.

Encouraging news: on December 27th, France administered its first COVID-19 vaccinations. Healthcare workers, first responders, and retirement home residents and employees have priority. No news about a general inoculation campaign but hopefully it is not far off.

Thursday 31 December

This morning, I Skyped with my German family, currently staying with Inge in Hainewalde. I worried about my comportment since every time Jürgen enters my thoughts I sob uncontrollably. Now, I have progressed to eyes welling up with tears that stream down my face. The family wanted to see me, and they wanted me to see the flowers I ordered from the village florist: a cheery red and yellow bouquet. I took half a Xanax with breakfast hoping to stay on an emotionally even keel during our chat.

Robert spoke first and provided details. In early December,

Jürgen had stopped by to wish a neighbor a happy birthday before driving to the grocery store. Several days later when Robert called, no one answered. His son drove from Dresden, a two-hour drive, and found Inge helpless and Jürgen very sick. He called an ambulance. After a few days in the hospital, Jürgen seemed better—as COVID-19 victims often do—and went home. A week later, he relapsed and returned to the hospital. Robert and Marita rushed from Potsdam to help on the 20th. On the 23rd, the hospital called to say that Jürgen was responding poorly to treatment and inquired about the extremes to which the family wanted to go to save him. They decided against intubating him, considering it the compassionate decision, and he passed later that day.

They refrained from calling on Christmas because they didn't want to ruin my day, although this year there was not much to ruin. They'll stay in Hainewalde for a few more days until our sister, currently working in Asia, arrives. I'm struggling with feelings of regret and helplessness mitigated by gratitude for the gift of an ersatz father, whose advice, love, and stories brought me such joy.

Chapter 12
January: Off to Antibes!

Tuesday 5 January

I spent New Year's Eve at Gabriel's. He invested significant effort into the preparations. For days, he quizzed me: did I like this kind of cheese, could I eat potatoes (my gluten intolerance has thrown him for a loop), could I eat a *Bûche de Noël*. Luckily, there is a pastry shop a ten-minute bike ride away in Vincennes, *Aux Merveilleux*, that offers meringue and *chantilly* delights I can eat in their entirety.

His apartment was immaculate, the table set with his best Cerulean blue, gold-rimmed china and etched crystal glasses; a stack of professionally wrapped presents awaited on the coffee table. Deciding how much to spend and what kind of gift to give is one of those vexing questions with which one grapples at the beginning of a relationship. I pursued the personal yet not intimate route: a box of Mococha chocolates, *The Snow Goose*, and a t-shirt I saw advertised on Facebook with an appealing graphic that read 'Pscyclepath' with a silhouette of a bicycle, appropriate for a cycling enthusiast like Gabriel. He has already bought one of my books, *An Introduction to Nineteenth-Century Art*, which I would have given him had I access to my cache or if the mail worked reliably.

Gabriel was more generous: a magnetic chess set made of wood with a drawer for storing pieces, an important book about the history of French women so heavy I could barely lift it, and a bottle of Chanel's Gardenia perfume. All wonderful, thoughtful gifts. When I confided that I only had two other bottles of perfume, a look of deep concern spread over his face as he exclaimed in English:

"Ooo la la! Zee woomaan must expwess zee *saisons* ond hair moodss. Yoo arrr leeving yoor laif wiz ay grahnd hondikep!"

Had he not looked earnestly worried about my well-being, I wouldn't have suppressed my laughter. Gabriel is very, adorably, French, with a diffidence, naivety, and sincerity that reminds me of a hybrid of Eyore and Pepé le Pew. Even if our relationship doesn't survive, I'll remember him for the rest of my life, or as long as the perfume lasts.

Yesterday, I relocated from Colette's in Menilmontant to Gabriel's in Fontenay-sous-Bois. It was one of those Parisian winter days when it's hard to tell upon waking if it's day or night. The weather has been dismal lately; I barely remember the experience of sunshine streaming through windows insistently prodding me out of bed. I bought flowers to welcome Colette when she arrives and arranged them in a vase on her Italian modern black and chrome dining table, which in the evening will have a backdrop of twinkling city lights. I also visited the *boulangerie* regarded by Internet voters as the best gluten-free one in Paris: Chambelland, a ten-minute walk and just south of Métro Parmentier. I was disappointed but not surprised to find no croissants, brioches, or baguettes and settled for an unadorned brick of focaccia and a delicious lemon meringue tart. I returned via place Maurice-Chevalier at the foot of Notre-Dame-de-la-Croix, a square that retains it village-like charm and has a café named 'Tomorrow is Far Away', a kind of *carpe diem* stop-for-a-drink-with-friends kind of haunt.

Gabriel and I spent yesterday afternoon exploring Menilmontant, an experience that has only whetted my appetite. Whenever we drive up the rue des Pyrénées, I peer down side streets, noticing enticing spots I hope to explore when the weather improves. Recently, I was looking out the driver-side window as we wound down the rue Belleville and noticed a plaque above a doorway inscribed with the words: "On the steps of this house was born in the very greatest destitution, Edith Piaf, whose voice later would astonish the world." We wandered down the rue de l'Ermitage, a street I have walked many times in winter darkness to attend musical events at Studio de l'Ermitage, Paris's premiere world music venue. I suppose it once was a hermitage; the pandemic has taught that you can live a hermit's life pretty much anywhere, even in Paris. Beside Studio is a lane of small, private houses with gardens, garages, and bikes leaning against picket fences. A plaque explains that before Menilmontant was incorporated into the City of Paris it had many such streets. Such informative signs visible everywhere in Paris transform an aimless wander into an enlightening history lesson that binds you even tighter to the city, in the way that learning more of a friend's or lover's history deepens your understanding of them and consequently your connection. I can imagine this little village vibrant in summertime. The plaque includes a photo of a communal dinner with jovial neighbors gathered at a single long picnic table that runs the length of the lane, evidence of their sense of community. Afterward, Gabriel helped me transport my worldly possessions to his car via elevator from Colette's eighth-floor apartment with its terrace and magisterial view of eastern Paris. I thrived there because I find myself happiest and most productive when I can occasionally glance up from my word-filled screen and rest my eyes for a moment on fields or forest, mountains or sea, a lovely garden or a sweeping cityscape.

For me, the year has begun with escalating activity. A Geman colleague asked me to assess two articles about world's fairs that she's considering publishing in a journal issue she's editing. The one on women and colonial subjects at the St. Louis Fair of 1904 fascinated, but the initially promising one about the influence of science on displays at London's Crystal Palace during the 1850s quickly became incomprehensible. I also did a sample edit of a Norwegian manual for youth leaders that hopefully will result in a paying gig from the Norwegian government.

A friend in Vienna was recently diagnosed with a second inoperable brain tumor. To cheer him up, several of us have organized a recurring Zoom rendezvous on Sundays. It's been comforting to catch up with these people regularly; we're rarely in the same place at the same time. Today, Stefan couldn't join because of the toll chemotherapy treatments had taken on him. We succeeded, initially, in avoiding discussion of the pandemic, which we all knew was where the conversation would end, and it was refreshing to talk about other topics. I mentioned my idea to spend a month or so in Hainewalde after returning from Antibes in mid-February. I regret my not being as helpful as a dutiful daughter should. I'd like to look after Inge until a suitable retirement home is found.

Hainewalde, nestled amidst the Zittau Mountains, is peaceful and beautiful. Although I've never worked much while there—I'm not even sure they have Wi-Fi—every window of my parental home offers sublime views of fields, forests, and the village church steeple, and I think I would be productive there. My friends thought travel could be problematic—if even permissible—since COVID-19 is spiraling out of control in the states of Thuringia and Saxony, where Hainewalde is situated. They advised against going under any circumstances and to book a first-class ticket if I do because those cars are less crowded. I would prefer to stay in France until vaccinated. I hope it's possible but realize I may have to repatriate to Stockholm for that. Until more definite information is available, there's no point in speculating.

I spoke to Kathy in Bregenz, where the situation is worsening. Austria is under lockdown, as are England and Scotland, following the recent development of a more easily communicable form of COVID-19. In France, the curfew has been lengthened from ten to twelve hours in many regions—from 6 p.m. to 6 a.m. instead of 8 p.m. to 6 a.m.—and journalists doubt this will change soon, at least in Paris.

Gabriel has been investigating the drive to Antibes. Under normal circumstances, I would want to make the most of such a long drive, taking a week to sightsee along the way, but now only parks and churches remain open. He's also having trouble finding accommodations, although he doesn't always seem familiar with

Internet searching. We'll break up our trip with two overnights, departing on Sunday around 3 p.m., with a need to find shelter before 6 p.m. One hotel he investigated accepts guests only on weekdays.

Dining also poses a problem. Only highway rest stop restaurants remain open, and I won't eat at them because of the poor food quality and lack of gluten-free choices. None of the quick-and-dirty travel-dining solutions—pizza, sandwiches, pasta—are possible for me. Gabriel did find an open hotel, but its restaurant is closed, although it offered to prepare and deliver meals to our room. I suggested investigating *gîtes*, the same principal as AirBnBs but existing long before. Previously unimaginable travel issues surface in these pandemic times.

If ever I had doubts about the wisdom of staying in France and not returning to teach in the U.S. for the spring semester, which begins in mid-January, the recently passed milestone of 350,000 deaths reassured me. Reports of depleted oxygen supplies in L.A. and generally exhausted and overextended medical personnel and facilities throughout the country bolster my decision. Video clips of rallies attended by overwrought, maskless yet baseball-cap-wearing, gun-toting hordes reinforced my assessment that returning to Purgatory was ill-advised. In normal times, I fear that town, inhabited as it is by twitchy, unpredictable meth heads, lethargic heroin and Fentanyl addicts, and a growing, destitute population of homeless and unemployed, among whom the Ku Klux Klan has a strong following. The more worrisome citizens possess caches of lethal weapons, and university employees receive active shooter training. Your typical mid-western town.

French news has been aghast at the notorious phone call Trump made to officials in the state of Georgia referencing close senatorial races and encouraging them to 'find' votes that would grant him the state's electors. A half-dozen Facebook friends have been posting obsessively for months about things political—mainly outrage and disappointment—commentating as if they were journalists, an activity that may be explained as a kind of self-care therapy but sounds more like ranting (except by lobbyists and campaign workers). Tomorrow, I get my teeth cleaned for the first time since November 2019. In France, dentists rather than dental hygienists (a non-existent profession here) perform this service.

Thursday 7 January

Yesterday turned out more exciting than expected. I had a chat date at 1 p.m. East Coast time with Joan in New York. She requested a delay until 1:30 p.m. because she was watching the Congressional counting of electoral votes. We chatted until around 2:30 p.m. Minutes later, she texted "watch CNN," so I turned on the TV. Gabriel and I watched, riveted by the drama unfolding at the U.S. Capitol. I wish I could add the adjective 'incredulous', but I'm not. An unmasked, armed mob broke into the Capitol building in Washington with the apparent intent of seizing control of the ballots and the government.

Today, the attempted *coup d'état*, as European media outlets call yesterday's Capitol infiltration, shared airtime with discussions of the COVID-19 vaccine rollout (managed partly by the European Union and distributed equitably to member nations), the dangers of the new, more communicable and virulent strain that has emerged in the UK, extended curfews in some French regions (from 8 p.m. to 6 a.m., including Antibes), and the superiority of France, the only Western nation offering free COVID-19 tests. Free and easily accessible: one can't walk more than five minutes in any direction without seeing a pharmacy or sidewalk tent advertising on-the-spot testing. Ad hoc sites have been set up in popular locations like Hôtel de Ville and place de la Republique on the Right Bank and place Saint-Germain and place Saint-Sulpice on the Left. I haven't sought testing because as long as I feel fine I can't see the point. I have, however, added zinc and increased Vitamin D to my morning supplements because medical experts believe they might discourage COVID-19 from taking hold if one becomes infected. I'm very much looking forward to strolls on the beach and natural Vitamin D infusions from the sun.

Sunday 10 January

Today, Gabriel and I left for Antibes. He spent the morning at a Masonic meeting while I packed and participated in the regular Zoom chat with my German friends. Two minutes in, Caroline texted.

"Urgent. Get in touch before you leave."

"Are you OK?"

"I'm fine. Just need to talk before you leave."

I now found myself distracted from the German conversation, which required all my concentration. Neither my French nor my German are good enough that I can listen casually. After the Zoom, much of which concerned the slow rollout of COVID-19 vaccines in Austria and Germany, I called. Caroline had secured a more comfortable apartment for us.

Since her arrival four days earlier, Caroline had texted repeatedly, reminding me to bring leggings and warm sweaters and that the kitchen had no heat. The luxurious seven-bedroom home had shrunken to three, with a kitchen and living area downstairs; apparently the rest of the 'house' occupied a building undergoing renovation on the other side of the garden. And the entire house was freezing, under fourteen degrees Celsius (fifty-seven degrees Fahrenheit). The owners had furnished an insufficient heater and were unwilling to do more. I suppose they have only stayed there in the summertime and never experienced the piercing cold of poorly insulated French dwellings. As a consequence, Caroline located another comfortable apartment, a three-bedroom triplex also located in the Old Town. Anything she decided was fine with me, I told her.

Gabriel and I drove on Autoroute A6 to the tiny village of Maconge, stopping for groceries enroute. We arrived after dark and are staying at a *chambre d'hôte* (room-for-rent) situated in a farmhouse in the village center. The *mairie* (mayor's office) is 50 yards away and a provincial Romanesque church stands across the road, its thick walls interrupted at intervals by tiny windows. Beside the *mairie*, stands an appropriately scaled town square—a modest lawn, really

—with a trough of running potable water and a Christmas tree decorated with blue lights. I wondered if our farmer host were the mayor, or if when the farmer became too old to farm and turned it over to his oldest son he was promoted to the position of Wise Old Mayor.

An unheated farmhouse, vacant in winter, stood beside the converted part of the barn where the farmer and his wife lived. We'll sleep in a poorly heated room up a steep stairway overlooking the church, *mairie*, and town square. Because restaurants and cafés remain closed until at least mid-February, we brought pasta, sauce, and grated cheese, which I prepared in the cramped kitchen—greasy sink, crumbs on the countertop, dirty floor—and we dined at an oak trestle table while our hosts watched a detective film in the adjacent living area. I befriended their thick-pelted Samoyed and wished I had not left my toasty fur coats in Stockholm and the U.S.

Monday 11 January

Last night, there was not a moment I wasn't uncomfortably cold. Wearing two pair of wool socks to bed didn't help, nor did Gabriel, who sleeps motionless on his back wearing a CPAP. I pulled the covers over my head, exhaling warm air, which helped marginally. The blankets on the bed were so heavy that I felt like I was trapped in a flower press.

After a breakfast of yogurt and bananas for me and a day-old baguette and bowl of milk-coffee for Gabriel, we departed for Chateauneuf-en-Auxois, a mountain village Gabriel had often passed and always wanted to visit. It was a crisp sunny morning, and we drove through fields of sheep and cows exhaling steam in the freezing morning air. Green fields coated with frost twinkled in the bright sunshine, and the village clustered around a closed château-fortress, now a museum, perched atop a high hill with a splendid view of the surrounding countryside. We wandered deserted streets, some more passageways than lanes, some too narrow for portly individuals to traverse. Several open onto the square, occupied by an enclosed market hall and *mairie* and animated by a lone dog walker conversing with a neighbor. Overlapping flat stones on one steeply inclined lane serve as a kind of stairway. Well-kept stone buildings dating from the fourteenth century and afterward have variously decorated window frames—one resembles a dollop of meringue— and there are many examples of decorative stonework and relief sculptures: Saint George astride his horse, for instance, and the cowled heads of monks.

Autun was nearby, so I suggested stopping there. I couldn't recall the significance of its twelfth-century cathedral, Saint-Lazare, but I remembered studying it in a Romanesque architecture course. Autun was founded by the Romans, and the first thing we encountered upon arrival was their gate to the city: a triumphal arch, the only visible remnant of the protective wall once surrounding the town. We drove to the center, a potpourri of architecture spanning the twelfth to nineteenth centuries, which exuded an urban vibe despite the vacant streets. On one side of the main square stands an Italianate theater and an imposing city hall, both in the ostentatious Beaux-Arts style of the late-nineteenth century. Because it was a Monday, most everything was closed, except the *tabac* (newsstand) and crêpe stand on the Champ-de-Mars.

We headed uphill, following signs through winding streets flanked by attractive half-timber houses and darkened store fronts, perhaps a third of which were empty and either for sale or rent: pandemic casualties. Houses spanning centuries line the deserted cathedral square with its medieval fountain. The visible absence of modernity encourages daydreaming about how this locale might have looked in times past: women in coarse linen dresses and woolen scarves, children playing, carts and horses, bustling shops, Christian pilgrims. I walked clockwise around Saint-Lazare, arriving at a broad terrace with benches and trees that led to the front steps of the cathedral. *Now* I remembered! The magnificent, Byzantine-style *Last Judgment* tympanum sculpted by an artist we know only as Giselbertus is the main attraction.

An enthroned Christ sits at center, his legs awkwardly splayed, as if the sculptor were unsure how to convey knees together in a sculpted relief. Incised lines, rather than rounded ridges, indicate the

folds of his robe. The Saved appear to his right and the Damned—
along with souls in the process of being weighed and judged—to his
left. My favorite figure is not really a figure at all, just a pair of long,
creepy, plier-like hands with pointy fingernails. This demon reaches
below the ground line and grabs the head of a terrified damned
soul, eyes wide and mouth agape. The face of each figure expresses
a particular emotion: boredom, patience, horror, fear, pain, contentment, happiness.

On the Judgment/Damned side, a kindly, smiling Saint Michael
accompanied by an angel stands closest to Christ and holds a
basket-like scale; he turns toward the undoubtedly terrified
Medieval visitor proffering a reassuring smile. Facing him stand a
pair of monstrous, slouching, and emaciated demons with heavily
textured reptilian skin and toothy gaping mouths that probably emit
frightful sounds. One holds a scale containing a soul, whose resemblance to its judges betrays its condemned spiritual status. I don't
remember much Latin, but I recognized the word 'horror' inscribed
on the band separating the long line of naked frightened souls
waiting for judgement. Three delicate columns, several of which are
beautifully decorated—one with alternating spiral bands of five-
petaled flowers, a second with leaves and vines, and a third, plain
with beveled edges—flank the door and support the tympanum. All
capitals depict biblical stories, with sizes of figures proportional to
their importance.

After stopping at the *tabac* to buy postcards and stamps, we
returned to the toll road. I drove while Gabriel searched the
Internet for lodging. I didn't understand why he had hesitated to
arrange Night Two when arranging Night One, but Gabriel doesn't
seem a convenience-fixated individual. After leaving messages at a
half dozen *chambres d'hôte*, at 5:15 p.m., forty-five minutes before
curfew, Gabriel succeeded in securing a room in a Grenoble suburb.

Upon our arrival, a kindly pair in their late seventies showed us
to a heated sunroom with an adjacent bedroom whose down pillows
augured a good night's sleep.

"You were lucky to find somewhere to sleep so late in the day,"
the man observed.

"I know, I know," agreed Gabriel. "This 6 p.m. curfew really complicates things."

"It has not changed our lives much since we mostly stay in during the winter. Our grandchildren are teenagers, though, and for them and their parents pandemic life is often stressful."

"I can imagine," I sympathized, happy that my child was independent.

"Have you already eaten, or would you like us to prepare you dinner?" the woman inquired.

I almost interrupted in my eagerness to respond.

"We'd be delighted if you could make us dinner. We haven't had a warm meal since yesterday."

"Ahh," she answered, "just give us twenty minutes to prepare. We'll serve you in the sunroom."

"Thank you very much," Gabriel replied.

I would have been happy with a slice of gluten-free quiche and a salad, but we were in France and our hosts belonged to the era when hospitality had strict rules. Thus, we enjoyed a splendid four-course dinner: potato-vegetable soup, duck breast with ratatouille, salad and cheeses, and bowls of fresh fruit topped by large succulent raspberries for dessert. The man put a newly opened Cabernet Sauvignon on the table and a tray with a bottle of cognac and two glasses on the coffee table. At no point was money discussed. I'm not sure if there are commonly understood hospitality parameters for *chambres d'hôte*, or if one just assumes that all behave in a fair and considerate manner. A restful night followed this welcome breath of civilization.

After breakfasting in the dining room while enjoying a spectacular view of snow-capped Alpine peaks, we embarked on the Route Napoléon toward the Mediterranean coast. In 2010, I picked up Hanna at the Nice airport, and we explored part of it heading north, in the direction of Digne. It appears much different in winter. Our first stop was Lake Laffrey and the 'Meadow of the Meeting', where Napoléon and the loyal followers who had welcomed him in Cannes after his daring escape from Elba encountered the French army on their northward march. Rather than following orders to arrest Napoléon, it accompanied him to Paris and helped him retake control of the government, an event known as the 'One Hundred Days'. An equestrian statue of Napoléon by Eugène Frémiet, the same sculptor who made the gilded equestrian *Joan of Arc* across from the Louvre at place des Pyramides, commemorates the event.

Tramping through a field knee-deep in snow to reach Napoléon reminded me that I hadn't walked in snow since departing the Quebec wilderness after New Year's 2020. It's one of my favorite outdoor experiences, especially when the sun shines and the snow is dry and fluffy. At Laffrey, tree branches held narrow shelves of snow, indicating that it had been wind-still since the snow had fallen. Further south, we paused at Les Barques, where Napoléon and his army spent the night before heading to Laffrey.

We stopped for lunch in Gap. Napoléon slept there, too, at an inn on a side street near the main square. In addition to an explanatory plaque that identifies the location, a painted frieze on the façade portrays the returning emperor on horseback, accompanied by cavalry, infantry, and local peasants. Unlike Autun, Gap felt inhabited, but then again, it was a Tuesday, when things are open. Enterprising restaurants and cafés offered easily portable eats, and we settled for crispy, hand-cut fries served with a choice of sauces, which we ate while seated on a snowy step in the bracing mountain air. I chose truffle mayo. Truth be told, I would eat almost anything topped with truffles.

Sufficiently fortified and having completed a quick walking tour, we piled back into the car and drove through charming Sisteron and up to its fortifications, which offer spectacular views of the surrounding countryside. As we continued southward, the road steepened and constricted into a tangle of hairpin turns; fortunately, it was neither snowy nor icy because we had no tire chains, required by law under such conditions (Gabriel had clearly not been a Boy Scout). At Senez, the road winds dramatically through a natural stone arch, and, shortly afterward, at Escragnolles, one spies a thin strip of azure sea beyond the irregular contour of pale blue mountains. From Grasse, the perfume capital of Provence, traffic became sluggish due partly to rush hour, partly to the approaching curfew.

Caroline met us at the edge of Old Antibes, closed to traffic except mornings between 7 and 10 a.m. ever since the 2016 Bastille Day attack in Nice. That day, a cargo truck driven by terrorists deliberately drove into a celebratory crowd on the always crowded Promenade des Anglais, the road separating the row of stately, Belle Epoque hotels from the beach. We lugged our possessions to the apartment, comfortably outfitted with both heat and a terrace with rooftop views. Caroline had found us a fabulous dwelling. The streets emptied by 6:15 p.m. save for stragglers heading home and a few dog walkers.

Saturday 16 January

Old Antibes lies beside the expansive Port Vauban (*vauban* indicates a partially closed, protected harbor) with its aquatic campground of fishing boats, sailboats, and yachts, ranging from the comfortably luxurious to the obscenely ostentatious. Ten-meter-high stone ramparts protect both it and Old Antibes. From its walkway to the west, one sees toney Cap d'Antibes, with some of the priciest real estate on the Côte d'Azur. To the east lies Fort Carré (Square Fortress), beyond which Cagnes-sur-Mer crouches beneath snow-capped peaks. There's something delightfully surreal about skiable slopes towering over an azure-blue sea and white sandy beaches. I'll be happy here. Arching around Old Antibes and Port Vauban lies modern Antibes, a hideously unattractive district unimproved by valiant attempts at landscaping.

Our street, the rue Migranier, curves to intersect with the main square, place Nationale, surrounded by tidy pastel-colored buildings with contrasting shutters and ornamental black wrought-iron balconies. Park benches line its perimeter, with one end dominated by an elegant gazebo, where I envision concerts animating warm summer nights. Specialty shops typical of Provence—ones special-izing in foie gras, truffles, lavender, and Provençal fabrics—pepper the narrow lanes leading to the sea, the port, and the *marché*. We're a

five-minute walk from the open-daily Marché Provencal, which
features vendors of local specialties: olives, cheese, honey, lavender
(and lavender-infused honey and cheese), flowers, cold-pressed
essential oils, greens, Corsican delicacies, and *socca*, an unleavened,
flat pancake of bread made with chick-pea flour, olive oil, water,
and salt. A couple sells it on weekends from a portable woodfired
oven, and it's delicious. They pour liquid dough into a round metal
form grilled atop burning embers for five minutes. When I saw the
line, I figured it was worth waiting for.

During *marché* hours—until around 1 p.m.—vendors occupy
most spots lining both sides of the hockey-rink-sized cement slab,
but otherwise, the space is sufficiently vacant for the Alvin Ailey
Dance Company to stage performances without inconveniencing
shoppers. On Saturdays, however, the *marché* bustles with an eclectic
mixture of spangly Russians, topsider-wearing British yachters,
awkward country yokels, and the reclusive rich of Cap d'Antibes.

On Thursdays, optimistic antique dealers set up by the gazebo
peddling furniture and silverware, lace and linens, porcelain and
ceramics, swords and toys. The paucity of customers transforms this
event into more of a pandemic social hour than a sensible commercial opportunity. Vendors chat among themselves because more
people patronize the two coffee shops on the square than browse
their wares. During the late afternoons, the coffee shops—one
attracting discerning snobs, the other, economical *gourmands*—
resemble London pubs after work, with small groups of the
unmasked mingling on the sidewalk outside.

On the block where one finds the old-fashioned Charcuterie
Lyonnaise and the stand selling delicious, gluten-free, buttercream-
frosted cupcakes, a lanky young man wearing a jaunty beret and
striped *marinière* busks on weekends. He plays the accordion with
professional proficiency and sings familiar *chansons* by Jacques Brel
and Edith Piaf in a sonorous voice and with an enthusiasm that
would infuse with joy even the crankiest pandemic sufferer. The
fingers of Amazing Accordionist dance over the buttons of his
instrument with assurance. He sways as he plays, occasionally
turning his face skyward, momentarily lost in the ethereal universe

of song. He smiles and nods at passersby, always offering a wide grin and a *"merci beaucoup,"* to those tossing coins or bills into his accordion case.

As I listen to Amazing Accordionist, I find myself crying; I'm relieved to be wearing sunglasses and a mask that conceal the tears rolling down my cheeks. His songs are not particularly sad —they certainly don't affect me emotionally when I hear them elsewhere— and neither is he; he appears happy, physically fit, and his clothes are clean and in good condition. Perhaps I have pent up emotions requiring liberation, or maybe I'm just triggered by this kind of beauty. Curious. It's as if his performance style—because it's not the lyrics—is an 'open sesame' command at which the gate to my soul, willingly or not, unbolts and flies open.

Before bed, but long after curfew, Gabriel and I stroll the empty streets and squares. With each evening we have become a bit bolder, lengthening our walks both temporally and geographically. Thankfully, local police enforce the spirit rather than the letter of the curfew. Swan-necked lamps affixed to buildings light our way. While many windows are shuttered, presumably the apartments of summer inhabitants, others glow with life. The hushed cobblestone maze of Old Antibes feels mysterious and otherworldly, especially the district between Marché Provençal and Port Vauban. I imagine Picasso, Jules Verne, Paul Gallico, and F. Scott Fitzgerald, glasses in one hand, cigarettes in the other, conversing quietly with friends under *marché* arcades or sitting on the gazebo steps of place Nationale.

From our terrace, I see rooftops and stars, a rare sight in cloudy, light-polluted Paris. On my second night, I was out stargazing and noticed the silhouette of a raven on the neighboring rooftop. I wondered if it were sleeping, resting, waiting, or searching for food. Then, I decided to speak to it. Why not? It turned toward me upon hearing my voice. I asked about its activities, what the word for 'human' was in bird language, if all birds understood one another, if there were various dialects of bird or were there distinct languages, and were the languages species-specific or regional? I thought it appropriate that birds don't have jobs, because their short life spans barely allow for recreational activities—in addition to eating and finding shelter—and realized that many humans are fortunate to have time for more diverse undertakings. It was a lovely imaginary conversation, and when I went inside, I wondered if we would meet again the following evening. I crawled into bed beside Gabriel exhausted and happy.

The next morning, I stepped onto the terrace and noticed the bird still there, motionless and made of metal. I had had an engaging one-way conversation with a sculpture! Not the first time I've made that mistake. One afternoon in the early 1980s, I went to Café Central in Vienna, in the days before it became a tourist attraction. I took the latest issue of *Wiener Zeitung* from the rack of bamboo-stick-mounted newspapers at the entrance, found a table along the wall of the rotunda, and ordered my usual *Melange* and apple strudel. An intense gaze disrupted my concentration. I glanced up and noticed a stocky bald man sporting a beret seated at a table across the room. He didn't flinch when my eyes met his. I returned to my reading. His piercing stare made concentration diffi-cult, and every time I looked up, there he was, eyes riveted on me. I scarfed down my strudel, inhaled my coffee, avoided the annoying man's aggressive stare, and left, thinking about how differently a man would react were the situation reversed. The following Sunday while strolling downtown, I again happened across Café Central, now closed. I peered into its windows and discovered the man *still* sitting at his table. I realized then that he was a life-size, realistically painted sculpture. I felt silly, but no one was around to notice my embarrassment.

A shade-seeking creature, I write on the terrace most mornings. When I look up, I see a panorama of rectangular salmon-colored tile roofs that, together with their palpable angular shadows, explain the inevitability of Cézanne and Cubism, both of which developed under sunny Mediterranean skies. After lunch, which the three of us eat together, I spend a few hours writing on the beach. If it's low tide and neither windy nor crowded, I go to the sand beach, which has a large stone that functions as a backrest. Otherwise, I repair to the pebble beach, open to the sea and usually empty. There, I discovered an elevated spot at the far end protected by a ring of boulders. It furnishes both a back rest and a spectacular sheltered vantage point for watching crashing waves sending sprays of foam into the air on windy days.

Regardless of my choice, I remove my shoes no matter how chilly the temperature and wiggle my toes in the sand or dig them underneath the pebbles in order to earth, to connect electrically with the earth. Skeptics may consider this a New Age delusion, but there's scientific evidence attesting to its salubrious benefits. I *feel* the energy of the earth reinvigorating me as I do when I touch an old tree: I tingle. After all, everything in nature is electrically charged and connected to the earth and that includes humans prior to the 1970s, when synthetic shoe soles became the norm, helpful in case of lightning strikes, but otherwise not as the Creator intended. During periods when I have been disconnected from the earth, I sleep poorly and am more susceptible to illness, so I am an earthing believer.

I have also always felt a profound spiritual need to be in direct contact with the earth and find comforting the smell of the sea and the sound of waves lapping the beach or crashing on the jetty. That's probably why I like lying on Greek beaches or on the soft moss carpeting the forests of southern Sweden and why I loved walking in the Lapland snow when temperatures hovered around -35 degrees Celsius wearing nothing on my feet but a pair of thin socks and my Finnish pressed-felt boots.

The boots are wool, a kind of high-top Nordic moccasin. After an hour of trekking through the woods, my eyelashes may have frozen, but the only cold part of my body was the tip of my nose. The experience of walking almost barefoot in the snow, feeling the contours of rocks and twigs beneath my feet, was fantastic. And such huge, rounded footprints I made! A few years ago, I realized that the winters I got sick, usually with chronic bronchitis and/or felt inexplicably exhausted for months, followed years in which I had little direct physical contact with the earth. I wonder if this modern tendency explains, at least in part, the escalation in physical, psychological, and social maladies from which humans increasingly suffer?

Could something as simple as running around barefoot make the world a better place?

Tuesday 19 January

Yesterday, Gabriel planned a wonderful itinerary that accommodated our collective interest in locations historical and beautiful with Caroline's urge to hike. We drove to Saint-Paul-de-Vence after breakfast, first along the beach, where the justification for the appellation *Côte d'Azur* became obvious. The Mediterranean, a calm blanket of intense turquoise blue, darkened toward the horizon. Just before the coastal road turns inland toward the mountains at Villeneuve-Loubet lies a hideous apartment building consisting of two horizontally striped rigid mountains of habitation that appear to tower above the snowy peaks behind them. Views from this prison-by-choice must be magnificent, with the sea on one side and mountains on the other. But it is an aggressive aesthetic affront to the cultural setting it occupies. Beyond it, the road to Saint-Paul winds upward in a circuitous manner, with tasteful villas dotting verdant hillsides.

The Fondation Maeght, a museum of modern art attracting visitors worldwide, was closed, as was everything else except the tourist office. Even the predominantly ex-pat community of art aficionados was absent. We picnicked at a table on the terrace of the pandemic-abandoned Café de la Place and envisioned crowds of culture mavens milling about in normal times. A workman on a ladder undecorated the lonely Christmas tree leaning against the ramparts. Absent the crooked lanes of impeccably kept, vine-encrusted stone houses, calligraphed shop signs, and window displays of pricey art, one might think the village abandoned. Some passageways are so steep that they had steps and handrails.

Afterward, we drove to 2,300 feet above sea level to a treeless landscape of rocks and patchy snow. Before departing in the morning, Gabriel advised bringing an extra sweater; I would have been miserable had I not. We followed a well-marked trail. Caroline jogged forward and back like an energetic Labrador, I walked briskly, and Gabriel strolled. We passed dilapidated farms, piles of feathers suggesting avian fights-to-the-death, and a few spots with views of the sea. Sunset coincides with curfew and the end of the workday, and we inched our way back to Antibes, taking forty-five minutes to travel four miles.

News that the factory of one of my favorite *chocolatiers*, Fabrice Gillotte, burned to the ground last evening in a village near Dijon saddened me, but probably not as much as it has Madame Chocolat on the rue Mouffetard. It's mostly his confections that I buy when I visit his exclusive Paris supplier, Mococha. I hope he rebuilds. His chocolates are just creamy enough, not too sweet, and with no weird ingredients—classic, in other words. I wonder if chocolate and alcohol sales have soared during the pandemic?

Today, Gabriel departed on the noon train to Paris. On the way to the station, he asked if I had discussed with Caroline staying in Antibes until the end of February.

"No," I replied. I had brought it up twice, but she was sufficiently vague that I booked a one-bedroom apartment elsewhere.

"Why not?"

"Because I thought it might be nice if we had a place to ourselves when you return. Don't you think so?"

"Yes, of course. Will it still be in Old Antibes?"

"Yes. And close to the *marché*."

"Ah!" Gabriel was often a man of few words.

Wednesday 20 January

Today is Inauguration Day, and D.C. looks like a militarized zone. It's disheartening to learn that all twenty-five thousand members of the National Guard security detail had to be background-checked to detect the handful with fascist sympathies. A worrisome number of Americans consider the election outcome illegitimate despite incontrovertible evidence that Biden won fairly. The U.S. seems increasingly fear-driven, with true contentment and security elusive. Never have I been happier to be in a tranquil Mediterranean town, listening to the waves lap the shore of a nearly deserted beach.

The U.S. has won the international COVID-19 sweepstakes with 400,000 deaths. India comes in a distant second with a bit over 150,000, although its numbers are rising at an alarming rate, and its poor live in the kind of crowded conditions that facilitate contagion. In positive news, eleven million Americans have received their first vaccinations.

Monday 25 January

Today, the air was chilly, but the sun warmed; Caroline and I decided on an excursion to the mountains. I prepared red lentil pasta spirals with pesto for lunch and brought along sugar-sweet cherry tomatoes and a bar of seventy percent chocolate. We drove along the spectacular coastal road to hideous Villeneuve-Loubet, continuing past Saint-Paul-de-Vence along a winding road interspersed with hairpin turns. Fifteen minutes later, we arrived in Tourrettes-sur-Loup, one of dozens of small, charming, well-maintained, medieval mountain towns situated within ten miles of the Mediterranean. Caroline deposited her container of pesto pasta, tomatoes, and chocolate in her day pack and jogged off to the trailhead.

I turned toward the village, walking along a meandering brook and under an old stone bridge. As in Saint-Paul, I found immaculate lanes flanked by walls of houses with facades formed by a higgledy-piggledy arrangement of irregularly shaped stones glued together by concrete. Individual residences are distinguished by the color of their pastel wooden shutters and doors and their plantings. Growing from stone troughs, buckets, and repurposed barrels, muscular ancient vines frame window casements and creep toward neighbors. The *boulangerie*, which also serves coffee, as they often do, was the only business open. Typical for a Monday.

Segments of the city wall remain, and many spots provide sea vistas. Tourrettes is not a wheelchair- or vehicle-friendly village, however. Stairs everywhere lead to house portals and connect lanes. Fountains of potable water create a pleasing sonic ambience, and the absence of vehicular or industrial noises and smells allowed nature a larger presence. It's lovely. The church, on the main square, contains a chapel displaying a nativity scene peopled by rustic wooden figures with painted facial features and dressed in natural fabric costumes sewn by villagers. In addition to the main characters —Mary, Joseph, Baby Jesus, three kings, and a few shepherds— villagers clad in the rural costumes of an earlier time engage in a variety of traditional activities—shepherding, smithing, spinning, milking, weaving, transporting in wheelbarrows and carts—are dispersed throughout the hilly setting. A plaque explains that due to the inhabitants' prayers to Our Lady of Lourdes, the village was spared occupation during World War Two. Grateful citizens contributed individual panels of appreciation now displayed on the walls. Since I was alone there and sheltered from sun and wind, I sat and wrote on my laptop until hunger drove me back to the car for lunch.

Afterward, I retraced my steps and settled at a restaurant, L'Ami Paul, across from the combined mayoral and post office, that had thoughtfully left chairs and tables on its terrace. The chairs were petite ladderback ones with rush seats held together by round wooden pegs. It seems unwise to leave wooden chairs out in the rain, frequent here in winter. But today was warm and sunny, and I peeled off layers: knee-length down coat, down jacket, cashmere turtleneck. When shadows overtook the square, I put them on again. And gloves. It reminded me of summertime in Sweden: chilly in the shade and sweltering in the sun. Although few people were around, most adults wore masks. Yesterday, I began double-masking when in close proximity to others for the first time and returned to always wearing glasses for protection outdoors, sobered by reports of the more virulent COVID-19 strains. I've been spared illness thus far and don't want to make errors I will later regret. In my weekly chat with German friends, the virologist among us warned that it could be another year before life returns to a semblance of normalcy.

For the past few days, French journalists have been mentioning the possibility of *re-confinement* as a measure to inhibit travel during France's upcoming, two-week-long winter sports vacation, which I really hope doesn't happen. If it does, though, what lovelier location is there to be in France than where, within one kilometer, I can find all necessary shops, a post office, a beach, ramparts, a marina, and spectacular views of the Mediterranean and snow-blanketed Alps? It now seems like a brilliant impulse to have come to Antibes.

Thursday 28 January

Le Monde reports that curfews have not impeded COVID-19 spread as envisioned. It might have, were it not for the new, more virulent and contagious strains. Macron will reveal new measures on Saturday evening.

Today would have been my father's 98th birthday. While sitting on a bench beneath Antibes's Fort Carré, a random, insignificant memory floated through my mind: my childhood family kitchen with its navy-blue wallpaper embellished by a pattern of white flecks, its yellow cabinets with black wrought-iron knobs and pulls. Outside the window over the sink, a flowering quince blossomed in springtime, and beyond, the side yard was enclosed by a hedge planted by my father. That was my view as I washed dinner dishes nightly. I remembered the kitchen table where Daddy and I played Scrabble in the evenings during my adult visits, scooping Bison Brand chip dip with Cape Cod crinkled potato chips. We drank— appropriately—Dad's root beer over ice cubes from iced tea glasses bearing the seals of Yale's various residential colleges. Daddy loved drawing and painting. Had he been with me in Antibes, he surely would have been beside me on the beach, his spiral pad open, sketching the contours of Old Antibes and its ramparts in the late afternoon sun.

I haven't noticed any sirens since I left Paris, a condition that promotes relaxation and, apparently, a false sense of security because ambulances here don't use sirens. In Paris, their waxing and waning alerted me to the state of the pandemic. I discovered early on—in April—that siren frequency correlated to the number of COVID-19 hospitalizations in Paris. It's blissfully, if misleadingly, quiet in Antibes, except for the hourly tolling of church bells and small streets noisy with the voices of school children at recess. This morning, I saw an ambulance in the post office square in front of the grocery store Carrefour, beside which lies the bar where mask-less locals and winter guests gather daily for a pre-curfew social hour of beer and hot wine. Mainly retirement-age folks gather, faces separated by less than the recommended meter, chatting carefreely in one of France's hardest hit regions. I figure either they have recovered from COVID-19 or are victims of the 'it won't happen to me' mentality.

Concerned by the communicability of the English strain, I ordered safer FN95 masks that should arrive on Saturday. I'll wear them over my Wuhan medical masks, seventy of which await, unopened, in Paris. Experts recommend wearing them no longer than four hours, longer than necessary in Antibes, anyway, and I air them out for at least twenty-four hours between wearings, a practice based on what makes sense to me rather than on scientific guide-lines. I haven't heard journalists or scientists discuss medical mask reusage.

Saturday 30 January

Today feels like the first day of summer: sunny and warm with people strolling jacketless. I wandered over to the *marché*. The spice stand is a work of installation art, with small, tightly woven baskets displaying tidy rows of mainly red and yellow powders. What happens when a gust of wind comes along? Market goers would look like revelers at Holi.

An oyster seller offers a half-dozen varieties. Although I adore lobster and crab, I've never understood the appeal of oysters (or clams or mussels). To me, they are wet, slimy bundles of saltiness, and I doubt I could appreciate the subtle differences among vari-eties. The Saturday and Sunday *marchés* are busy social scenes, with small groups conversing, nibbling *socca*, and sipping coffee at the cafés lining the *marché*'s outer perimeter. After buying greens, Gouda, and a bouquet of buttercup-yellow mimosa to brighten the apartment, I headed to Naturalia via two shop-lined cobblestone lanes and the two major Old Antibes squares.

Shopping completed, I felt an impulse to walk down the ugly

street beside Naturalia, half expecting, for no particular reason, I would be happily surprised by something. But I wasn't. It *was* ugly: a tall wall enclosing a school yard, projecting air conditioner units, and functional metal doors that looked like the back entrances to businesses. I continued around the block to the pedestrian street that leads back to the post office square, and there he was, Amazing Accordionist, installed across from Charcuterie Lyonnaise. Smiling, swaying as he sang, head high, performing enthusiastically to Saturday shoppers. *There* was my happy surprise! I listened to two songs, my teary face protected by both sunglasses and mask and gave him €5. I usually give musicians €1 or €2, but since I would gladly pay a €20 cover charge to hear him play indoors, €5 seemed a modest token of appreciation. And I remembered, as I often do, my mother's wise words when it comes to moments when spending gives one pause: "Will you miss that money in one year? If not, do it!" If only she could know how much hedonistic pleasure that advice—shared when I was in my forties—has given me and how much anxiety it has alleviated.

I stopped by the cupcake stand and bought the vanilla model (the other option is chocolate) with 'red fruits' buttercream, which the vendor packed into a festive paper carrying box. The charcuterie displayed colorful vegetable terrines in the window. I bought two—one white, one orange, both decorated with cucumber rounds —to accompany the foie gras Caroline bought for Sunday dinner. Later, I thought, *If I hadn't walked down that ugly little street, I would never have encountered Amazing Accordionist or the terrines. How lucky that I followed my whim.* It reminded me of the importance of 'cat' days: days when I do exactly what I want when I feel like it and switch activities as impulse dictates. Occasionally, it involves skipping in public or hugging trees, gestures that attract quizzical glances.

Tonight, Prime Minister Castex spoke, putting to rest speculation about upcoming COVID-19 restrictions. A 6 p.m. to 6 a.m. curfew has been imposed on the entire country beginning today and will last for at least two weeks. Ski resorts are closed, parks are open. Retail spaces larger than twenty thousand square meters (such as malls and department stores) will close indefinitely as of Monday.

That seems fair because they no longer restrict the number of shoppers, and *petits commerçants* have been suffering terribly for almost a year; this will hopefully give single-proprietor establishments an opportunity to survive.

While the hospital situation isn't dire, nowhere in France is the rate of infection less than 50 per 100,000 inhabitants, with around 16,000 new cases reported daily. Officials currently feel that curfews effectively impede virus spread but exhibit great wariness about the highly communicable variant that England is sharing, a vengeful parting gift as it leaves the EU, journalists comment sarcastically. Castex also reported the tightening of EU borders, with a negative test required for those boarding inbound flights and ships. New arrivals are also required to quarantine for seven days with a negative PCR test required for release, although exactly how that will be enforced wasn't specified. Greater restrictions apply to Brits coming to France; they must quarantine at their own cost in a hotel chosen by the French government, even if that directive seems ignored by those arriving on yachts.

Schools remain open, with strict hygienic precautions enforced in school cafeterias; all group physical activities, indoors and out, are suspended. High schools remain on the hybrid model in effect since early November. Many university students and professors complain about the deleterious effects of isolation, both psychologically and on their research and studies. Castex also announced the first stage of public vaccinations, beginning with those seventy-five-years and older and those with "health-compromising" conditions. These guidelines are in effect during the two-week winter school vacation occurring between February 6th and March 8th, staggered by region.

Chapter 13
February: Making Choices

Tuesday 2 February

Today, Caroline and I made our weekly excursion to the mountains. We followed the route to Saint-Paul-de-Vence before turning onto the white-knuckle road to Courmes, filled with switchbacks and flanked by a protruding wall of rock on one side and a vertigo-inducing drop on the other. I was glad to be driving and not sitting helplessly in the passenger's seat, leaning away from the certain death that pulls me toward it.

Adjacent to the small municipal parking lot in Courmes lie two *pétanque* courts. In fact, every flat, fine-graveled spot in France is one. There, mostly older folks play, while in Stockholm, the activity attracts a younger demographic. *Pétanque* reminds me of horseshoes, a social activity that's vanished from the American scene. My uncle had a pitch in his backyard, where he and my father played on warm summer evenings. It's been decades since I saw anyone play, or a pitch, for that matter.

Aside from a few cars, this barely-a-village encircled by sheer rockfaces with angled striations indicating ancient, violent geological activity seemed deserted. I followed Caroline up a steep hiking trail that someone long ago had thoughtfully furnished with stone steps. A narrow path veered to the right between two ancient, deformed trees through a meadow. *Where does it lead?* I wondered. I followed the path to a pair of bunker-like stone buildings with locked metal doors from whose interiors I could hear running water. A sewer, I guessed. The path continued, and I heard more water, louder as I proceeded. After a few minutes, I reached a mountain stream. Jagged, snow-dusted peaks glistened in the distance. I left the path and descended to the stream, strewn with emerald-green, moss-covered rocks. I felt as though I'd walked through a magical portal to the land of *Darby O'Gill and the Little People*.

Small cascades threaded their way down the mountain. I thought of *Näcken*, the Scandinavian Water Sprite. *Näcken* was an ally of Lucifer and cast out of Heaven with him (do angels and demons have genders, or should I 'they' them?). He landed in the forests of Scandinavia. Awash with regret, *Näcken* frequents streams and lakes singing and playing plaintive melodies on his fiddle. Forest wanderers drawn to his music—as I was to the sound of water—drown, incidents that intensify the Water Sprite's shame and, ironically, the beauty of his music. This legend once explained the disappearance of people wandering alone in forests.

I returned to Courmes and strolled its half dozen streets. A tiny cemetery the size of a Brooklyn backyard, with just two rows of gravestones, lies across from the tiny church. Inside the church, a Neoclassical-style altarpiece painted in 1783 by an unfamiliar artist named A. Sussin depicts a Madonna and Child seated on a cloud, surrounded by putti. Below them, a gatekeeper angel bars humans from disturbing their tranquility. She firmly grasps the forearm of an elderly man trying to communicate with the holy pair. I wondered if the painting were intended to reinforce the Roman Catholic protocol stipulating believers could only access the divine indirectly through the agency of a priest and not directly, as Protestantism asserted and as the elderly man tries to do. Protestantism's spiritual liberty encouraged individuals to ignore long-established hierarchies, behavior that eroded religious and social order in the decade preceding the French Revolution.

At the edge of the village, I discovered the laundry, an enormous stone basin protected by a wooden roof and fed by a mountain stream. It empties into a smaller basin for rinsing before continuing its downhill trajectory. Beside it, underwear, socks, and pants dried on clotheslines. I've never seen a 'medieval' laundry still in use before. Do Courmes inhabitants lack washing machines?

Caroline returned early because a hovering cloud descended, making visibility difficult. So off we went to another picturesque town, Gourdon. After surviving the harrowing return to the 'main' road, we exited onto a twisty-turny road better engineered for motorized vehicles. Gourdon is charming, well-kept, and visibly more affluent than Courmes; its château identifies it as the former residence of a nobleman. The town laundry, with its giant stone basin, was constructed on the arcaded ground floor of a small, two-story stone building with pale, blue-grey shutters. Before it stands an elegant quatrefoil fountain from whose center a stone column rises, surmounted by a sphere. Four male heads, whose mouths drool water, form the column base. A sign warns that the water is non-potable.

The château chapel doubles as the village church, whose large iron bell hangs in the belfry, suspended by leather straps from thick wooden beams. When it chimes the hour—loudly for such a small village—the sound reverberates for almost a minute. Clouds descended there too, first concealing the panoramic view that extended to the Mediterranean. They quickly obscured the charming lanes, enveloping Gourdon in the eeriness of a 1940s suspense film set. Tourist-oriented artisanal shops—glass (blowing), candy (making), perfume (manufacturing)—remained optimistically open for the few pandemic winter tourists. Gourdon must resemble a congested open-air museum during normal times.

Saturday 6 February

Yesterday, I received an e-mail notifying me of my eligibility for a COVID-19 vaccine in Purgatory. If only I could tele-transport. Just briefly. Who knows how long I'll have to wait in Europe. Thus far, there's no discussion of vaccines for France's under-seventy-five population. In the shorter term, I hope I can spend time in

Hainewalde. I find the abrupt cessation of decades-long visits and rituals with Inge and Jürgen distressing. I miss our breakfasts on the porch, excursions—to nearby Poland to see the Norwegian stave church in Karpacz and to the Czech Republic to visit Wallenstein's palace in Frydlant—and forays through villages of *Umgebindehäuser* to Oybin, the Gothic monastery ruin immortalized in the paintings of Caspar David Friedrich. I will especially miss our candlelight discussions of life, literature, and history lubricated by bottles of *Weißburgunder*. Perhaps I can return in June.

The only certainty now is that I must return soon to Paris to have a Power of Attorney notarized at the American Embassy. I've sold my rental condo, the proceeds of which will go into a bank account that will allay concerns about survival until paychecks resume. I must give my real estate agent power of attorney to complete the transaction, and apparently the lawmakers of Purgatory don't trust foreign notaries, attorneys, or bank officials to verify a signature. I proposed signing over Zoom or sending a video, but that, too, was a no-go. This lack of trust seems endemic to American bureaucracy, a system in which college students owing money to their institutions are denied diplomas despite having successfully completed their studies.

In contrast, an American friend who lived illegally in Sweden for thirty years was immediately given citizenship, a small pension, and health insurance the moment his daughter reticently presented his case to Swedish authorities. Their response was 'Oh no! You shouldn't have been living in fear and without proper social services for all these decades. How can we help'? I'm pretty sure were this to have happened in the U.S. he'd have been expeditiously deported.

Since I've prepaid for another month at Grande-Chaumière, I guess I'll spend March there, although I'd love to be elsewhere during April. Paris, when overcast, chilly, and closed-up like a tomb, is not nearly as pleasant as the sunny Mediterranean, with the sea on one side and forests and mountains on the other. Maybe I should return to Antibes. Gabriel mentioned the possibility of our renting a house at Étretat, but considering the French penchant for under-heated homes and Normandy's ceaselessly cloudy skies and bone-chilling humidity, it doesn't appeal, even if Claude Monet painted there (certainly never in wintertime).

The Grande-Chaumière apartment is warmed only by a portable electric heater purchased by the owner. I've never spent so much time in fuzzy leggings, yoga pants, and several layers of cashmere sweaters as I have during fall and winter in Paris. Scandinavians keep their homes much warmer in winter than do the French and English. North of the Alps, air-conditioning is a luxury provided only for tourists. Even the most luxurious Parisian penthouse is sweltering in summer. Of course, the rich can lower the blinds and decamp to their country houses, but teensy apartments with poor ventilation are virtual saunas during the summer months.

Wednesday 11 February

Yesterday, Caroline and I decided on a coastal—rather than a mountain—adventure and headed westward, past Juan-les-Pins, Cannes, and Mandelieu-la-Napoule, to Théole-sur-Mer. It's a small village squeezed between an escarpment and the sea. Just beyond is the park Pointe de l'Aiguille (Eye of the Needle). We parked at the trailhead, and Caroline, as usual, stuffed her plastic lunch container of Michelle salad into her daypack and trotted off on the path that wraps around the peninsula. I contented myself with leisurely exploration in both directions and then side-stepped my way down to the sea on the vertiginous path flanked by scrubby greenery.

There, needle-like red sandstone outcroppings hug the shore. Between towering boulders, small pebble beaches open to the sea. While the day was not especially windy, the incoming tide created waves that crashed against the rocks, launching clouds of white spray, or eddied and swirled in cavities worn hollow after millennia of erosion. I tested several spots, remaining until either my backside became sore, or the aquatic performance, predictable. Differently configured spots kept me entertained for hours.

People enjoy nature in varying ways. To me, using nature trails as pedestrian motocross courses feels wasteful. Can people who do that engage deeply with the aromas, vistas, flora, and fauna of a particular location? Couldn't they just as well be sprinting around the track at the local high school? I become immersed in the nuances of a site: the presence or absence of wind and how it gusts, the rustling of leaves, the activities of insects and animals, the shifting scents depending on the surrounding vegetation and wind. And water. I never tire of hearing waves crash or of studying the water's transparency as it sweeps over rocks, its fluctuating patterns both dynamic and still. I need 'nature slow'.

Tonight, as I surveyed the street-lit lane beneath my window, I witnessed a scene so banal that it probably happens simultaneously thousands of times around the globe, yet so wonderful that it made me smile. A young couple was walking home with their unleashed dog (way past curfew, around 11 p.m.). When they arrived at their front door, the dog took off like a shot and the couple instinctively crouched, slapped their thighs, and whispered as loudly as they could, "*Viens! Viens! Arrêtes! Hermès! Arrêtes!*" Hermès, dashing at full speed, ignored them, as poorly trained dogs will. When it reached the bend in the lane, it froze, glanced over its shoulder, and then galloped back, just as fast as it had run away. 'I gave them a fright,' I imagined it thinking. The man then turned the key in the door, Hermès and his owners entered, and the door closed quietly behind them.

Thursday 18 February

Gabriel arrived by train in the rain on Monday, and I insisted he quarantine for three days, a modest request, I thought, considering the standard COVID-19 quarantine lasts two weeks. He complied reluctantly and stayed at Port Vauban in a small boat with no indoor plumbing. Clearly, we have differing criteria when it comes to weighing the merits of economy versus comfort. We spent time outdoors during the day: shopping in the *marché*, walking to the beaches and parks of Juan-les-Pins, and hanging by the Château, now the Picasso Museum. Gabriel practiced accordion, and I wrote with an unfettered view of the sea, seated on a cushiony succulent growing on the museum's low wall. I'm not sure I would sit there in normal times (or if it would even be permitted), but with all cafés and the public library off limits it's the best option. Today, after his negative test, Gabriel moved to my new apartment, a light-filled, newly renovated, third floor walk-up with spectacular views from the skylight of port Vauban, place Nationale, and the Picasso Museum.

There, we had our first argument. He complained that I didn't seem happy with his presence. And he was right. I wasn't unhappy, but I did prefer being alone. Caroline is also, I sense, frustrated by my need for solitude. I kept Gabriel waiting at the train station, admittedly inhospitable behavior. It's one of the very few times I've done that to someone. I delayed leaving until the last minute, not exactly a demonstration of eagerness to see one's beloved. I then panicked when I made several wrong turns and couldn't see the easily identifiable red building that I knew was just beyond the port and Old Antibes. Had I made no navigational errors, I would barely have arrived on time. The question is: if I find him irritating, why do I keep seeing him? It isn't loneliness because I, the increasingly reclusive, don't even want to spend time with Caroline, my only friend in Antibes.

Last night at bedtime, Gabriel wanted to discuss my relationship indifference, but I refuse to have emotionally or intellectually demanding discussions at bedtime. He deferred but suggested he depart on Sunday. I said OK and felt relieved that he was making the decision to end our relationship. Short discussion, no drama. I slept poorly, nonetheless. I've also decided to return to Antibes for at least March and possibly April, mainly because I feel terrific here: energized and happy. I enjoy freedom and sunshine at a time when Paris is dreary and mostly closed. Lovely views out my windows here enable me to concentrate, and the enticing range for procrastination-wandering is limited.

I've always considered myself a people person. However, since my solitary stay in Quebec at New Year's 2020, I've found that solitude generates the greatest sense of well-being. Previously, romantic partners constituted the center of my world, my center of gravity. No wonder I lived in a state of emotional, psychological, and spiritual imbalance. Lately, I've felt my center returning to me, where it belongs. It comes and goes, but when it's 'home' I feel its presence.

Friday 19 February

Today, Gabriel woke up, apparently having forgotten his decision to depart. He announced he was going to do laundry. There's a machine in the apartment, which is not always the case. He loaded it, told me he was washing at 30 degrees Celsius (86 degrees Fahrenheit), a temperature considered cold—hot is 90 degrees Celsius (194 degrees Fahrenheit), almost boiling—and asked me if I wanted to wash anything. *Ah, he's domestically competent,* I thought. But then, as I returned with my dirties, he stood in the kitchen holding up my one-kilo bag of collagen powder, spelled in French exactly as in English.

He inquired, "I use zeess for cleening zee clozez?"

"Uh, no," I replied in English, as I try to do whenever he—often confusingly incorrectly—speaks it to me. "You found that in the food cupboard, so it's food. You've seen me drink it every day. It's not laundry detergent. Check under the sink, where the cleaning supplies are."

I wonder what happens if one washes clothes with collagen?

Monday 21 February

To my delight, Amazing Accordionist played all day long both weekend days. I wish he were audible from my window because I get antsy watching him for more than ten minutes. We passed him on Sunday afternoon, when Gabriel and I walked to Juan-les-Pins, adjacent to Antibes. We followed the shore, where a railing separates the pedestrian walkway from the rocks and sandy beach. Along the route, plaques display reproductions of views painted by artists—Monet, Picasso, Renoir, Sisley—from the exact location where you stand. Like the numerous historical markers throughout the country, they draw attention to the significance of place. Strollers pause to compare modern vistas with views painted long ago. Often, they look surprisingly the same, except, perhaps, for details like the kind of flowers in bloom or the color of shutters flanking windows.

Today at breakfast, I asked Gabriel if he still wanted to visit mountain villages, and he said yes, so we did. We headed toward Italy on the high corniche to Mons, an overgrown near-ghost town east of Monte Carlo. Well-kept inhabited houses alternate with dilapidated ones for sale. The streets, most too narrow for cars, consist of tidy, brick-shaped, granite blocks into which are embedded two paths formed by wider, longer stones sanded smooth to enable carts to pass more easily. In the town square, a green-pati-naed fountain topped by a granite bowl of flowers dispersed water from two downward-turning pipes that resemble limp oversized phalluses protruding from the mouths of leonine heads.

It was Monday, so most businesses were closed. A metal baker's rack stood outside the *boulangerie,* whose pale, peeling, green double doors needed a coat of paint. The parking lot/*pétanque* court at the edge of town occupies an escarpment that would have offered stunning panoramas had it not been overcast. In its center stands a large powerful 'freedom tree', planted in many towns beginning with the revolution of the 1790s and continuing throughout the nineteenth century. They signified a town's allegiance to the Republican principles of the French Revolution: freedom, equality, solidarity. Its thick branches support thinner ones that spring skyward, creating the impression of a leafless, spiney fan. From there, we drove to Callian, whose main attraction is a fortified château restored by a wealthy dilettante Belgian sculptor.

Sunshine yellow mimosas bloomed on the hillsides. As usual, we didn't talk much and often wandered separately, careening around the towns like double pinballs. On the way back to Antibes, we stopped by a lake. No one was around, and we parked. The sharp pointy stones typical of Provence that lined the path down to the lake jabbed the soles of my sneakers, nudging me off balance; I longed for the soft friendly dirt paths and rounded rocks of Sweden and Quebec. I stood beside the lake and cried; Gabriel seemed not to notice. The soft lapping of the water and the irregular shoreline with no signs of human habitation and surrounded by trees evoked memories of my favorite lakes. Most evenings during summers in Sweden, I walked to the shore of Lake Tolg. There, I sat and listened to loons cooing and waves lapping while watching fish jumping and yo-yo bugs bouncing up and down mid-air in the tranquil luminosity of Nordic summer evenings.

Wednesday 24 February

Today, Gabriel and I made our last mountain-town outing. Our objective was Èze Ville, perched on a mountain top seven miles inland from the beach of Èze Mer. Instead of the quicker corniches cut through the mountains at higher altitudes, we took the meandering coastal road. We drove down the Promenade des Anglais in Nice. While urban sprawl has tarnished Nice to a greater degree than other towns on the Côte d'Azur (except Marseilles), the old part appeared reassuringly unchanged. The Sun Fountain dominates place Massena, a circular plaza paved in a black-and-white checkerboard pattern at the center of Nice's Old Town. The fountain features an oddly androgenous nude Apollo with rounded thighs and a jaunty contrapposto stance. The sculpture has raised questions ever since its installation in the 1950s: why are Apollo's four horses crowning his head instead of drawing a chariot? Why did the sculptor reduce the size of Apollo's penis after the marble sculpture was installed? I also wondered if place Massena had been designed by a freemason, for whom a black-and-white checkerboard symbolizes the Temple of Solomon (which allegedly had such a floor) and the contrast between ignorance (black) and enlightenment (white). Apollo would fit as a bringer of light. For me, though, place Massena's reddish buildings punctuated by white-framed windows with green shutters conjured fond memories of quiet summer evenings enjoying a glass of rosé by the sea after a day of research in local archives and libraries.

Gabriel and I stopped on the east side of Nice to survey the town from the escarpment overlooking the port, beach, and Promenade. A few miles distant lies Villefranche-sur-Mer, whose fortress now houses government offices and a rose-garden memorial to

World War Two resistance fighters and victims of deportation. A sign with a yellow-filled black triangle warned of heightened security following the 2016 Bastille Day terrorist attack in Nice. That response reminds me of the 'Shoelace Bomber' incident, an isolated event that has resulted in airline passengers in the U.S. having to remove their shoes at security checkpoints decades after shoelace bombing no longer seems a viable threat, if ever it was. It's fascinating how that event prompted the swift enactment of preventative measures by U.S. officials whereas school shootings haven't. As a consequence of the 2016 attack, formidable walls of bullet-proof glass now protect the Eiffel Tower. Visitors can no longer stroll beneath its huge arches without undergoing a security check, tainting what once was one of the grand casual pleasures of a visit to Paris.

Beyond Villefranche lies Beaulieu-sur-Mer, and it is a *beau lieu* (beautiful spot), indeed. We stopped to admire its small Romanesque church, whose exterior walls are a mosaic of irregularly shaped smooth stones. We picnicked at Èze Mer, the beach I frequented on earlier visits to Nice. Aside from one enviable residence—a golden-colored, classical-style villa with a red-tile roof set amidst a grove of palm trees—one sees only the sea. The stone beach was much narrower than I remembered. It's odd how time distorts memory.

Afterward, we zig-zagged up to Èze Ville, a magnet for charm-seeking foreigners. It's impeccably preserved with exclusive restaurants and hotels, all closed, tucked along steep lanes, some with stairs and handrails. There, I saw my first group of Chinese tourists since March 2020: a half-dozen, young adults who had arrived by public bus and sat on a bench in front of the *boulangerie* sampling *pains aux raisins* and *pains au chocolat*.

Thursday 25 February

Today is my 66th birthday. Last year, between my return from Costa Rica and my departure for Paris, friends in Cleveland and New York arranged small, surprise celebrations. Normally, nothing much happens on my birthday aside from the deluge of Facebook messages and a call from Hanna. But last year was different and wonderful. In both locations, at the end of restaurant meals—with Walt at Edward's in Cleveland, a sedate French restaurant that employs (and educates) only the formerly incarcerated, and with Joan and Sydney at MoMA in New York—waiters brought small, gluten-free desserts inscribed 'Happy Birthday, Michelle'. Love endorphins coursed through my veins, and I flushed with happiness on both occasions.

This morning after breakfast, Gabriel left to serenade passersby at the port; he's uninhibited about playing accordion in public. I shopped for lunch and bought two of my favorite, red-fruit butter-cream cupcakes. The proprietor nestled them in the round holders of the custom-made box with the care of a jeweler setting precious gems. When I returned, I left the box on the kitchen counter and began packing for tomorrow's departure for Paris. By the time Gabriel returned, I had prepared our salads. We ate, and he cleared the table.

"Wha dis deese?" he inquired.

"Cupcakes," I replied.

"Bet why?" he wondered.

"For my birthday."

"E tees today?"

"Yes."

"*Ah, zut!*" which translates roughly as 'oh shit'! He grabbed his wallet and bolted for the door.

"Don't go. Don't get me anything! We're leaving tomorrow," I implored. He was agitated, embarrassed, stressed.

"Please don't worry about it. I don't expect presents. No one is giving me any," I reassured.

This, of course, was the scenario I had hoped to avoid by giving Gabriel multiple advance warnings that my birthday was approaching. I was surprised by the failure of what felt to me an almost infantilizing effort. Was he dumb or just didn't care? Is there another option? Early onset dementia? Even Trocadéro Man, who truly didn't care, remembered my birthday the one time it occurred during the period we were a thing. He wrote me a poem. After drinking coffee and eating the cupcakes, Gabriel rushed out to buy a dozen red roses.

In the afternoon, we drove to Cap d'Antibes, the neighboring peninsula. It looks near, but the attractive part is one hour by foot through the suburban sprawl of Juan-les-Pins or along the coastal road. Eventually, you reach leafy gated estates and small patches of publicly accessible coastline. I wanted to see the gardens of the famous Hôtel du Cap-Eden-Roc which, we realized upon arrival, don't open until April. We followed the lane hugging the hotel property to a small cove with a comfortable spot for wave-watching among the rough, white, volcanic rocks. The sky was cloudless. Gabriel left to explore while I studied the domino effect of white caps as they formed, always from east to west at the horizon, where the steel blue Mediterranean meets the beau blue sky. By the time the waves reached the cove, they lost their momentum, reduced to mere ripples.

I wasn't alone: a snorkeler in a wet suit paddled about, attached by a cord to a tiny rubber raft that held harpoon-fishing supplies. I thought of my good fortune to be luxuriating beside the Mediterranean; I'll choose liberty over salary any day. When he returned, Gabriel wondered what I had been doing because I brought neither bathing suit nor book. He couldn't imagine being fully occupied with observing seagulls coasting on air currents, the rise and fall of waves on the sea, and a snorkeler. We have dissimilar ways of being in the world; he's more of an activist-doer and I, a hedonist-observer.

We returned to Antibes and parked beside Marché Provençal. Gabriel left to buy *boudin blanc* (veal sausage) that he planned to prepare for my birthday dinner, along with a few side dishes from Charcuterie Lyonnaise. He also picked up a half bottle of champagne, a gesture that seems weirdly stingy. I went one last time to see if the shop on place Nationale had received the waxed-cotton fabric I had promised to buy for Hanna's kitchen table. No. I found myself waiting for Gabriel in the small street bordering the *marché*, now long emptied of commerce and washed clean by the post-

marché sanitation crew. It would be a fabulous party space, with its open walls and permanent roof.

I sat on the steps of the recently opened CBD boutique across the street. Cars passed occasionally, heading home for the 6 p.m. curfew. They slowed to avoid being launched skyward by a speed bump. In German, these are called '*Farthinder*', literally 'speed-hindrance', and there are few moments in beginning German class that trigger eruptive laughter more than the introduction of this new vocabulary word. In French, it is a '*ralentisseur*', a 'slower-down-er', which is not funny at all.

An unremarkable, dark-grey Peugeot containing four twenty-something men approached. The fellow in the front passenger seat leaned out as they passed and yelled in English "Happy Birthday!" to my surprise and bewilderment. No one else was nearby, so he couldn't have been addressing anyone else. The only people in Antibes aware it was my birthday were Caroline and Gabriel and neither knew—or would have sent—a carload of party-ready dudes to deliver such a message. I asked them both, just to be sure. It was simply one of those bizarre synchronicities that reaffirm the happy benevolence governing the universe.

Sunday 28 February

We left Antibes around 10 a.m. on Friday. I wanted to see Saint-Raphaël because I imagined it charming, and Gabriel wanted to drive to Saint-Tropez if we had time, which we didn't. We packed the car and the salads I had made and drove on the coastal road west of Cannes to Saint-Raphaël. We quickly surveyed the historic center. There's a magnificent Romanesque church—its square belltower intact—with a spacious shady plaza on one side. The densely sculpted portal of Cave des Caryatides, a wine shop, caught my eye. Two male caryatids with worried expressions flank the door. Each has one hand placed on their head, atop which is a carved stone cushion on which a portrait-head-and-putti encrusted entablature rests; their other hands appear to hold swathes of cloth concealing their nether regions. The

formidable oak door is a thickly carved work of art, with compartments framed by bark-and-stalk-textured squares that contain
symmetrically positioned, open-petaled flowers. The colors of buildings in Saint-Raphaël, sand-colored or pale yellow with Greek blue or
pale turquoise shutters, differ from those elsewhere. I wonder if locals
can identify regions or towns by the colors of their architecture the
way Bavarians can identify folk costumes worn in particular villages?

After picnicking on the Saint-Raphaël beach along the peninsula leading to Saint-Tropez, we turned north toward Avignon
because Gabriel had long wanted to visit the nearby mountain
village of Gordes. We arrived there as the setting sun bathed the
town—which dribble down the mountainside—in an intense light
that heightened the geometry of sand-colored rectangular buildings
and red-tile roofs punctuated by arcades and occasional cylindrical
towers. After pausing to admire the view from across the valley, we
headed to the lodgings Gabriel had reserved: a small motel on a
noisy truck route with a currently off-limits dining room.

A middle-aged woman answered the door. Her exposed roots
and wispy beehive hairdo reminded me of an earlier decade or a
character on *Trailer Park Boys*. She grudgingly put on a mask at my
request and sullenly showed us to our room on a short, dark
corridor painted bright red and decorated with a gilded mirror to
which had been affixed white feathers. It looked like a brothel; I
could imagine trucker trysts. Optimistically, it was a rococo night-
mare. One which got worse. 'Our' room had purple walls and
silver/chrome embellishments, including a silver, crushed-velvet
bedspread and pillows with spangly tassels.

"Is there a Wi-Fi code?" I inquired of the woman.

"No."

Gabriel went downstairs to fill out the requisite paperwork. I felt
uneasy. After five unsuccessful minutes of trying to connect to Wi-
Fi, I went to another room to try my luck. No Wi-Fi there, either. I
went downstairs to report the problem and found Gabriel seated at
a table in the vacant dining room masked and filling out a registra-
tion form as the again unmasked woman and her unmasked
husband looked on. I figured if they were that cavalier about masks,

other hygienic conditions were also suspect, not to mention the vulgar décor and inconvenient lack of Wi-Fi. I stood for a moment, incredulous. Then, I snapped.

"Gabriel, we're leaving."

Gabriel stopped writing and looked quizzically over his shoulder toward me; I got the impression that the three of them considered me a foreign 'princess and the pea'. That he found neither the maskless proprietors nor the generally tacky, uninviting ambiance problematic stunned me. We clearly operate according to very different tolerance standards. Thankfully, Gabriel obeyed without a word, following me into the parking lot and into the car.

"I can't stay in a hotel operated by owners who show no respect for the health of their clients," I explained, "and I'm shocked that you found it acceptable."

Gabriel is a conflict averse fellow who aims to please, but I would still have found it reassuring had he shared my appraisal. He refrained from responding.

"What shall we do now?" he wondered. By then, it was 7:30 p.m., ninety minutes past curfew.

"I'm guessing there's an Ibis or Holiday Inn or some chain hotel open in Avignon."

"How will we know?"

I tried not to roll my eyes in exasperation.

"If you search 'Ibis Avignon' you should find phone numbers and then you can call and ask. I'll drive."

It took fewer than three minutes to book a room just outside the fortified wall surrounding the town.

"This is really nice, isn't it?" Gabriel commented when we got to the room.

I wasn't sure if he meant nicer than the motel or *really* nice. I knew from experience that I sometimes phrased such clarifying questions in a manner that past partners have found offensive, so I avoided asking. I don't consider any boilerplate chain hotel room nice, but it was certainly clean, quiet, and pleasant.

"Yes, it's a huge improvement," I answered diplomatically, wondering to what kinds of accommodations he was accustomed.

In the morning, we crossed the street and entered the once papal stronghold through one of the portals capped by a crenellated tower and explored Avignon. I remembered it vaguely, especially the square with the beautiful carrousel (they're everywhere in France) where Mother and I sat at a café in the late afternoon after touring the cavernous unfinished Papal Palace. The carrousel's name is 'La Belle Epoque', and its crown is painted with scenes of the town: the Palace, the skyline, and the river, including the famous *pont*, where—according to the song—people dance. It was a horse-only carrousel with a few benches installed for those not wishing to pump up and down. The Palace was closed and the expansive plaza before it, usually teeming with tourists, empty. We crossed a bridge that offered a good view of the *pont* fragment. Only three arches remain, and the bridge now extends only to mid-river, functioning more as a strollers' jetty. Turning thirty degrees toward the town, I realized that Avignon's silhouette could not have changed much since the Middle Ages.

Before returning to the car, we stopped at a *charcuterie* and bought a few vegetable salads and slices of roast beef, which Gabriel doesn't yet remember that I don't like. Afterward, we stopped for homemade ice cream. I ordered my usual, mint chocolate chip, and it was delicious. The first taste transported me back to the visit with Mother. We dined that evening at an excellent restaurant in the center of town, and all I remember from that meal is the restaurant's interior (traditional Provençal, that we sat at a table close to the side entrance), and the mint chip ice cream. The memory of its flavor is etched in my culinary memory, like the delicious, spit-roasted pork Hanna and I relished on our visit to Meteora, Greece. I thought of mentioning these memories to Gabriel, then realized I didn't have the vocabulary to convey their Proustian power. We ate in silence as I reminisced.

We then returned to Gourdes, guided by meticulously main-tained low stone walls. Many of its narrow lanes lead to the edge of town at various elevations and offer stunning vistas. One steep street leading up to a town portal was designed with narrow steps in the center, making the climb easier for man and beast. It's flanked by two smooth cobblestone tracks placed cart-wheel distance apart, a beautiful mosaic of various-sized grey stones in a field of green moss. I wondered about the citizen who originated the idea of engineering the street in this clever and functional way and what discussion it generated.

Spring had arrived, and the air was fragrant. Apple trees blossomed. Little was open. First, we walked up to the Florentine Renaissance-style church of Saint-Firmin, named after a third-century Spanish saint. Its rounded nave arcade and semicircular apse—embellished by a decorative pattern of sandstone-colored Greek crosses set into paler quatrefoils against a slightly darker background—shouted eighteenth century. That was when the town's population outgrew the original Romanesque church and required the demolition of a neighborhood to accommodate the enlarged structure. We picnicked beside an apple tree just outside the city wall and enjoyed the warming sunshine, aromatic air, and stunning views of the countryside. We continued to the nearby twelfth-century Cistercian abbey of Notre-Dame de Sénaque, a tourist destination judging from its interactive video displays and expansive gift shop. There, one could buy honey, lavender, and candles made by resident monks as well as items produced by monasteries elsewhere in France. Sénaque lies isolated at the bottom of a deep, narrow valley and is surrounded by extensive gardens and rugged escarpments.

Our next stop, several hours distant, was Cluny, home of France's most famous Benedictine abbey, established in the tenth century and destroyed during the French Revolution. We arrived after dark and searched for *Maison romane* (Romanesque House), where we would spend the night. Built in 1136, it's located on a small square and reputedly the second-oldest domestic dwelling in France. The owners have lovingly restored it and outfitted their two guest rooms with tasteful antiques from near and far and with modern comforts like thick terrycloth towel and down duvets. Our corner room overlooking the square was magnificent.

Over the bed hangs a beautifully preserved Renaissance tapestry in earth tones. Two large fields containing prancing, open-mouthed griffins flank a narrower one with two pale-green winged horses seated back-to-back. The entire scene is framed by a border of stylized large-eyed roosters, no two exactly alike. The two windows squares cut into the eighteen-inch-thick walls, each has a pair of wooden shutters embellished with leaded glass roundels and wrought iron fittings instead of curtains. I unfastened one to look out only to discover there is no glass. Just like in the twelfth century! The walls preserve remnants of frescoes—a dragon and agricultural scenes—flecks of smoothness and color on an otherwise rough grey stone wall.

Our hosts prepared a lavish dinner beginning with an *amuse bouche* (an 'entertain the mouth'— a small appetizer offered by the establishment to tickle your tastebuds), followed by foie gras with toast points, roast chicken with potatoes and green beans, local cheeses, salad, chocolate tart, then coffee, all served at the elegant, claw-footed table-for-two in our room along with three different wines. After all, we were in Burgundy, the center of French viticulture, where such details are important. On Sunday morning, we investigated the charming town and the remnants of the monastery. The museum—including the monastery's inner precinct—was closed.

From there, it was off to Beaune, Burgundy's capital. The main attraction there is the fifteenth-century hospital (now a museum) that, until the 1960s, served all citizens, regardless of social status or ability to pay. Its gaily colored tile roof advertises the wealth of its benefactors, Guigone de Salins and her husband, Nicolas Rolin. Now a museum, it, too, was closed, but the numerous wine shops, often the property of vineyards or consortia, were open. One could taste wines, and signs advertised advantageous shipping deals for minimum purchases of one case. I would have enjoyed tasting and learning, although in my semi-nomadic state buying would not make sense. Gabriel, apparently not particularly fussy about what he consumes, didn't express any interest. We stopped for ice cream again, but that delicious mint chip flavor seems to be a specialty of Provence.

We arrived at Fontenay-sous-Bois around 7 p.m. and dined on

boxed soup. It was nice to see the miniscule Eiffel Tower glowing in the distance again, but neither that nor Gabriel's kindness and good intentions exert a strong enough influence to keep me in his sixth-floor walkup for the week I will stay in Paris before returning to Antibes. It seems like we are now activity buddies with benefits more than partners. This, for me, is a new category of friendship.

Epilogue
The Path Forward—March 2022

I spent March and April 2021 in Antibes living a happily solitary and routinized life. My top-floor apartment was in the flight path of seagulls: when I stuck my head out the window, I heard the beating of wings and felt the air currents they produced. The space was luminous, big enough to jump rope, and furnished in restful shades of white and moss green. On weekends, when I opened the windows, the strains of a Romany accordionist wafted in. I visited the *marché* several days a week and bought myself a cupcake on Saturdays, usually after listening to Amazing Accordionist.

As the weeks progressed, Antibes's sandy beach attracted increasing numbers of bathers, volleyball players, and families. I spent my time in my elevated refuge on the pebble beach, except on windy days when I would have been soaked by the spray of crashing waves. Afternoons, I was often joined by two men: a young muscular Russian, who divided his time between swimming and throwing stones into the water, and a lanky, seedy-looking, grey-haired, possibly homeless gentleman, who collected interesting stones and driftwood and arranged small sculptural installations atop the walls of my refuge. Cruel children sometimes destroyed his fragile, whimsical works shortly after their construction. We spoke several times, agreeing on our good fortune that despite increasing numbers of tourists we continued to have a beach almost to ourselves.

Most evenings, I took a post-curfew stroll through the empty streets, sometimes accompanied by Caroline. The number of illuminated apartment windows attracting my curiosity grew steadily as seasonal visitors began arriving. I often stopped for a few minutes on the steps leading down to the sea on the west side of the archaeological museum, where I watched the starry sky and waves lapping the shore or crashing on the rocks. Moonlit nights were especially beautiful. I dreaded the end of my idyllic time in Antibes just as I dreaded the pandemic ending. It was a wondrous time in a temporary modern world that I wished were permanent: little traffic, negligible air, noise, or light pollution, a sense of space, people not too harried to be friendly, plenty of solitude. I experienced the distasteful feeling of having to leave in the midst of a really fun party. When I considered my life back in Purgatory, it seemed to belong to someone else even if I remembered many details: weekend dinners at the home of Serbian friends, teaching, morning swims at the Y, Thursday evenings at the Comedy Attic.

I thought about how different my life would now be had things worked out with Mark. I would have relocated to New York last August, taught both semesters from his three-bedroom duplex, been vaccinated by St. Paddy's Day, and have had distanced outdoor meetings with friends. That path seems unreal now: like a dream or a story from someone else's life. I was thoroughly happy alone in Antibes although I enjoyed chats with Gabriel, who told me about the history of Troy and his wheat growing experiment at the family farm in Champagne. Caroline gave up on my providing sufficient companionship and found several Anglo-American expat groups. March and April in Antibes flew by. I got my first dose of the Pfizer vaccine on April 12th at the center in Antibes and returned a month later for my second dose.

I spent May at rue de la Grande-Chaumière; it felt good to be home, back in my neighborhood. The 9 p.m. curfew antagonized theater and restaurants owners and patrons. I returned to my routine of writing in le Luco, shopping at Marché Monge on

Wednesdays, and meeting friends or going to the theater in the evenings. Hanna came for a week, and we did our favorite things: wandering, seeing friends, hanging in le Luco. We often stayed until closing because we both love when the guards circulate, blowing their whistles and calling '*Fermature! Fermature du jardin!*'. With Americans banned until June 15th, Gabriel and I profited by visiting Versailles, in whose gardens we wandered in virtual solitude and were alone, except for a single guard, in the majestic Hall of Mirrors.

In June, I spent a week with Gail at her bucolic gite in Normandy and kitty sat for the rest of the month at her apartment in the heart of Paris's unusual red-light district, where sex shops occupy the ground floors of elegant co-op apartment buildings. Instead of writing in le Luco, I sat in nearby Montmartre Cemetery, whose tombs functioned well as desks and seats. The artistic highlight there is François Rude's magnificently moving bronze *gisant* of the early nineteenth-century politician Godefroy Cavaignac, while the touristic highlight is the tomb of Vaslav Nijinsky, where a bronze effigy of the Polish dancer in the guise of Petrushka sits and ruminates, like Rodin's *Thinker*.

My last forty-eight hours in Paris were unexpectedly emotional and eventful. While I was staying at Gail's, I invited Jim over for dinner. He noticed familiar looking photographs on the walls. Not by anyone famous like Atget or Cartier-Bresson, but ones resembling those taken long ago by his artist-friend Aristide. I called Gail, still in Normandy, to inform her of this coincidence, and she was speechless upon hearing Aristide's name. She had met him in New York in the 1970s, and he lived with her briefly. When Gail visited Aristide in Paris, he introduced her to her ex-husband. These friends had not seen each other since 1999. Gail harbored fond memories and was eager to see him after such a long time. In the meantime, Jim had mentioned Gail to Aristide and he, too, experienced a visceral reaction. He couldn't wait to reconnect with her and invited the three of us for dinner on the eve of my departure. I was pleased to facilitate such a meaningful and unanticipated reunion. Aristide went to work planning a wonderful dinner. The evening prior, Jim called.

"I have bad news," he began.

"What?" I couldn't imagine because my last evening in Paris promised to be an intimate and fascinating one.

"Aristide died today."

That was the last news I expected. After a moment of stunned silence, I inquired what had happened.

"Aristide had just returned from shopping for our dinner. He hadn't even put away all the groceries. He must have been ravenous because he made himself an omelette. A friend found him a few hours ago lying on the sofa. It seems like a heart attack."

When I told Gail, she let out a shriek and then fell into a sobbing heap. Instead of feeling delighted that I had almost facilitated such a momentous meeting, I felt sad and regretful. Gail, not I, will have to live with all the 'what ifs' and never-answered questions. We three met for dinner anyway, and Gail spoke of Aristide's time in the U.S. and Jim caught Gail up on his life in recent decades. It was a strange and bittersweet last evening in Paris.

I left Paris on July 1st and returned in September for the historic final project of Christo and Jean-Claude, *L'Arc de Triomphe, Wrapped*. I went with Harriet, the friend with whom I first visited Paris in 1974. She knew the Christos, and thanks to her we had guest passes that allowed us privileged access. Gabriel became interested and documented the pre-wrap preparations as well as the dismantling of the project after its three-week run. Christo fever gripped the city. Thousands flocked from across the globe, many from Germany who fondly remembered the *Wrapped Reichstag* of 1995 and wanted to re-experience a Christo event and share it with loved ones. Gabriel tagged along much of the time, enjoying his participation in this historic art event. Former student, now friend, Alberto, joined from Madrid to share this once-in-a-lifetime experience.

Although life in France changed dramatically during my final four months—the country opened (except for bars and discos); tourists, pickpockets, busses, and water sellers returned; traffic increased and air quality worsened—my interior life maintained a cheerful stability that embraced life's dynamism and uncertainty. A new and exhilarating feeling flourished: awareness of interior change as it happens. I haven't just come to some significant realizations; I'm a fundamentally different person than I was at the pandemic outset: happier and more self-assured.

I find myself on a joyful journey still in progress, one I now pursue with certainty and confidence rather than doubt and hesitation. I've rediscovered my inner compass, learned how to read it, and to follow its guidance. I think. The voice within no longer whispers but speaks distinctly, and I follow its counsel. It has piped up at regular intervals throughout my adult life, but the screeching of cultural, economic, and societal pressures drowned it out, often with lamentable results. My emotional center of gravity, long dis/misplaced onto romantic partners, has shifted back to me, and I feel empowered. Although thoughts of Trocadéro Man arise occasionally, I no longer wish we were together. I recognize that the purpose of our meeting was to jolt me into a spurt of spiritual growth. Together with ayahuasca, it instigated a transformation, functioning as a kind of slow-release psycho-emotional-spiritual remedy.

I always thought people, especially women, who asserted they preferred the single life, could not possibly feel that way; I assumed they were just making excuses for their inability to secure partners. Now, I find myself making exactly that choice out of self-love, out of feeling Time's winged chariot, as my father used to say. I want to live life on my terms—when and how I like—without having to explain or manage or compromise. I've always liked being alone: rowing in Casco Bay, cross-country skiing with dog Jessica in the woods of upstate New York, wandering Europe during long summers in graduate school, picking blueberries in the forests of Sweden, staying at Trocadéro Man's Quebec chalet, living on the Costa Rican beach, living in France during the pandemic.

I enjoy solitude more than ever. The path ahead seems clear although one is never sure where it leads. I have changed *how* I spend my time and am working on changing *where* I spend it. While I adore Paris and Antibes—and I may well land in one of those locations—I'm more concerned with the quality of my milieu. It should be sunny, offer beautiful views and chiming church bells throughout the day; a place where my daughter, the Mediterranean, and forests are not far. Paris and Antibes will always be there, but it's not necessary for me to be. Maybe I will encounter Mr. Right, but for now, I am all the company I need.

CPSIA information can be obtained
at www.ICGtesting.com
Printed in the USA
BVHW040531141122
651679BV00012B/38